*home
and family*

ANGELAKI

issue editor:
Sarah Wood

executive editors:
Charlie Blake
Pelagia Goulimari
Aletta J. Norval
Barry Stocker
Sarah Wood

general editor:
Pelagia Goulimari

managing editor:
Gerard Greenway

contributing editors:
Linnie Blake
Josep-Anton Fernández
Nick Groom
Sara Guyer
Gary Hall
David Howarth
Forbes Morlock
Timothy S. Murphy
Ben Norland
Yanna Popova
Mozaffar Qizilbash
Roy Sellars
Robert Smith
Robert White
Mike Whitworth

design and art direction:
Ben Norland

production and design:
John Peacock

Printed in Great Britain
by Antony Rowe Limited

© ANGELAKI 1995
ISBN: 1 899567 03 8
ISSN: 0969 725X

CONTENTS

Introduction
Sarah Wood 5

On the Psychology of the Uncanny
Ernst Jentsch 7

Doubly Uncanny
Forbes Morlock 17

Privatising Culture: Reflections on Jean-François Lyotard's "*oikos*"
Bill Readings 23

This Is Not a Book Review. Esther Rashkin: *Family Secrets and the Psychoanalysis of Narrative*
Nicholas Royle 31

Missing a Generation: The Rat Man and *Hamlet*
Robert White 37

Albeit Eating: Towards an Ethics of Cannibalism
Sara Guyer 63

Imaginary Homelands: Notes on *Heimat* and *Heimlich*
Stephen Keane 81

Homes Without *Heimats*: Jean Améry at the Limits
Dan Stone 91

Traversing Identity: Home Movies and Road Movies in *Paris, Texas*
Roger Bromley 101

Noah's Ark
Pictures by Marcus Wood 119

Fourier's "Familism" Against the Household
René Schérer 125

Home Exercises
Pictures by Sotirios Athanasiou 133

Luce Irigaray – At Home with Martin Heidegger?
Alison Ainley 139

Home Economics/Household Words: Disciplining Rhetoric and Political Economy
Forbes Morlock 147

The Art of Doing Nothing
Fran Sendbuehler 169

Theory on the Toilet: A Manifesto for Dreckology
Roy Sellars 179

Notes on the Contributors 198

  Angelaki Information 200

  Forthcoming/Back Issues 201

  Ordering Information 208

ANGELAKI 2:1

home and family

edited by sarah wood

home and family
is dedicated to the memory
of bill readings (1960-1994)

EDITORIAL INTRODUCTION

sarah wood

HOME AND FAMILY

Everybody knows what "Home and Family" means, don't they? This issue of *Angelaki* was born out of curiosity about what work might be happening on the subject. How much of it would coincide with my own interest in household words and family secrets? What would become of the disciplines marked as *Angelaki*'s own (philosophy, literature, and the social sciences) when put in contact with this private and domestic theme? After reading the work sent in response to the call for contributions, these questions looked rather naive and insufficient. The theme itself had produced all sorts of possible confusions, so that "Home and Family" seemed to bring with it traces of a disorder in relation to knowledge. One set of effects, briefly sketched here, must stand for others.

This issue's title covers addresses paid to home and/or family by the household names of modern thought: Marx, Freud, Heidegger, Lyotard, Kristeva, Irigaray. Less familiar names are still identifiable in terms of known projects and debates: Fourier, Jentsch, Améry, Abraham and Torok, Rashkin. These lists suggest some kind of continuity, but two tendencies oppose the assimilativeness of the emphasis on a shared theme, or "projects and debates". One is the incompatibility of the forms and placements of change enacted or proposed in each piece. But the discontinuity is more than spatial: a more fundamental hitch lies in the informality of the topic "Home and Family". The issue cannot be a place saved for thought alone: it never becomes possible to simply discount the ineducable pathos that the language of home and family bears. This pathos, both a resource and a limitation, divides each piece from itself from the start. None can forget that the terms of this language (its nouns, certainly, but also its conjunctions and figures) are liable to experiential interpretation. *Angelaki*'s exchange with René Schérer clearly dramatises the persistence of this effect. It is the deliberate loosening of associations, whether through negation ("This Is Not a Book Review") or through extension ("*Dreck*" and its rhetorical outfall), that powerfully resists the collapse of thinking into a process of definition. Much of the interest of this issue lies in the traces of conflict that affect "Home and Family" from and through its adoption as the theme of a theoretical journal. The hope remains, that "confusion between the pathos of direct experience and the knowing of this experience", can come together with attempts to produce a knowledge that is not "immediate, intuitive, experienced knowledge".[1]

The pieces and images included here need not be read thematically and they do not lie side by side. On the contrary, individuals call out to other individuals, a wall stretches

home and family

between certain pieces: these are not clean relationships classifiable in advance.2 The terms to describe the unity or division of the issue as a whole are not determined, although the vocabularies of several disciplines are made available ... but why continue to disturb the seclusion of your reading?

Station House, January 1995

notes

1 Negation and extension do not always draw attention to themselves with negative words or new words. In a 1964 review of William Barrett's *What is Existentialism?* by Paul de Man, de Man points out that Heidegger "uses the word 'existential' to mean exactly the opposite" of the popularized version of the same word, referring to "philosophically conscious knowledge as opposed to immediate, intuitive, experienced knowledge" (p104).

2 "Relationships" is a word perhaps not sufficiently distinct from its familiar sense to describe the way that writing threatens the idealistic distinction between form and content.

bibliography

de Man, P., "Heidegger Reconsidered" (1964), *Critical Writings 1953-1978*, ed. and intr. by L. Waters (Minneapolis: Minnesota University Press, 1989) p102-106.

*In his famous essay on the uncanny, first published in 1919[2], Freud begins by complaining that aesthetics has not paid much attention to the aberrant and the repulsive. This complaint is also an expression of anticipatory pleasure, in so far as the uncanny in particular has no "literature" with which he will have to contend – but Freud has to admit that there is one exception, namely the essay translated below (*Standard Edition *vol. 17, 219). Jentsch emphasises that the uncanny arises from a certain experience of the uncertain or the undecidable, and this seems to be intolerable for Freud. Freud decides, in other words, that the undecidable cannot be tolerated as a theoretical explanation, but it nonetheless recurs in his own essay, undecidably (221, 230-31). He also pays close attention to Jentsch's argument about the uncanniness of automata (226-27, 233).*

The two passages of this article quoted by Freud in "The Uncanny" are here italicised, with references to the Standard Edition *of Freud's works.*

*Ernst Anton Jentsch was born in 1867. A doctor by profession, he wrote several books of psychology and pathology, including a study of mood (*Die Laune, *1902) and a two-volume work on music (*Musik und Nerven, *1904-11); he also edited a volume of Havelock Ellis in German (1907).*

Thinking the home involves thinking the un-homely, the un-heimlich, *that calls into question the opposition between the unknown and the known. Reference is sometimes made to Jentsch's essay, in the vast secondary literature on the Freudian uncanny, as if its content were known – familiar in advance, and therefore not requiring to be read. But especially since (as far as we can see) the essay has never before been translated into English, it might be more appropriate to call its appearance here "uncanny".*

Roy Sellars

ernst jentsch

ON THE PSYCHOLOGY OF THE UNCANNY (1906)[1]

I

It is a well-known mistake to assume that the spirit of languages is a particularly acute psychologist. Thanks to this spirit, gross errors and astonishing naiveties are often quite readily disseminated, or at least supported – errors and naiveties which are rooted partly in the uncritical tendency of observers to become caught up in their own projections, and partly in the limited lexical material of a particular language. Nevertheless, every language still often provides particular instances of what is psychologically correct or at least noteworthy in the way in which it forms its expressions and concepts. In a psychological analysis, it is always a good idea to make the terminology clear in one's own mind; something can often be learned thereby, even when one cannot always make use of the result of the investigation.

With the word *unheimlich* ["uncanny"]

on the psychology of the uncanny

the German language seems to have produced a rather fortunate formation. Without a doubt, this word appears to express that someone to whom something "uncanny" happens is not quite "at home" or "at ease" in the situation concerned, that the thing is or at least seems to be foreign to him. In brief, the word suggests that a *lack of orientation* is bound up with the impression of the uncanniness of a thing or incident.

No attempt will here be made to define the essence of the uncanny. Such a conceptual explanation would have very little value. The main reason for this is that the same impression does not necessarily exert an uncanny effect on everybody. Moreover, the same perception on the part of the same individual does not necessarily develop into the "uncanny" every time, or at least not every time in the same way. But this does not mean to say that it would be impossible to give a working definition of the concept of the "uncanny", since one can perhaps suppose that the impression which generates the feeling will be constituted along the same lines for a certain psycho-physiological group. In the present state of individual psychology, though, one can scarcely hope for a step forward in knowledge by this path.

So if one wants to come closer to the essence of the uncanny, it is better not to ask what it is, but rather to investigate how the affective excitement of the uncanny arises in psychological terms, how the psychical conditions must be constituted so that the "uncanny" sensation emerges. If there were people for whom nothing whatsoever is uncanny, then it would be a question of psyches in which such fundamental conditions are completely lacking. But since (with the exception of these conceivable extreme cases) opinions as to what in this or that case can be described as having an uncanny effect will greatly diverge, it is a good idea provisionally to limit the posing of the problem even further, and merely to take into consideration those psychical processes which culminate experientially in the subjective impression of the uncanny with some regularity and sufficient generality. Such typical events can be singled out from the observation of daily life with some precision.

If one takes a closer look at everyday psychology in this sense, it can easily be seen that a quite correct and simply confirmable observation underlies the image used by language that was noticed at the outset.

It is an old experience that the traditional, the usual and the hereditary is dear and familiar to most people, and that they incorporate the new and the unusual with mistrust, unease and even hostility (misoneism). This can be explained to a great extent by the difficulty of establishing quickly and completely the conceptual connections that the object strives to make with the previous ideational sphere of the individual – in other words, the intellectual mastery of the new thing. The brain is often reluctant to overcome the resistances that oppose the assimilation of the phenomenon in question into its proper place. We will therefore not be surprised that misoneism will be weakest where these resistances are smallest, where for example associative activity in a corresponding movement is particularly prompt and lively, or where it takes its course in some particular way: in the case of youth, of high intelligence, or of a permanent aversion to the well-tempered fashion of judging things and reacting accordingly (as happens in a hysterical disposition, for instance).

That which has long been familiar appears not only as welcome, but also – however remarkable and inexplicable it may be – as straightforwardly self-evident. No-one in the world is surprised under usual circumstances when he sees the sun rise in the

ernst jentsch

morning, so much has this daily spectacle crept into the ideational processes of the naive person since early childhood as a normal custom not requiring commentary. It is only when one deliberately removes such a problem from the usual way of looking at it – for the activity of understanding is accustomed to remain insensitive to such enigmas, as a consequence of the power of the habitual – that a particular feeling of uncertainty quite often presents itself. In the example mentioned above, this happens when one remembers that the rising of the sun does not depend on the sun at all but rather on the movement of the earth, and that, for the inhabitants of the earth, absolute movement in space is much more inconsequential than that at the centre of the earth, and so forth. The feeling of uncertainty not infrequently makes its presence felt of its own accord in those who are more intellectually discriminating when they perceive daily phenomena, and it may well represent an important factor in the origin of the drive to knowledge and research.

It is thus comprehensible if a correlation "new/foreign/hostile" corresponds to the psychical association of "old/known/familiar". In the former case, the emergence of sensations of uncertainty is quite natural, and one's lack of orientation will then easily be able to take on the shading of the uncanny; in the latter case, disorientation remains concealed for as long as the confusion of "known/self-evident" does not enter the consciousness of the individual.

Apart from the lack of orientation arising from the ignorance of primitive man, an ignorance which under usual circumstances is therefore hidden from him to a great extent by the everyday, some stirrings of the feelings of psychical uncertainty arise with particular ease either when ignorance is very conspicuous or when the subjective perception of vacillation is abnormally strong. The first case can easily be observed in children: the child has had so little experience that simple things can be inexplicable for him and even slightly complicated situations can represent dark secrets. Here is one of the most important reasons why the child is mostly so fearful and shows so little self-confidence; and bright children are in fact generally quite the most fearful, since they are clearer about the boundaries of their own orientational abilities than more limited children are – although, as must of course be added, the latter can become particularly impertinent and cheeky once they have managed to achieve a certain intellectual mastery over a particular area.

As a rule, a certain insight with regard to the estimation of one's own intellectual capacities in the assessment of a situation is generally present in healthy people, as long as strong passions or psychically harmful factors (such as narcotic substances, exhaustion, and so on) are not involved. Such insight can be reduced, since excessive associative activity – and also, for example, a tendency to unusually strong reflexivity – do not allow one to complete the formation of a judgement at the appropriate time. But one's insight can be especially reduced because of a rampantly proliferating fantasy, as a consequence of which reality becomes mixed up in a more or less conscious way with the additions of the apperceiving brain itself. In the latter case, confusion must of course be the result in how one regards things and, equally, in how one intervenes appropriately in one's environment.

It is certainly not necessary that the processes in question be articulated very clearly in order for the well-characterised sensation of psychical uncertainty to be aroused. Indeed, even when they know very well that they are being fooled by merely

on the psychology of the uncanny

harmless illusions, many people cannot suppress an extremely uncomfortable feeling when a corresponding situation imposes itself on them. In games, children strive by means of grotesque disguises and behaviour directly to arouse strong emotions in each other. And among adults there are sensitive natures who do not like to attend masked balls, since the masks and disguises produce in them an exceedingly awkward impression to which they are incapable of becoming accustomed. This abnormal sensitivity is not infrequently a phenomenon accompanying a generally nervous disposition. It should therefore ultimately not make a great difference whether the affective availability of a certain class of moderately unsettling influences that do not generally or persistently concern healthy people is to be ascribed to a particularly intensive and rapid proliferation of the potential chain of consequences of the phenomenon in question, or whether, in more causal terms, their availability represents an excessive combination of more or less apposite unsettling reasons for the origin of the images exciting the affect. In any case, a stronger tendency to bring about such sensations of uncertainty under certain external circumstances is created in the case of an abnormal disposition or merely of a psychical background deriving from an abnormal base, as for example in light sleep, in states of deadening of all kinds, in various forms of depression and after-effects of diverse terrible experiences, fears, and in severe cases of exhaustion or general illness. The breakdown of an important sense organ can also greatly increase such feelings in people. In the night, which is well known to be a friend to no man, there are thus many more and much larger chicken-hearted people than in the light of day, and many people are much relieved when they have left a very noisy workshop or factory floor where they cannot make out their own words.

This entire group of states of psychical uncertainty, already determined in many subsidiary ways by abnormal conditions, can show similarities with or transitions to the general disorientation that appears in psychical illnesses.

The affective position of the mentally undeveloped, mentally delicate, or mentally damaged individual towards many ordinary incidents of daily life is similar to the affective shading that the perception of the unusual or inexplicable generally produces in the ordinary primitive man. This is the source of that characteristic wariness in relation to unusual people, who think otherwise, feel differently, and act otherwise than the majority, and in relation to processes that for the time being elude explanation or whose conditions of origin are unknown. It is not always just the children who watch the skilled conjurer – or however he calls himself now – with a certain nervous feeling. For the more clearly the cultural value of an enigmatic process strikes one, the more strongly the sensation aroused doubtless approaches the pleasant and joyful feeling of admiration. The appearance of this stirring always presupposes the individual's insight into a certain higher form of expediency of the phenomenon in question. So the remarkable technique of a virtuoso or a surgeon is simply admired, while an "artist" who has huge stones crushed on his head, swallowing bricks and petrol, or a fakir who has himself buried or walled up, do not receive the genuine admiration of the majority but rather leave behind a different impression. A slight nuance of the uncanny effect does also come to light now and then in the case of real admiration, and can be explained psychologically in terms of one's bafflement regarding how the conditions of origin for the achievement in question were brought about, on

ernst jentsch

account of which such a nuance is generally lacking in those who are special experts in the field at stake.

II

Among all the psychical uncertainties that can become an original cause of the uncanny feeling, there is one in particular that is able to develop a fairly regular, powerful and very general effect: namely, *doubt as to whether an apparently living being is animate and, conversely, doubt as to whether a lifeless object may not in fact be animate* (*SE 226*) – and more precisely, when this doubt only makes itself felt obscurely in one's consciousness. The mood lasts until these doubts are resolved and then usually makes way for another kind of feeling.

One can read now and then in old accounts of journeys that someone sat down in an ancient forest on a tree trunk and that, to the horror of the traveller, this trunk suddenly began to move and showed itself to be a giant snake. If one accepts the possibility of such a situation, this would certainly be a good example to illustrate the connection indicated above. The mass that at first seemed completely lifeless suddenly reveals an inherent energy because of its movement. This energy can have a psychical or a mechanical origin. As long as the doubt as to the nature of the perceived movement lasts, and with it the obscurity of its cause, a feeling of terror persists in the person concerned. If, because of its methodical quality, the movement has shown its origin to be in an organic body, the state of things is thus explained, and then a feeling of concern for one's freedom from personal harm arises instead – which undoubtedly presupposes, however, a kind of intellectual mastery of the situation for the sake of all other forms of intensity.

Conversely, the same emotion occurs when, as has been described, a wild man has his first sight of a locomotive or of a steamboat, for example, perhaps at night. The feeling of trepidation will here be very great, for as a consequence of the enigmatic autonomous movement and the regular noises of the machine, reminding him of human breath, the giant apparatus can easily impress the completely ignorant person as a living mass. There is something quite related to this, by the way, when striking or remarkable noises are ascribed by fearful or childish souls – as can be observed quite often – to the vocal performance of a mysterious being. The episode in *Robinson Crusoe* where Friday, not yet familiar with the boiling of water, reaches into simmering water in order to pull out the animal that seems to be in it, is also based on an inspiration of the writer that is psychologically very apposite. Likewise, the timidity of many animals may originate in the fact that they actually see the living object of their terror (the principle of the scarecrow), and the impression concerned produces in this case a particularly baroque effect, since the associative activity which usually provides a transition into another affective sphere is here very slight. This "weakness" in beasts of burden is therefore treated successfully by, for instance, presenting or holding out to them the suspicious object so that they can see it or smell it, whereby a kind of intellectual classification of the object exciting the affect is undertaken by the animal and the object is at the same time turned into something familiar which, as mentioned above, easily loses its terrors for them. So when a few years ago, on the occasion of a great carnival procession, some tame elephants forming part of it took to their heels and created considerable confusion when faced with the dragon Fafner spewing fire and flames, this

on the psychology of the uncanny

does not seem so remarkable in view of the fact that the elephants had not read the trilogy [in which Fafner appears].

The unpleasant impression is well known that readily arises in many people when they visit collections of wax figures, panopticons and panoramas. In semi-darkness it is often especially difficult to distinguish a life-size wax or similar figure from a human person. For many sensitive souls, such a figure also has the ability to retain its unpleasantness after the individual has taken a decision as to whether it is animate or not. Here it is probably a matter of semi-conscious secondary doubts which are repeatedly and automatically aroused anew when one looks again and perceives finer details; or perhaps it is also a mere matter of the lively recollection of the first awkward impression lingering in one's mind. The fact that such wax figures often present anatomical details may contribute to the increased effect of one's feeling, but this is definitely not the most important thing: a real anatomically prepared body does not need in the least to look so objectionable as the corresponding model in wax. Incidentally, it is of considerable interest to see in this example how true art, in wise moderation, avoids the absolute and complete imitation of nature and living beings, well knowing that such an imitation can easily produce uneasiness: the existence of a polychrome sculpture in wood and stone does not alter this fact in the least, and nor does the possibility of somewhat preventing such unpleasant side-effects if this kind of representation is nevertheless chosen. The production of the uncanny can indeed be attempted in true art, by the way, but only with exclusively artistic means and artistic intention.[3]

This peculiar effect makes its appearance even more clearly when imitations of the human form not only reach one's perception, but when on top of everything they appear to be united with certain bodily or mental functions. This is where the impression easily produced by the automatic figures belongs that is so awkward for many people. Once again, those cases must here be discounted in which the objects are very small or very familiar in the course of daily usage. A doll which closes and opens its eyes by itself, or a small automatic toy, will cause no notable sensation of this kind, while on the other hand, for example, the life-size automata that perform complicated tasks, blow trumpets, dance, and so forth, very easily give one a feeling of unease. The finer the mechanism and the truer to nature the formal reproduction, the more strongly will the special effect also make its appearance. This fact is repeatedly made use of in literature in order to invoke the origin of the uncanny mood in the reader. Not the least pleasure of a literary work (or of a play, and so on) lies in the empathy of the reader or audience with all the emotional excitements to which the characters of the play, novel, or ballad, and so forth, are subject. In life we do not like to expose ourselves to severe emotional blows, but in the theatre or while reading we gladly let ourselves be influenced in this way: we hereby experience certain powerful excitements which awake in us a strong feeling for life, without having to accept the consequences of the causes of the unpleasant moods if they were to have the opportunity to appear in corresponding form on their own account, so to speak. In physiological terms, the sensation of such excitements seems frequently to be bound up with artistic pleasure in a direct way. However strange it may sound, there are perhaps only very few affects which in themselves must always be unpleasurable under all circumstances, without exception. Art at least manages to make most emotions enjoyable for us in some sense. For we can observe in children that they often show a certain preference for ghost stories. Horror is a thrill that with care and specialist knowledge can be used well to increase emotional effects in general – as is the task of poetry, for instance. *In storytelling, one of the most reliable artistic devices for producing uncanny effects easily is to leave the reader in uncertainty as to whether he has a human person or rather an automaton before him in the case of a particular character. This is done in such a way that the uncertainty does not appear directly at the focal point of his attention, so that he is not given the occasion to investigate and clarify the matter straight away; for the particular emotional effect, as we said, would hereby be quickly dissipated. In his works of fantasy, E.T.A. Hoffmann has repeatedly made use of this psychological artifice with success (*SE 227*)*. The dark feeling of uncertainty, excited by such representation, as to the psychical nature of the corresponding literary figure is equivalent as a whole to the doubtful tension created by any uncanny situation, but it is made serviceable by the virtuosic manipulation of the author for the purposes of artistic investigation.

Conversely, the effect of the uncanny can easily be achieved when one undertakes to reinterpret some kind of lifeless thing as a part of an organic creature, especially in anthropomorphic terms, in a poetic or fantastic way. In the dark, a rafter covered with nails thus becomes the jaw of a fabulous animal, a lonely lake becomes the gigantic eye of a monster, and the outline of a cloud or shadow becomes a threatening Satanic face. Fantasy, which is indeed always a poet, is able now and then to conjure up the most detailed terrifying visions out of the most harmless and indifferent phenomena; and this is done all the more substantially, the weaker the critical sense that is present and the more the prevailing psychical background is affectively tinged. This is why women, children and dreamers are also particularly subject to the stirrings of the uncanny and the danger of seeing spirits and ghosts.

This possibility will be especially close, once again, when the imitation of an organic being is itself given. The boundary between the pathological and the normal is crossed here with particular ease. For people who are delirious, intoxicated, ecstatic, or superstitious, the head of a pillar (or the figure in a painting, and so on) comes alive by means of hallucination: they address it, carry on a conversation with it, or mock it, showing familiar traits. These means of arousing uncanny effects are also often exploited by poets and storytellers. It is a favoured and quite banal trick to come up with the most hair-raising things and then to reveal all that happened to the reader in three lines at the end as the content of a wild dream vision – favoured, because in this case it is possible to push the play with the reader's psychical helplessness very far with impunity.

Another important factor in the origin of the uncanny is the natural tendency of man to infer, in a kind of naive analogy with his own animatedness, that things in the external world are also animate or, perhaps more correctly, are animate in the same way. It is all the more impossible to resist this psychical urge, the more primitive the individual's level of intellectual development is. The child of nature populates his environment with demons; small children speak in all seriousness to a chair, to their spoon, to an old rag, and so on, hitting out full of anger at lifeless things in order to punish them. Even in highly cultivated Greece, a dryad still lived in every tree. It is therefore not

on the psychology of the uncanny

astonishing if that which man himself semi-consciously projected into things from his own being now begins again to terrify him in those very things, or that he is not always capable of exorcising the spirits which were created out of his own head from that very head. This inability thus easily produces the feeling of being threatened by something unknown and incomprehensible that is just as enigmatic to the individual as his own psyche usually is as well. If however there prevails sufficient orientation with respect to psychical processes, and enough certainty in the judgement of such processes outside the individual, then the states described – under normal psycho-physiological conditions, of course – will never be able to arise.

Another confirmation of the fact that the emotion being discussed is caused in particular by a doubt as to the animate or inanimate nature of things – or, expressed more precisely, as to their animatedness as understood by man's traditional view – lies in the way in which the lay public is generally affected by a sight of the articulations of most mental and many nervous illnesses. Several patients afflicted with such troubles make a quite decidedly uncanny impression on most people.

What we can always assume from our fellow men's experiences of ordinary life is the relative psychical harmony in which their mental functions generally stand in relation to each other, even if moderate deviations from this equilibrium make their appearance occasionally in almost all of us: this behaviour once again constitutes man's individuality and provides the foundation for our judgement of it. Most people do not generally show strong psychical peculiarities. At most, such peculiarities become apparent when strong affects make themselves felt, whereby it can suddenly become evident that not everything in the human psyche is of transcendental origin, and that much that is elementary is still present within it even for our direct perception. It is of course often in just such cases that much at present is generally accounted for quite well in terms of normal psychology.

But if this relative psychical harmony happens markedly to be disturbed in the spectator, and if the situation does not seem trivial or comic, the consequence of an unimportant incident, or if it is not quite familiar (like an alcoholic intoxication, for example), then the dark knowledge dawns on the unschooled observer that mechanical processes are taking place in that which he was previously used to regarding as a unified psyche. It is not unjustly that epilepsy is therefore spoken of as the *morbus sacer*, as an illness deriving not from the human world but from foreign and enigmatic spheres, for the epileptic attack of spasms reveals the human body to the viewer – the body that under normal conditions is so meaningful, expedient, and unitary, functioning according to the directions of his consciousness – as an immensely complicated and delicate mechanism. This is an important cause of the epileptic fit's ability to produce such a demonic effect on those who see it. On the other hand, the hysterical attack of spasms generally has a limited alienating effect under ordinary conditions, since hysterics usually retain consciousness, falling over and hitting out so that they do not (or only slightly) harm themselves – whereby they reveal precisely their latent consciousness. Then their type of movement again frequently reminds one of hidden psychical processes, in that here the muscular disturbances follow a certain higher ordering principle; this stands in relation with the dependence of their fundamental affliction on processes of imagination (in other words, processes that once more are psychical).

ernst jentsch

In the case of an expert, the corresponding emotion will occur only rarely or perhaps be completely lacking, for to him the mechanical processes in the human mind are no longer a novelty; and even if he is still exposed in particular cases to numerous errors with regard to their course, at least he knows that they exist and rediscovers their trace so often elsewhere that their appearance no longer has the power to affect him to any extent. The situations mentioned are also naturally quick to lose their emotional effect if someone is or has become otherwise used to such incidents, as is the case with a nurse, for instance, and – if one can speak of them in this way – with sick people themselves.

The uncanny effect which an insight into the deranged system of a sick person produces for most people is doubtless also based on the fact that a more or less clear idea of the presence of a certain urge to associate – that is, a mechanism – appears in man which, standing in contradiction to the usual view of psychical freedom, begins to undermine one's hasty and careless conviction of the animatedness of the individual. If clarity regarding the relevant conditions is established, then the special character of the peculiar emotional state disappears – a state whose roots are to be sought simply in people's current disorientation with regard to the psychological.

The horror which a dead body (especially a human one), a death's head, skeletons, and similar things cause can also be explained to a great extent by the fact that thoughts of latent animatedness always lie so close to these things. Such a thought may often push its way into consciousness so that it is itself capable of giving the lie to appearance, thereby again setting the preconditions for the psychical conflict that has been described. It is well known that such stirrings tend more or less to become lost in the case of those belonging to particular professions who are continually exposed to the corresponding impressions. Apart from the force of habit, the associative working through of the awkward affect that mostly occurs in such cases plays a very significant part in the affect's disappearance. Whether this working through is factual or not is of no great importance, as long as its final result is accepted by the individual. In intellectual terms, for example, the superstitious person also masters in his fashion a great part of his imaginative field, and he too has his doubts and his certainties: the inappropriateness of his entire judgement does not alter this psychological fact at all.

The human desire for the intellectual mastery of one's environment is a strong one. Intellectual certainty provides psychical shelter in the struggle for existence. However it came to be, it signifies a defensive position against the assault of hostile forces, and the lack of such certainty is equivalent to lack of cover in the episodes of that never-ending war of the human and organic world for the sake of which the strongest and most impregnable bastions of science were erected.

Translated by Roy Sellars

notes

1 "Zur Psychologie des Unheimlichen" was published in the *Psychiatrisch-Neurologische Wochenschrift* 8.22-23 (1906) p195-98, 203-05. (The bibliographical references in the Freud editions, incidentally, do not make it clear that Jentsch's essay is spread over two separate issues of the weekly.) As far as we can tell, the essay has never been reprinted.

2 "The 'Uncanny'" in *The Standard Edition of the*

on the psychology of the uncanny

Complete Psychological Works of Sigmund Freud, vol. 17, ed. and tr. James Strachey et al. (London: Hogarth, 1955) p217-56; or in *The Pelican Freud Library,* vol. 14, ed. Albert Dickson, tr. James Strachey (Harmondsworth: Penguin, 1985) p335-76. For Freud's German text, see the *Gesammelte Werke,* vol. 12, ed. Anna Freud et al. (London: Imago, 1947) p227-68; or the *Studienausgabe,* vol. 4, ed. Alexander Mitscherlich et al. (Frankfurt: Fischer, 1970) p241-74.

3 [At this point Jentsch's essay breaks off, to be resumed in the next issue of the *Wochenschrift.* Trans.]

forbes morlock

DOUBLY UNCANNY
an introduction to "on the psychology of the uncanny"

Ernst Jentsch's essay "On the Psychology of the Uncanny" [1906] is "in reality nothing new or alien, but something which is familiar and old-established".[1] It forms the starting point, the point of disagreement, for Sigmund Freud's celebrated essay "The Uncanny" [1919]. In that essay, the form as well as the argument of which explores doubt and uncertainty at every turn, the one thing that is certain is the inadequacy of Jentsch's account of the uncanny (as the product of intellectual uncertainty).

Freud's essay has attracted a great deal of attention in recent years. For Harold Bloom "it is the only major contribution that the twentieth century has made to the aesthetics of the Sublime" (101). Readers as well-known and as careful as Hélène Cixous, Samuel Weber, Sarah Kofman, Jeffrey Mehlman, Neil Hertz, and Maria Torok have worked through its text brilliantly and at considerable length. In most cases, the analysis of E.T.A. Hoffmann's tale "The Sandman" – Freud's essay's first and most elaborate example – has formed the basis of their readings, readings which have staged provocative encounters between psychoanalysis and literature.

And yet the only "literature" Freud can find to read before writing "The Uncanny" is Jentsch's "On the Psychology of the Uncanny". As many of the readers above return to "The Sandman" and the other literary examples Freud deploys, they refer to Jentsch and his essay's argument. They refer to it without themselves returning to it.[2] They quote it but only to quote Freud quoting it.[3] With only one exception in the vast "literature" that has built up around "The Uncanny", Jentsch's essay has remained unread.[4]

The repressed, however, always returns – the uncanny in "The Uncanny" is about nothing else – and the return of Jentsch's text now may be timely. Freud, after all, frames his own essay as an encounter not between psychoanalysis and literature but between psychoanalysis and aesthetics. Freud's essay has long been read within the domains of psychology, literature, and philosophy[5]; today, as it acquires readers in architecture and the fine arts, it may return to the broader domain of aesthetics with which it opens: is the uncanny, for example, a property of the object perceived? does it belong to the perceiving subject? or does its essence lie, rather, in a relation between the two? Here a reading of Jentsch's text, which draws on an entire aesthetic tradition in exploring the question of imitation, may help to move Freud's essay across disciplines.

Jentsch's essay forces us to look again (and this time askance or obliquely) at Freud's essay. From its own title it poses the question of Freud's title: "The Uncanny

doubly uncanny

[*Das Unheimliche*]". The position of the uncanny in "The Uncanny" is less than certain: in effect, Freud asks both, What is the uncanny? and, more difficultly, Is the uncanny? How does the uncanny exist? How is its nature to be determined – through the collections of words that inhabit the dictionaries of European languages or through the collections of experiences that inhabit memory, individual and collective (in the latter case in the form of fiction)? Not only is it hard to identify a concept of the uncanny in Freud's essay, but it is also by no means certain that there can be a concept of the uncanny in that essay. "Uncanny [*unheimlich*]" as an adjective appears regularly in Freud's writings from his letters to his future wife Martha in the early 1880s to his last published work, *Moses and Monotheism*, but the substantive "the uncanny [*das Unheimliche*]" appears on only a few occasions – outside "The Uncanny", that is. Is the substantiation of the uncanny in "The Uncanny" (and after Freud we speak routinely of the "theory of the uncanny") in any way related to Freud's relation to Jentsch? Jentsch is both the first to take the path towards [*zur*] the psychology of the uncanny and the last to suggest that he can speak of the "essence" of the uncanny.

If "The Sandman" has become the critical counterpoint to Freud's essay, the literary pendant to that psychoanalytic work, this doubling has often been effected in Jentsch's name. Freud quotes Jentsch at the point in his essay where he introduces Hoffmann's text, and he argues for a reading of the tale which he insists is opposed in every way to Jentsch's. What is interesting about the return of Jentsch's essay, then, is its reading of "The Sandman" – for, of course, Jentsch makes no mention of Hoffmann's story by title, name of character, or event of plot. Indeed, the essay mentions Hoffmann only once, precisely in the passage quoted by Freud. After reading Jentsch, the ostensible occasion for Freud's extended analysis of "The Sandman" (his fullest exposition of the equation between the loss of the eyes and castration) and the justification for the elaborate and highly-charged defences surrounding it almost disappears. As readers have already suggested, the explanation for "The Sandman"'s position at the head of "The Uncanny"'s long parade of examples must be secreted elsewhere.[6]

If "The Sandman" is surprisingly absent in Jentsch's essay, an absence less unexpected from that text is the phenomenon of the double. On this subject Freud's debts to Otto Rank's *The Double* [1914] and to his own contemporary writings (to be published as *Beyond the Pleasure Principle* [1920] and *Group Psychology and the Analysis of the Ego* [1921]) are visible and marked. Under the sign of the double, Freud will formulate the death drive, which he broaches for the first time in "The Uncanny"'s "compulsion to repeat" (238). "The Uncanny" attends surprisingly little, however, to the complexities of the double in (and to the doublings of its own argument around) "The Sandman". Reading the absence of the double in Jentsch would seem not to help Freud's reader here.

And yet there is something familiar about Jentsch's essay, more familiar than Freud's limited use of it might lead the reader to expect. It begins with an appeal to the German language, to the dictionary and to etymology before turning to collect experiences of uncanny phenomena. Again and again, it finds these experiences in children and in "primitive men". Even as it presents its parade of examples, it seems to lack a certain drive, a drive to conclude, to thematize, to conceptualize: each of its efforts to understand the central characteristics of the

forbes morlock

uncanny is dissipated in an assortment of instances. These features of Jentsch's "On the Psychology of the Uncanny" find themselves inhabiting, haunting, Freud's "The Uncanny".

The etymological connection between double and doubt is itself doubtful. Yet, in aspects of its form, even as it is certain that the uncanny is not linked primarily to uncertainty or doubt, Freud's essay is the double of Jentsch's. All that Jentsch's essay lacks is the relentless bifurcation of argument and rhetoric of doubling which leads Freud's along its course. The only thing certain about "The Uncanny" is that the uncanny is not about doubt or intellectual uncertainty, and "The Uncanny" is certain of this certainty more than once. In its own defence against Jentsch's argument, by its very performance of doubling "On the Psychology of the Uncanny", "The Uncanny" is able to articulate a theory of the double: in the double, the "assurance of immortality" becomes "the uncanny harbinger of death" (235). Certainly, the double in "The Uncanny" has been taken as the harbinger of a death drive. As itself a double – the double of Jentsch's essay – Freud's text became the harbinger of another death, the death "[Of] the Psychology of the Uncanny". Assuring Freud's "The Uncanny" of immortality – its own name preserved in death by that text's life – Jentsch's "On the Psychology of the Uncanny" returns and remains to be read.

notes

1 Sigmund Freud, "The Uncanny", tr. A. and J. Strachey, *Standard Edition*, vol. 17, p217-256 – p241.

2 Hélène Cixous, for example, wonders if Jentsch does not "say more than what Freud wishes to read", without herself seeming (to wish) to read Jentsch's essay – p534.

3 As Freud himself quotes only those parts of Hoffmann's tale already in quotation marks – Hertz p105.

4 Vidler p23.

5 In the case of philosophy, notably in the work of Jacques Derrida. Derrida's first reference to "The Uncanny" ends "(To be continued)" – "The Double Session" p220. Any attempt to pursue this reference, to continue along the lexical and conceptual path of the *unheimlich* in Derrida, would lead the reader through most of his published writings. Perhaps anticipating such a course, Sarah Kofman entitles her early essay on Derrida, "Un philosophe 'unheimlich'".

6 In the case history of the Wolf Man (Cixous, Rand), the story of Freud's "uncanny" relation with Victor Tausk (Hertz), or the encrypted structure of the family secret and Freud's own family history (Rand and Torok).

At least one more tale of "The Sandman"'s home within "The Uncanny" – a story that would begin with Freud's opening reference to Offenbach's opera, *Tales of Hoffmann*, and the Freuds' (Sigmund and Martha's) first home in a haunted (apartment) house – remains to be told.

bibliography

A selection of the discussions across various disciplines in English and French of Freud's essay "The Uncanny". Those works that refer to Jentsch are marked with an asterisk. Dates given in square brackets are those of original publication in the original language.

Bach, S., "Narcissism, Continuity and the Uncanny", *International Journal of Psycho-Analysis*, vol. 56 pt. 1 (1975) p77-86.

Bergler, E., "The Psycho-Analysis of the Uncanny", *International Journal of Psycho-Analysis*, vol. 15 pts. 2-3 (April-July 1934) p215-244.

doubly uncanny

Bloom, H., "Freud and the Sublime: A Catastrophe Theory of Creativity", *Agon: Towards a Theory of Revisionism* (New York: Oxford University Press, 1982) p91-118.

*Cixous, H., "Fiction and Its Phantoms: A Reading of Freud's Das Unheimliche ('The Uncanny')" [1972], tr. Robert Dennomé, *New Literary History*, vol. 7 no. 3 (spring 1976) p525-548.

Derrida, J., "The Double Session" [1970], *Dissemination*, tr. B. Johnson (Chicago: University of Chicago Press, 1981) p173-268, esp. p220, 248, 268.

Derrida, J., *The Post Card: From Socrates to Freud and Beyond* [1980], tr. A. Bass (Chicago: University of Chicago Press, 1987) esp. p270, 342-343, 361, 420-422, 426-427.

Derrida, J., *Specters of Marx: The State of the Debt, the Work of Mourning, and the New International* [1993], tr. P. Kamuf (New York: Routledge, 1994) esp. p133, 173-174, 195-196.

*Dolar, M., "'I Shall Be with You on Your Wedding-Night': Lacan and the Uncanny", *October*, no. 58 (fall 1991) p5-23.

Foster, H., *Compulsive Beauty* (Cambridge MA: MIT Press, 1993).

Freud, S., *The Standard Edition of the Complete Psychological Works of Sigmund Freud*, 24 vols., ed. J. Strachey (London: Hogarth Press and the Institute of Psycho-Analysis, 1953-1974).

Granoff, W., "L'inquiétante étrangeté", *La pensée et le feminin* (Paris: Minuit, 1976) p268-287.

Hertz, N., "Freud and the Sandman" [1979], *The End of the Line: Essays on Psychoanalysis and the Sublime* (New York: Columbia University Press, 1985) p97-121, 246-248.

Jackson, R., *Fantasy: The Literature of Subversion* (London: Methuen, 1981) p63-72.

Jones, E., *Sigmund Freud: Life and Work*, 3 vols. (London: Hogarth Press, 1953-1957).

*Jones, M.V., "'Der Sandmann' and 'The Uncanny': A Sketch for an Alternative Approach", *Paragraph*, vol. 7 (March 1986) p77-101.

Kofman, S., "Un philosophe 'unheimlich'" [1973], *Lectures de Derrida* (Paris: Galilée, 1984) p11-114.

Kofman, S., "The Double Is/And the Devil: The Uncanniness of *The Sandman* (*Der Sandmann*)", *Freud and Fiction* [1973], tr. S. Wykes (Cambridge: Polity Press, 1991) p119-162, 185-190.

Krell, D.F., "*Das Unheimliche*: Architectural Sections of Heidegger and Freud", *Research in Phenomenology* vol. 22 (Deconstruction and the Architecture of the Uncanny) (1992) p43-61.

*McCaffrey, P., "Freud's Uncanny Woman", *Reading Freud's Reading*, ed. S.L. Gilman et al. (New York: New York University Press, 1994) p91-108.

*Mehlman, J., "Poe Pourri: Lacan's Purloined Letter" [1975], *Aesthetics Today*, rev. ed., ed. M. Philipson and P. J. Gudel (New York: New American Library, 1980) p413-433.

*Meltzer, F., "The Uncanny Rendered Canny: Freud's Blind Spot in Reading Hoffmann's 'Sandman'", *Introducing Psychoanalytic Theory*, ed. S.L. Gilman (New York: Brunner/Mazel, 1982) p218-239.

*Milner, M., "'L'inquiétante étrangeté' (1919)", *Freud et l'interprétation de la littérature* (Paris: Société d'Édition d'Enseignement Supérieur, 1980) p245-299.

*Møller, L., "'The Sandman': The Uncanny as Problem of Reading", *The Freudian Reading: Analytical and Fictional Constructions* (Philadelphia: University of Pennsylvania Press, 1991) p111-139, 151-153.

Rand, N., "La traduction-conseil. De l'occulte dans l'*Unheimliche* de Freud", *Cahiers Confrontation*, no 10 (automne 1983) p173-177.

Rand, N. and M. Torok, "*The Sandman* Looks at 'The Uncanny': The Return of the Repressed or of the Secret; Hoffmann's Question to Freud", *Speculations after Freud: Psychoanalysis, Philosophy and Culture*, ed. S. Shamdasani and M. Münchow (London: Routledge, 1994) p185-203.

forbes morlock

*Rubin, B., "Freud and Hoffmann: 'The Sandman'", *Introducing Psychoanalytic Theory*, ed. S.L. Gilman (New York: Brunner/Mazel, 1982) p205-217.

Schur, M., *Freud: Living and Dying* (London: Hogarth Press and Institute of Psycho-Analysis, 1972) p333-339.

*Todd, J.M., "The Veiled Woman in Freud's 'Das Unheimliche'", *Signs*, vol. 11 no. 3 (spring 1986) p519-528.

*Vidler, A., *The Architectural Uncanny: Essays in the Modern Unhomely* (Cambridge MA: MIT Press, 1992).

Weber, S., "The Sideshow, or: Remarks on a Canny Moment", *MLN*, vol. 88 no. 6 (December 1973) p1102-1133.

*Wigley, M., *The Architecture of Deconstruction: Derrida's Haunt* (Cambridge MA: MIT Press, 1993).

Wright, E., *Psychoanalytic Criticism: Theory in Practice* (London: Methuen, 1984).

bill readings

Bill Readings died, at the age of 34, in the plane crash between Indianapolis and Chicago on 31 October 1994. The essay below is one of the many to be published in the wake of this event – and, as he wrote in the Glossary to his *Introducing Lyotard: Art and Politics* (London: Routledge, 1991), an event is "the fact or case that something happens, after which nothing will ever be the same again" (xxxi). This issue of *Angelaki* is dedicated to his memory.

Bill had already emerged as one of the outstanding thinkers of his generation. At the time of his death he was Associate Professor of comparative literature at the university of Montreal. A graduate of Oxford, he had also taught at Syracuse and Geneva, and was known throughout Europe and the U.S. as a lecturer and debater, as well as a mentor who combined rigour with caring. At least one collection of memorial essays on his work is currently being produced, and a foundation to aid graduate students has been set up in his name at Montreal. His book on the fate of the university will soon be published by Harvard (see "For a Heteronomous Cultural Politics: The University, Culture and the State", *Oxford Literary Review* 15 [1993]), and most of his equally path-breaking work on Milton has still to be published. "Privatising Culture" forms part of his interrogation of the cultural-political economy after Lyotard and Adorno. There are no words to describe the event that has cut off this work so prematurely. Bill knew the problems of the unspeakable and the immemorial; but he always remained committed to reading. Now read on.

Roy Sellars

bill readings

PRIVATISING CULTURE
reflections on jean-françois lyotard's "oikos"[1]

Let's say we are all interested in culture. But how is culture to be understood, as public or as private? The question is not as simple as it might seem, for all that we are inclined to understand the question as one of a choice between the euphoric democratisation of a public culture (the carnivalesque, as it is generally invoked) and the merely private culture of the gentleman for which Newman called.[2] In modernity, culture has named the becoming-public of the private, the point at which an intimate feeling of ethnic belonging becomes the object of a rational-historical discourse: this is Schiller's argument in *On the Aesthetic Education of Mankind*.[3] And Arnold, in opposition to Newman, sought along with Schiller to make culture into the organic ground of a national belonging that would be accessible to reason.[4] If a certain tradition of Enlightenment thinking on culture has begun to lose its grip, Lyotard's is one of the names that is most associated with that weakening.[5] In discussing briefly his essay *"oikos"*, I want to look at how he inflects the notion of the private as a way of understanding the contemporary horizon of the kind of question that modernity called "cultural". What interests me in Lyotard's argument is how, in response to a conference on ecology, he invokes the *"oikos"* to trouble the Enlightenment distinction between the public and the private. And he does so in a way that has little to do with the current discourse of ecology, motivated as it is by a call to public concern for the domestic economy of the planet:

> [T]here is a relation of language with the logos, which is not centered on optimal performance and which is not obsessed by it, but which is preoccupied, in the full sense of 'pre-occupied' with listening to and seeking for what is secluded, *oikeion*. This discourse is called 'literature', 'art', or 'writing' in general. (*PW* 105)

Thus does Lyotard make a distinction between economics on the one hand, which belongs to the public sphere, as the optimal regulation of goods, values, and services, and eco-logics, on the other, as the discourse of a secluded thing, which is not public, which is not a matter for communication, which is structurally not part of any system. The public logic of economics organises elements as virtual units within a closed system, so that language is considered as the means of communicating bits of information. Hence operations are performed to make language more efficient, in view of this goal. This is a story as old as Plato's well-known warnings against rhetorical ornament, in *Gorgias*.[6] The attempt to give law to the household, to provide a *nomos* for the *oikos*, is an attempt to make it public, as a system. As a system, economics would be in principle a general law, one that can be transferred elsewhere, applied to all households.

privatising culture

This is, of course, the horizon of our existence, at the end of the Cold War. The world is no longer held together by the tense fiction of superpower rivalry, by the conflict between two competing economic systems, each attempting to give its law to the households of the planet. So we hear a lot about global issues, primarily "ecology" and "development". Lyotard's "*oikos*" was given as a lecture at an "ecology" conference, and doubtless his attempt to make of ecology something other than a discourse on optimal planetary balance, something other than an economics of planetary survival, aroused some opposition. In thinking about his essay, I want to move it more explicitly into the context of "development".

"Development" implies the global imposition of a general law of maximum return on investment in all fields, a law whose observance requires neither moral fortitude nor political will but efficient management. It is not an ideological colonization, nor a political imperialism, since it applies both to the metropole and to the empire. Parts of the West are currently being left behind by development, along with the vast majority of Africa. It is, however, asymmetrical, since the permeability of social systems to cost/benefit analysis is differentially inflected around the globe. "Development", as a notion which implies a certain kind of systemic logic, is not merely an issue for economists. Rather, I would argue that the systemics of development (I will henceforth rely on the reader to inflect the term for herself, having already sufficiently marked my suspicions) are now the general horizon under which, whether we like it or not, all forms of life are being subsumed.

Hence, where once the superpowers engaged in cultural rivalry, we now speak of degrees of cultural development. Thus, for Marco Antonio Rodrigues Dias, head of the Higher Education Division of UNESCO, "with the end of the Cold War, the main problem in the world is 'underdevelopment'".[7] And this applies to the field of what used to be called "culture". "Culture" was once held to be the expression of a symbolic life whose ideological role was political rather than economic. Culture served to tie the subject to the nation-state, a political benefit held to outweigh economic considerations (hence, for instance, the state funding of non-competitive national airline carriers). In the systemics of global development, there is no longer any economic alternative to the free market economy, so that there is no longer a political imperative to cushion the savagery of its functioning, and remind each member of the populace that they are *all*, as political subjects, better off than in the Soviet Union. Nowadays, areas of the world can be allowed to collapse, if they are "uneconomic", without fear that they will fall into the communist bloc, without fear that they will be lost to culture.

For culture is itself subject to the systemic laws of the economic market. Western European countries attempt to "develop" their cultural heritage for internal tourism, while external tourism becomes a significant mode of appropriation of "underdeveloped" countries. Incidentally, the structure of profit in tourism is interestingly parallel to that which holds for manufacturing industry. Raw materials are exported to be processed in First World countries, and the labour of processing is remunerated at ten times the level of the labour of extraction. Tourism packages or processes the raw material of cultural difference, and the major profits accrue to First World tour organisers rather than to local economies.

The implication of this is that those of us who work in the field of the humanities are no longer primarily servants (or critics) of a national ideology of "culture". We are rather, as Adorno argued later in his life, caught up in a cultural system that is unipolar, within which critique merely reinforces the system. I say "cultural system" in order to avoid confusion with the more direct assault on mass culture which Adorno (and Horkheimer) engaged in under the name of the "Culture Industry" in *Dialectic of Enlightenment*.[8] While there was still an outside, a true vision of culture, implicit in the diatribes of *Dialectic of Enlightenment*, this is no longer the case in "Cultural Criticism and Society"[9], which recognizes such critique as reinforcement of the system. This complex essay traces the breakdown of traditional forms of cultural critique in the face of contemporary culture's abandonment of ideological pretence. Neither the anti-exclusionary assault on high culture as the (bourgeois) part standing in for the whole nor the assault on mass culture as "bread and circuses" masking the true nature of expropriation will do. In this context, the critique of culture as an ideology becomes obsolete (CCS 33), since there is no outside to cultural ideology. Culture no longer hides anything, there is nothing behind culture for ideology critique to find, although "the materialistic transparency of culture has not made it more honest, only more vulgar" (CCS 34). This means that the analysis of culture can no longer assume a stable ground, can no longer assign its products to the machinations of particular vested interests:

> Today, ideology means society as appearance. Although mediated by the totality behind which stands the rule of partiality, ideology is not simply reducible to a partial interest. It is, as it were, equally near the centre in all its pieces. (CCS 31)

As Adorno points out, either the cultural critic assumes a transcendent position that criticises culture as false or unnatural (without realizing that the notion of the "natural" is itself generated by the culture under critique), or s/he takes up an immanent position which offers culture a self-consciousness that it already possesses, that increases its vulgarity rather than its honesty:

> There are no more ideologies in the authentic sense of false consciousness, only advertisements for the world through its duplication and the provocative lie which does not seek belief but commands silence. (CCS 34)

The critique of culture depends on the assumption that culture is organized in terms of truth and falsehood rather than in terms of successful or unsuccessful performance. Critique depends on the idea that there is a quasi-religious belief in the icons of culture, and it loses its force once the system is prepared to make any cultural icon the site of economic profit. So the British royal family becomes a soap opera rather than an ideological excuse for popular submission, while on MTV Beavis and Butthead can perform semiotic analyses of gender roles in video-clips for the amusement of those viewers whom cultural critique presumes are the blind dupes of these same video-clips.

Hence the problem of cultural studies: its analyses of culture do have an effect, but as a site for further investment by a system that is no longer "cultural" in the traditional sense. Rather than posing a threat to it, the analyses performed by "cultural studies" risk providing new marketing opportunities for the system. Practices such as punk music and dress-styles are offered their self-consciousness in academic essays, but the dignity that they acquire is not that of authenticity but of marketability, be it in the cinema, on MTV, or as a site of tourist interest for visitors to London. The travel guide is a prime example of the way in which cultural particularity no longer offers an authentic alternative to the market system but is in fact a form of access to the status of the commodity. It has no referent, that is, outside the system in which it circulates. To put it bluntly, the shock value of punk is not *lasting* in a cultural sense, since it soon becomes possible to be "profitably punk". To say that it is not lasting does not mean that there is no point in trying to do something new, only that it is naive to presume that in so doing one gains access to a real culture outside the system.

In speaking of the *oikos* as the secluded, then, Lyotard is trying to suggest something that might resist entry into the system. Not a true culture, for the word "culture" has always been caught up in the public sphere, merely functioning as an element of *political* economy (the calculations of ideology) – rather than of the market. If our present conjuncture is marked by the disappearance of the relative autonomy of the political (both the nation-state and its adjunct "public sphere"), then culture will not save us. The thought of culture, since Dryden first began speaking of the "cultivation" of the individual to refer to the sphere of arts and letters, has always been the attempt to produce a political economy of symbolic life. It reached its apogee in German Romanticism, where it came to define the place of the State institution as the regulator of markets in the interest of national culture. The end of "culture" is marked by deregulation and "privatisation", by the progressive decline of the influence of the nation-state as an instance over the functioning of societies. The progressive "privatisation" of the media is a strong instance of this, one which it would be frankly foolish to try to understand as inherently progressive (liberating from state control) or reactionary (exposing culture to the law of free-market capitalism). The temporal trajectory of progressive and reactionary is simply not appropriate to such a conjuncture, because its unilinearity depends upon the instance of the nation-state (the very instance that is disappearing) in order to give it expression.[10] As Lyotard puts it:

> In the *Umwelt* I am describing, all politics is certainly nothing other than a program of decisions to encourage development. All politics is only (I say 'only' because I have a revolutionary past and hence a certain nostalgia) a program of administrative decision making, of managing the system. (*PW* 101)

So we have two modes of privatisation. On the one hand, the everyday use, in which the term expresses the removal from political-ideological control of the operations of certain aspects of the economy. Traditionally, these operations concern infrastructural elements (transportation or communication networks) whose establishment had required state intervention. It is in the sphere of communication and information technology that this process is perhaps most evident: as in the debate over the "information superhighway" in the United States, where the reference to the highway system evokes not only the question of transportation but also the historical role of the State as builder and maintainer of transportation networks in the modern period. Here, "privatisation" names subsumption under the systemic logic of the economic.

And on the other hand, we have Lyotard's sense of privatisation: an *aneconomic* sense of the private. It would be very easy to confuse this with a Romantic vision of culture. If Habermas insists on the private sphere as the site of the elaboration of avant-garde practices, prior to their entry into the public sphere, it is in terms of such a romanticism. A romantic feminism seeks to make public, make political, the private experiences of women among themselves: their diaries, their journals, their conversations. The problem here is not in the nature of the object but in the claim to be able to make them public. The assumption is that publicisation does not alter their essential nature, merely corrects an external censorship, a repression, that had up to now excluded women's private thoughts from serious consideration in the male public sphere. And this assumption is false. For, and here I follow Lyotard, what is private in the strong sense is the structurally secluded; like the Unconscious, it will not be made public as such, it is systemically dysfunctional:

> ... [F]unctionally speaking, the unconscious (to use Freudian terminology) is the dysfunctional entity par excellence. It provokes only trouble, that is, paradoxes and even silences or noises, which are the same thing. (*PW* 100)

Paradox, silence, noise, all are interruptions or aporias in communication, in the systemic regulation of discourse in the public sphere. They cannot be made public. Not at the time.

> Afterward, yes, when the work is written, you can put this work into an existing function, for example, a cultural function. Works are doomed to that, but while we are writing, we have no idea about the function, if we are serious. (*PW* 100)

Here Lyotard names the "cultural function" as precisely the systemic economy of the recuperation of the shock of the private for public discourse. The privacy of the *oikos*, which is not (need it be said?) the property of a subject, is at odds with the cultural function, which seeks to make public its privacy, to make its incommunicable noise the object of a communication. Economics inscribes privacy within a system of subjects, who know their privacy only as the ground of individual economic calculation of private interests – calculation as to the kind of functionality about which Lyotard contends that serious writers have no idea. Privacy belongs to no one, since it is the point at which the relation between the individual singularity and the system becomes *incalculable*. To listen to this incalculable privacy is to engage in a singular kind of writing, which Lyotard wants, perhaps too quickly, to call "literature". For literature is not the other to the system. After all, Paul Auster is literature, and he writes, as Wlad Godzich has pointed out, in the language of systemic global communication, the textual equivalent of the mid-Atlantic accent of the rock singer: "Auster does not write in American, nor even in English, but in Global".[11] Perhaps "writing" is a better term for the particular encounter with an incalculable otherness that language involves. To write is to speak in a language that comes from elsewhere, a language that precedes writing, of things that have not yet found their expression, that are not yet communicable, for they are private. The space of public discourse, of communicability and translatability, is both preceded by, and precedes writing – that untimely activity. We are not yet ready to think of literature in untimely terms, for literature is born along with the possibility of a literary history, of a public discourse between ancients and moderns.

Nonetheless, if we are to understand the question of writing as a question that cannot wholly be answered in terms of development, of cultural functionality, it is to an activity of writing that we must turn, an activity that is not essentially literary but which has sometimes been conducted under the rubric of literature. This I will call, for the moment, the writing of privacy (which is the sense in which I take Lyotard to be inflecting the possibility of an *oiko-logos*, an ecology). Privacy does not here occupy the position of the

privatising culture

Unconscious in a liberatory discourse (in the style of Wilhelm Reich), as something that subjects might occupy, inhabit, as an alternative to the system. Privacy, that is, is not open to development as an alternative. It can, however, be maintained as a question, something that holds open the frictions that refuse to be functionalised by the systematics of global development, frictions such as gender difference, which are both marginal and central at the same time. "*oikos*" reminds us that, precisely because writing is a domestic activity that is always *unheimlich*, our accounts with language can never be settled. And it is in the unsettling quality of those unbalanced accounts, rather than in the communicative rationality of the public sphere, that a space appears which is neither that of political utopianism nor of economic despair. It is not a space to be built, for it has always been there – it does not require of us heroic militancy in its name, nor cynical detachment at the fact of its failure. All it requires is an exercise of listening, an exercise that is both difficult (complex) and simple (direct), the kind of direct yet complex attention that we usually pay to such household matters as the question of what constitutes a good relationship, a good life, etc. The kind of attention that appears when we reflect on these unanswerable, everyday, philosophical, questions. They are questions that public discourse tries to answer, with statistics, polls, and laws. They are questions that, in the privacy of the household, appear as unanswerable questions in the light of which we nevertheless have to live. Unanswerable questions to which we are nonetheless answerable. The questions of the *oikos*.

notes

1 The essay "*oikos*" is published in Jean-François Lyotard, *Political Writings*, trs Bill Readings and Kevin-Paul Geiman (Minneapolis: University of Minnesota Press, 1993) p96-107. Further references to this text will be incorporated as (PW).

2 On the private culture of the gentleman, see John Henry Cardinal Newman, *The Idea of a University: Defined and Illustrated* (London: Longmans, Green and Co., 1925) especially p208-211.

3 Friedrich Schiller, *Letters on the Aesthetic Education of Mankind* (1793), eds and trs E.M. Wilkinson and L.A. Willoughby (Oxford: Clarendon Press, 1967).

4 Matthew Arnold, *Culture and Anarchy* (1868), ed. J. Dover Wilson (Cambridge: Cambridge University Press, 1932).

5 Most obviously, in relation to his publication of *The Postmodern Condition*, trs Geoffrey Bennington and Brian Massumi (Minneapolis: University of Minnesota Press, 1984). See also *The Postmodern Explained*, trs Julian Pfanis et al. (Minneapolis: University of Minnesota Press, 1993).

6 Plato, *Gorgias*, tr. Walter Hamilton (Harmondsworth: Penguin, 1971) p38-48.

7 "Preface" to Alfonso Borrero Cabal, *The University as an Institution Today* (Ottawa and Paris: IDRC and UNESCO, 1993) pxv.

8 Theodor W. Adorno and Max Horkheimer, *Dialectic of Enlightenment*, tr. John Cumming (London: Verso, 1979).

9 Theodor W. Adorno, "Cultural Criticism and Society" in *Prisms*, trs Samuel and Sherry Weber (Cambridge, Mass: MIT Press, 1983) p17-34. Further references will be incorporated as (CCS). See also "Culture industry reconsidered" in Theodor W. Adorno, *The Culture Industry*, ed. J.M. Bernstein, tr. Anson G. Rabinbach (London: Routledge, 1991).

10 For a more detailed discussion of the process of "depoliticisation" see my remarks in the Foreword to *Political Writings*, entitled "The End of the Political".

11 Wlad Godzich, "The Seduction of Words" p199-201.

bibliography

Adorno, T.W., "Cultural Criticism and Society" in *Prisms*, trs S. and S. Weber (Cambridge, Mass: MIT Press, 1983).

Adorno, T.W., The Culture Industry, ed. J.M. Bernstein, tr. A.G. Rabinbach (London: Routledge, 1991).

Adorno, T.W. and M. Horkheimer, *Dialectic of Enlightenment*, tr. J. Cumming (London: Verso, 1979).

Arnold, M., *Culture and Anarchy* (1868), ed. J. Dover Wilson (Cambridge: Cambridge University Press, 1932).

Dias, M.A.R., "Preface" to A.B. Cabal, *The University as an Institution Today* (Ottawa and Paris: IDRC and UNESCO, 1993).

Godzich, W., "The Seduction of Words" in J.-F. Lyotard, *The Postmodern Condition*, trs G. Bennington and B. Massumi (Minneapolis: University of Minnesota Press, 1984).

Lyotard, J.-F., *The Postmodern Explained*, trs J. Pfanis et al. (Minneapolis: University of Minnesota Press, 1993).

Lyotard, J.-F., *Political Writings*, eds B. Readings and K.-P. Geiman (Minneapolis: University of Minnesota Press, 1993).

Newman, J.H. Cardinal, *The Idea of a University: Defined and Illustrated* (London: Longmans, Green and Co., 1925).

Plato, *Gorgias*, tr. W. Hamilton (Harmondsworth: Penguin, 1971).

Schiller, F., *Letters on the Aesthetic Education of Mankind* (1793), eds and trs E.M. Wilkinson and I.A. Willoughby (Oxford: Clarendon Press, 1967).

nicholas royle

THIS IS NOT A BOOK REVIEW
esther rashkin:
family secrets and the psychoanalysis of narrative

Isn't the genre of the book review necessarily at odds with itself, starting from the fact that every book review, by signalling itself as belonging to that genre, does not simply belong? At the same time, to say that there can be no book review, no "critical examination" or "critique" (*Chambers*) that would be merely a "looking back" or "retrospect" is to start towards an acknowledgement that the review participates in the very emergence of the book and may be at least as much prospective as retrospective. The identity of a book review is at once constituted and divided within itself by a logic of grafting. It may be dependent, like offspring, on the book under review; but this dependency cuts in different ways. The practice of the book review is bound by the double business or obligation on the one hand to provide a faithful account of the book under examination (in which case the book review aspires towards the condition of self-effacement, ideally having nothing to do but recite), and on the other to break not only with this account (and everything that it implies about the secondarity of the review, as of a translation) but also with the very genre and institution of the book review in order to dream, perhaps, of something altogether other.

To categorize and compartmentalize in terms of the book review, in a journal, magazine or newspaper, is to keep things in their place with a rigour so obvious we are perhaps blind to it. Such compartmentalizing no doubt constitutes, in considerable measure, the *homeliness* of the publication of which it is part, the larger form and enabling structure of what is known as house-style. One might speculate on a dissemination of the book review, on the effects of breaking up the family or house-breaking, for instance in terms of how, say, *The New York Times Book Review*, *The London Review of Books* or the *Times Literary Supplement* might *read* if these publications were no longer structured around the rubric and conventions of the book review.

Is all of this by way of preamble to a quite conventional book review, focused on Esther Rashkin's *Family Secrets and the Psychoanalysis of Narrative*? Yes and no. The title of the present text plots the paradox. It declares a non-belonging dependent precisely on the identification of that to which it purports to be other. As already indicated, there is nothing unusual about this: every book review can be defined according to the principle of a genre-clause (whether or not this is made explicit) which identifies the text as book review while, in this very clausality, not belonging to that text. At once in and outside the family. The impossibility of a book review is highlighted in the case of Rashkin's work because in certain fundamental respects *Family Secrets* is *not a book*.

31

family secrets

Of course conventions demand to be negotiated: *Family Secrets* is a fascinating and provocative study which takes off from the psychoanalytic theories of Nicolas Abraham and Maria Torok and elaborates readings of texts by Conrad (*The Secret Sharer*), Villiers de l'Isle-Adam (*L'intersigne*), Balzac (*Facino Cane*), James (*The Jolly Corner*) and Poe (*The Fall of the House of Usher*). It offers us some of the strange fruits of attempting to consider literary texts in terms of Abraham and Torok's notions of the crypt and phantom. A crypt is an unspeakable secret, often linked to the death of a loved one and the refusal or inability to mourn. It is lodged in an individual, neither conscious nor unconscious but rather, like a foreign body, interred "in" the unconscious. More peculiar still, a phantom is a crypt-effect, the manifestation of the *transference* of a crypt. To see a phantom or ghost is uncannily to bear witness to the presence within oneself of the crypt of *another*. A crypt, in other words, can be passed down a family line; a phantom can appear to a number of generations, before finally disappearing.

Rashkin gives an account of this and other aspects of Abraham and Torok's work in the opening chapter of her book, "For a New Psychoanalytic Literary Criticism", an essay originally (and in a slightly different form) published in *Diacritics* and still perhaps the finest short exposition of Abraham and Torok's work. Rashkin quotes Abraham:

> Should a child have parents 'with secrets', ... the child will receive from them a gap in the unconscious, an unknown, unrecognized knowledge – a *nescience* ...
>
> The buried speech of the parent will be (a) dead (gap) without a burial place in the child. This unknown phantom returns from the unconscious to haunt its host and may lead to phobias, madness, and obsessions. Its effect can persist through several generations and determine the fate of an entire family line. (27)

This kind of formulation proves extraordinarily *generative* (in more than one sense of that word) for thinking about literary works – especially those which are variously concerned with the uncanny, ghostly and unspeakable. But it is not only pertinent to an apprehension of the strangeness and power of literature: it unsettles the very distinctions between the literary and non-literary, between the textual and non-textual, between culture and nature. In these respects *Family Secrets* is perhaps a more radical work than it thinks it is or even than it wants to be.

Hence the apparent craziness of suggesting that *Family Secrets* is not a book. It is not a "book" insofar as one might understand by this a fixed and determinate volume of words. It deranges the space of the book; it evicts all assumptions about what is and is not "in" a book (and, no doubt by the same logic also, "in" a book review). Rashkin proceeds by remarking that "[t]his book is a study of the haunting effects of family secrets on characters in narrative" (3), but the narrowness of her focus goes alongside "a reconsideration of extant conceptions of narrative limits and textual boundaries and a rethinking of the notion of textual origins" (5). On one level, then, *Family Secrets* is engaged with close readings of a quite small number of nineteenth- and twentieth-century short stories all of which contain evidence of crypts or phantoms. On another level, however, it becomes impossible to confine the implications of Rashkin's readings to the texts analysed. Nowhere is this more obvious perhaps than in the turn performed by her concluding sentence:

32

Finally, the phantom potentially offers a new perspective from which to analyse the transmission and transformation of literary theories themselves as well as the resistance, within the literary/critical community, to certain approaches to interpretation. (165)

It becomes clear, in other words, that no account *of* the cryptic or phantomatic can be readily dissociated from the *effects* it seeks to examine and describe. Rashkin observes:

> [V]iewing the text as bearing within it the traces of its own missing complement means that the text we encounter on the printed page is not yet realized as the text. (161)

But who decides on what this "missing complement" is and how to delimit it? Could this "missing complement" ever completely "realize" the text? Will there not always be the possibility of a supplement?

Rashkin's are not simply close readings: they ask us, in effect, to rethink the entire issue (again, in more than one sense) of "closeness". We are drawn to wonder, for example: "close" to *what*? In their attention to the anasemic (to what is *this* side of meaning) and to the cryptonymic (to words that hide), one might say that Rashkin's readings are – to invoke the title of a fragmentary cryptic text by Allon White – too close to the bone. But they are also, to recall the words of little Miles in *The Turn of the Screw*, "miles and miles away". In this sense they touch on more than what is in the family cupboard. These are close readings which engage with forces of relationless relation and distance without distance but which repeatedly seem to disavow it. Rashkin reads with an astonishing, one could say monocular, eye for detail. Of the word "monocle" for example, which she regards as crucial to an understanding of the haunted character of Spencer Brydon in Henry James's *The Jolly Corner*, she writes:

> When we pronounce in French this word (whose meaning and spelling are identical in French and English), we hear suspended in this spectacle the name of the man issued from the concealed cuckolding, the identity of the offspring born (or imagined to be born) from an adulterous union and palmed off as a legitimate heir. We hear in *monocle*: *mon oncle*, 'my uncle', the brother of Spencer's father. (118)

Or again, Rashkin reads with a sort of obsessive, single-track concern to discover lines of relation. Thus in the chapter on Poe she isolates the phrase "the lady Madeline of Usher" and asserts:

> It names Madeline as *the lady* (who) *Made* (the) *line of Usher*, as the incarnation or spirit of the woman who installed the fissure in the Usher House and replaced the lord Usher as the maker or progenitor of the Usher line. (136)

These instances may suffice to suggest what seems to the present reader a weird discrepancy between the potentialities opened up by Rashkin's largely expository reading of Abraham and Torok and the attempted unfolding of that reading in relation to specific literary texts. In this context it is a matter not so much of whether or not Rashkin's monoculism is convincing or even interesting, but rather of the more general paradox whereby she acknowledges the "theoretically infinite" processes "by which meanings are carried or borne from one place, state, or form to another" (79) but repeatedly argues for readings which (allegedly) shut down these processes and close off these "infinite" possibilities. The cryptic resonances of such shutting down and closing off are perhaps not fortuitous: they would comport with Rashkin's final speculation about the phantoms at work in "the transmission and transformation of literary theories themselves" (165).

family secrets

In its attunement to the ways in which texts work not simply in terms of "words on a page" but in terms of "a variety of lexical relationships including homophony, paronomasia, synonymy, interlinguistic synonymy, and anagrammatization" (79), *Family Secrets* is, then, a more disruptive, housebreaking book than it seems prepared to admit. It plunges reading into a new and uncanny thinking of what it means to be "in" a text. It phantomizes the present of reading through its foregrounding of linguistic shadowlands and "past dramas". *Family Secrets* reverses the temporality of clairvoyance, turning us towards the dizzying prospects not of "telling the future" but telling the past. Rashkin rejects the apparently commonsensical view that a psychoanalysis of fictive characters is absurd. It is not, she says, "that talking about a fictive character's past means treating that character as human and his or her past as 'real'" (7). She goes on:

> The past dramas I reconstruct from short stories and to which I trace characters' behavior have the same fictional status as the characters themselves. Both the 'life' of the character as it is presented in the text and the past I conjecture are fictive, which is not to say fictitious. The familial dramas that can be reconstituted as motive forces in each story are not without textual basis but are inscribed and readable in the narrative. It is thus not a question of inventing a false, fantasized past for a character but of understanding that the text, in each instance, calls upon the reader to expand its apparent parameters to include scenarios that are rhetorically, semantically, phonemically, cryptonymically, and symbolically inscribed within it. (7-8)

Reading involves expanding the parameters and redrawing textual boundaries which, Rashkin notes, "are not static but move constantly outward" (8). One expansion here might be to reconsider the temporal plotting of the phantomatic: in other words, could one not after all equally construe texts in terms of *fictive futures*? In a sense no doubt such a hypothesis is already inscribed within the temporal "falls" of the House of Fiction announced by the theory of the crypt. Another expansion might be in terms of the notion of a sort of extended family or rather *plus de famille*. Rashkin's study is constrained by (mostly tacit) assumptions about the purity of concepts of family and legitimacy. In this respect it may indeed seem that the concern with illegitimacy seemingly encrypted in many of the stories Rashkin reads is not ultimately separable from the *issue* of the legitimacy of her *readings*. This concern is inscribed in *Family Secrets*, for instance at the moment when she writes:

> While I would maintain that there is no concrete textual evidence to support an interpretation of incest in [*The Fall of the House of Usher*], it can *legitimately* [emphasis added] be proposed that the interlocking relationship [between Roderick and Madeline] ... is conducive to an incestuous rapport. (144)

The uncertainty of distinguishing here between "an interpretation of incest" and "incestuous rapport" perhaps serves to embellish a more basic observation, namely that Rashkin repeatedly circumscribes her analyses, stopping herself short with stipulations about "the absence of textual evidence" (see also, for example, 85, 183, 199), yet it is at precisely such points that her work broaches what is most radically generative and insightful. The law is cryptic. There is no pure space of the family, or of textual genealogy, or of presenting and passing judgment on "textual evidence".

34

nicholas royle

The phantom, after all, does not exist. It cannot accede to presence, even if conversely there can be no presence without phantoms. In her conclusion Rashkin proposes that the phantom

> is a *conceptual possibility* [emphasis added] with implications for evaluating the behavior of certain fictive characters in narratives from a nondevelopmental, nonphallocentric, nonparadigmatic perspective that preserves intact the specificity of those characters and the distinctiveness of their narratives. (157)

But this final acknowledgement of the phantom as "conceptual possibility" sits uneasily with Rashkin's opening assertion that "Not all texts have phantoms. Those that do do not all involve families or illegitimacy" (12). To this one feels compelled to ask: Don't they? How could one know? Isn't it possible that every text, including a book review, has phantoms?

Esther Rashkin, *Family Secrets and the Psychoanalysis of Narrative* (Princeton: Princeton University Press, 1992). Pages: 228. ISBN: 0-691069-51-4. Price: £17.50/US$29.95.

> It is self-evident that you must guard the secret of my indiscretion strictly and for all time.
> *Ferenczi to Freud, 19 October 1911*[1]

> Eternal discretion goes without saying!
> *Freud to Ferenczi, 21 October 1911*[2]

> He was hungry and was fed.
> *Freud, "Original Record" of the analysis of the "Rat Man"*[3]

robert white

MISSING A GENERATION
the rat man and hamlet

Could a book – a text – raise the dead? Or the questions of the dead? In this article I wish to discuss several texts which explore the consequences of the death of a father. I will discuss some lines in *Hamlet*, a reference Freud makes to *The Tempest* and in particular Freud's case history of the Rat Man. I want to attempt to indicate the more or less uncanny ways in which these texts seem to be affiliated. To this end, I will refer to Jacques Derrida's reading of the work of the psychoanalysts Nicolas Abraham and Maria Torok. Abraham and Torok have analysed how the family as an intelligibly historicized entity can become susceptible to being disrupted by events, memories, traumas which defy the sequence of generations, which despise the conventions of genealogy. Sometimes, when mourning fails or when the dead return to trouble the living, an individual cannot get free of the ancient history of his or her family. Sometimes the present cannot get over the past; sometimes the family collapses in on itself because it cannot lay its ghosts to rest. My premise is that such a collapse – whatever its existential manifestations – may evidence itself as a textual phenomenon or a performance between texts, and that this has implications for a study of Freud's writings at large.

Freud was fascinated with the interrelationship between the life of the individual and the larger history of the species. For Freud ontogenesis recapitulated phylogenesis, but this recapitulation could equally reverse itself in a strange contortion of mimesis, a perversion of historiographical logic. The motivation for such thinking could be said to derive from a sense of the historicity which infects the most intimate parts of the individual's life, of the way in which the life of the individual reaches into the ancient experience of previous generations. For the most part, this "Lamarckism" tends to a proliferation of heuristic narratives. Freud was prone to explaining away individual behaviour in terms of a phylogenetically transmitted disposition to acquire certain characteristics or experiences which would intervene where individual experience was wanting (with regard, for instance, to weaning, the dissolution of the Oedipus complex, or the witnessing of a "primal scene"). But he was equally convinced that a typical ontogenetic narrative could be trans-

missing a generation

ferred to human prehistory, and could uncover some of the repressed events in this history. This historiographical aporia tends to all kinds of confusions of understanding, and particularly to the inconclusiveness of individual texts. So, in *Totem and Taboo* (1913 [1912-13]), one of the few texts of which Freud was unequivocally proud, he uses ontogenesis (that is, the psychoanalytic theory of individual development) as a guide to the past – but only in order to assert that the life of the individual is irrevocably subject to the disturbance of history, and above all to the persistent but displaced effects of a sense of guilt relating to the prehistoric murder of the "primal father" by his sons:

> [T]he elimination of the primal father by the company of his sons must inevitably have left ineradicable traces in the history of humanity; and the less it itself was recollected, the more numerous must have been the substitutes to which it gave rise.[4]

Disguised in the failure of memory is the ominous return of the dead, the capacity of the dead to intensify their influence on the living. But anthropological speculation and historiographical virtuosity are not the only explanatory resources which allow Freud to come to this conclusion. As if all the detailed arguments and analyses which precede this assertion were insufficient to demonstrate it convincingly, Freud refers the reader to some lines from Shakespeare; to lines spoken by Ariel, half air, half body, Prospero's ageless surrogate child:

> Full fathom five thy father lies;
> Of his bones are coral made;
> Those are pearls that were his eyes;
> Nothing of him that doth fade
> But doth suffer a sea change
> Into something rich and strange.[5]

Ariel speaks these words to Ferdinand, whose response is: "[t]he ditty does remember my drowned father".[6] Ferdinand's father is, of course, not dead. Freud's interest in referring to these lines consists, one assumes, in their representation of the transformations to which a dead father is subject, the strange regeneration which death may instigate. The father in some form lives on, albeit in a different context, his body altered. In a rather similar fashion, Shakespeare is revived in another context, granted a vague, intuitive intelligence which obscurely anticipates psychoanalytic insight. But these lines appear in a footnote, at the bottom of Freud's page; they appear on the bed of the page, one might say, and one should not necessarily be surprised if they too "suffer a sea change". The literary collaboration Freud invokes may not quite be subordinate to what it "shores" up.

Freud was often confronted with the consequences of the death of a father, and the propensity of this event to cause all kinds of disturbances and unexpected effects. Not least among these effects was a creative productivity. Freud recalls that, for him, the composition of *The Interpretation of Dreams* (1900) was indissociably bound up with his reaction to the death of his father, "the most important event, the most poignant loss, of a man's life".[7] And even though he would later cast doubts upon the legitimacy of *Hamlet*, or rather raise questions about the identity of its author, Freud's well-known reading of that play (a reading to be found in the book on dreams) is predicated upon the fact of its being written very shortly after the death of Shakespeare's father, a coincidence which makes the play explicable for Freud.[8] The death of a father inaugurates diverse texts, texts which commemorate this event. The same incident looms large in the case history of the Rat Man, "Notes upon a case of

38

Obsessional Neurosis" (1909). The Rat Man responds to his father's death with a repetitive, ritualistic verbosity, and a troubled but keen capacity for anticipating a return of the dead:

> He used to arrange that his working hours should be as late as possible in the night. Between twelve and one o'clock at night he would interrupt his work, and open the front door of the flat as though his father were standing outside it; then, coming back into the hall, he would take out his penis and look at it in the looking-glass. This crazy conduct becomes intelligible if we suppose that he was acting as though he expected a visit from his father at the hour when ghosts are abroad [*Geisterstunde*]. He had on the whole been idle at his work during his father's lifetime, and this had often been a cause of annoyance to his father. And now that he was returning as a ghost [*wenn er als Geist wiederkam*], he was delighted at finding his son hard at work. But it was impossible that his father should be delighted at the other part of his behaviour; in this therefore he must be defying him. Thus, in a single unintelligible obsessional act, he gave expression to the two sides of his relation with his father.
>
> (N 204; 425-6)

The prospect of the return of the dead coincides with "a single unintelligible obsessional act"; the Rat Man's intellectual integrity is compromised, his behaviour given over to putting on a display of conflicting acts, perpetuating what is problematic about his relations with another generation. The possible return of the father ensures that what is outstanding between generations can continue not to be resolved; an ambivalence between son and father is renewed rather than dissipated. The Rat Man performs a kind of totemic ritual, at once placating the dead father and defying him. But if this suggests – in whatever way – a facility of transgenerational communion in which the dead are able to endure, this communion is shrouded in an overdetermined unintelligibility. The return of the father, the extraordinarily enduring influence of the dead, is achieved at the price of expository fluency, of the ability to act or communicate intelligibly. The Rat Man can renew contact with the dead, but this contact tends not to the efficiency of understanding between generations, but to irresolution, to an uncertain communication which does not exhaust itself in a definitive reconciliation of the parties involved.

The death of a father, it could be said, establishes a degree of uncertainty and indirectness of influence which nevertheless testifies to the strength of this influence. Some kind of disguise, metamorphosis or recontextualization accompanies the continuing influence of the dead. Moreover, this continuing influence is the pretext for textual productivity as well as a kind of methodological irresolution and a sense of immediate unintelligibility. The return of the dead is not obvious and coincides with certain interruptions of communication which nevertheless indicate an uncanny communicative power. Faced with the appearance of the ghost, in the first scene of *Hamlet*, Horatio is reduced to an elegant protestation of the breakdown of his interpretative abilities:

> In what particular thought to work I know not,
> But in the gross and scope of mine opinion
> This bodes some strange eruption to our state.[9]

Overcome by interpretative disarray, Horatio can only indicate that a breach has occurred in the fabric of things. And when the impossible happens, when the dead father speaks, this same problem is reprised:

missing a generation

But that I am forbid
To tell the secrets of my prison house,
I could a tale unfold whose lightest word
Would harrow up thy soul, freeze thy young blood,
Make thy two eyes like stars start from their spheres,
Thy knotted and combined locks to part,
And each particular hair to stand on end
Like quills upon the fretful porpentine.[10]

> The dead return, by this account, labouring under the pressure of an injunction not to disclose certain secrets. The ghost must skirt around the issue, hold something back. He cannot speak definitively. For the disclosure of secrets from beyond the grave would split open the head of the individual to which they are divulged, force out its organs of perception, transfix and petrify its corporeal organicity and integrity. The hair would attain a cutical hardness, almost like bone or dead coral. The ghost speaks eloquently about a knowledge which could violate the body, introducing alien material into the flesh. I note in passing that such a metamorphosis, such a violation of the flesh, would seem to be the precondition for the transformations imagined by Ariel ("[t]hose are pearls that were his eyes"). And the effect of the eruption of the dead with an incommunicable knowledge would be, to make a final preliminary point, a kind of obsessive secret memory which would be reminiscent again of textuality:

Remember thee?
Yea, from the table of my memory
I'll wipe away all trivial fond records,
All saws of books, all forms, all pressures past
That youth and observation copied there,
And thy commandment all alone shall live
Within the book and volume of my brain,
Unmix'd with baser matter.[11]

If this is not quite the same kind of memory as Freud envisages in *Totem and Taboo*, it shares at least an apprehension of the painful durability of another generation. Hamlet's obsessively guarded knowledge – not to mention the verbal copiousness it will induce – marks the persistence of another generation's barely spoken secret crimes. But the textual memorialization of these secrets, too. The dead father is (in) the book.

II

I will return later to these texts, what they share, how they are interimplicated, but it may now be appropriate to take up in a more theoretical way one question which is raised by them all. How would it be possible for there to be communication, however abrupt or abbreviated, across generations – a communication indifferent to death? The work of the Hungarian psychoanalysts Nicolas Abraham and Maria Torok may be said to be predicated on this question (a question which, however, is formulated specifically by Freud).[12] Abraham and Torok are concerned to account for the persistence of contact between generations, although not in the sense of any overt extension of mutual understanding. What Abraham calls "transgenerational haunting"[13] is a process by which family secrets are passed down from a parent (or a grandparent and so on) to a child. The hidden torments of one generation can be re-established in successive generations. Such secrets are preserved but not necessarily revealed or even understood. They are comprehended as Derrida puts it, gathered within, in order perhaps not to be understood (xiv, xl).[14] The most noticeably radical aspect of the work of Abraham and Torok is a rethinking of certain of Freud's topographical descriptions of the mind. Having postulated the process of "preservative repression" (as opposed to "constitutive repression")[15], the means by which a secret is interned in the mind, Abraham and Torok are faced with giving a metapsychological account of the location of what is interned. They do so by speculating upon the "presence" of a "crypt", or "innermost safe", *within the ego* of the individual.[16] The crypt preserves a secret which has been transmitted from the unconscious of an other where it had been buried (xxxi). This theory is extraordinarily interesting and, although a short account of its implications is unlikely to do it justice, in the present context an attempt should be made to examine some aspects of it. I would like to do so in a somewhat illegitimate, bastardized, Freudian fashion, in terms of topography, historiography, and economy.

The theory of an inclusion within the ego which in some sense encompasses the topography of an other (xxx-xxxi) does not allow for a duplication or displacement of the logic of the priority of consciousness over the unconscious (or vice versa); the crypt "no longer rallies the easy metaphors of the unconscious (hidden, secret, underground, latent, other, etc.)" (xiii). The crypt is neither integral to the ego (the "Self" as Derrida chooses to put it) nor foreign to it. It has a place in the topography where it is maintained as a "foreign body" (xvii),[17] both alterior and intimate to the "cryptophore", the one who bears the crypt.[18] The crypt is artificial and in every logical sense pernicious to the stability of the individual's psychical architecture. And yet it is secreted with the greatest care, magically and lovingly (xvii), by the most secure incorporative manœuvre. The crypt is preserved in this way because its unrecognised contents are shameful and incriminating – not necessarily for the cryptophore, but for a loved one;

the encrypted secrets are those to which a loved one cannot admit or which a loved one cannot absorb and therefore the crypt "is lodged, like a 'false unconscious', like the prosthesis of an 'artificial unconscious'" in someone else.[19] Preserved in this way, the crypt becomes a disturbing monument to the failure of any attempt to destroy for good what is most distressing. What is so painful as to be disavowed in the most strenuous way is locked away right at the cryptophore's heart, or right in the head. The crypt, however, is an intruder within the ego, not easily accommodated there. It is kept safe by being intimately preserved, but – being intimately preserved – cannot fail to make its presence barely felt, although never quite invisibly nor explicitly. The crypt, to put this another way, is "a wound that the subject does not know how to heal"[20]:

> [F]or the cryptophore, a desire already directly fulfilled, lies buried, equally incapable of rising or of disintegrating. Nothing can undo its having been consummated or efface its memory. This past is thus present as a *block of reality*; it is referred to as such in denials and disavowals. The reality cannot quite die, nor can it hope to revive.[21]

Or, as Derrida writes – gesturing towards the paradoxical psychical architecture of the cryptophore – the crypt "is erected by its very ruin, held up by what never stops eating away at its foundation"(xxiii):

> The crypt is always an internalization, an inclusion intended as a compromise, but since it is a parasitic inclusion, an inside heterogeneous to the inside of the Self, an outside in the domain of general introjection within which it violently takes its place, the Cryptic safe can only maintain in a state of repetition the mortal conflict it is impotent to resolve. (xvi)

Such would be the topographical disturbance to which the cryptophore is subject, the almost impossible interruption or eruption of otherness into the ostensible homogeneity of the ego. This interruption is harboured in the self, maintained as if it were a guarantee of integrity. The crypt, the prosthetic excluded intrusion (xiii, xix) thus hardens within, as it were, the flesh of the ego; it is:

> [A] parasitic inclusion, an inside heterogeneous to the inside ... the inside as the outside of the outside, or of the inside; the outside as the inside of the inside, or of the outside, etc. (xvi, xix)

But this foreign body is not unwanted, simply alien. It is also of inestimable value; it is a keystone indispensable to the topographical edifice even if it is flawed and dangerously destabilizing. The crypt stands as a precarious monument to the shame or the prohibited passion and illicit desire vicariously precious to the cryptophore. And despite the fact that the crypt is an artificial inclusion, it is vital to the extent that it preserves the living-dead (xxxvi). The crypt is, perhaps, like a pearl – like a pearl in the I – something precious but parasitic (whose excavation will kill what hosts and nurtures it) to be found in the shell: "a pearl is a hidden treasure that had to be looked for in its shell" (O 274). It is something dear, beloved but costly, in the inner external shell, the shell which Derrida remarks (reading Abraham) is not simply outside but must "always face on two fronts".[22] It might also be said that the metapsychological "supplements" and "additions" which Abraham and Torok have introduced into the body of Freud's metapsychology would be like a foreign body there, dependent but distinct (xliii).[23] But would Abraham and Torok encrypt Freud's work, or would their thinking be parasitic upon this work? It becomes difficult, as Derrida says, to stop switching around the "dizzying topology" (xix), to get a view from outside it, be clear of its maze-like lures.

III

Aside from this radical topography the work of Abraham and Torok is all the more sophisticated, and in an important sense confused, for encompassing or engrafting a temporal, historical, or historiographical dimension: the cryptophore is theorized as embodying or receiving a history that is effectively alien and undecipherable despite being composed of specific events, and despite all the material for its decipherment supposedly being accessible. This history presses to be revealed or unlocked, but the conditions for its disclosure and corroboration are not proper to the cryptophore in whom this discontented and disconnected history nevertheless survives. History is an included but occluded area of the cryptophore, forgotten or unknown but at the very site of consciousness. Cryptophores are informed by the secrets of others, the secrets of other generations, of which they are to some extent unaware despite always testifying that somewhere there is a massively overdetermined gap within. Something has passed silently across generations by means of a supereffective comprehension or secret-transference. The consequence of this process is the raising of a "phantom", a "heterocryptic ghost" perhaps, according to what Derrida names "the law of *another generation*"(xxxi):

> What haunts us are not the dead, but the gaps left within us by the secrets of others ... [w]hat comes back to haunt are the tombs of others.[24]

The secrets which are encrypted are not, "in the first place" (whenever or wherever that is or was), known as such. They represent an intimate unknown knowledge, what Abraham calls "nescience".[25] They are always already entombed, entombed long ago, and therefore absent from present understanding. This remarkable formulation problematizes everything about the phantom which might, in a perverse way, be comforting. The phantom is not a figure who plays the part of a more or less displaced interlocutor, reassuringly present to pass on information. One cannot reapply to the dead who return a model of effective communication based on presence, unless such a model could assume a simultaneous exposure to the abyss of history. The phantom cannot be interrogated. The phantom is always elsewhere, despite its radical topographical proximity to the cryptophore. The cryptophore does not conceal "truth", to put this another way, but what is already a lie; thy father('s) lies: "[a] ghost returns with the intention of lying: its would-be 'revelations' are false by nature".[26] This is as much as to say that communication with a phantom – if one can talk of such an enterprise – would also be subject to "phantom-effects", to the unavoidable pressure of a disingenuous knowledge, of knowledge whose destiny is to be made unknown even as its almost determinable place in the psychical topography intimates the possibility of it being tracked down definitively.

For, according to Abraham and Torok, the cryptophore acts according to the imperative that the tomb entombed within, the secret secret, must above all be prevented from seeing the light of day. The secret-bearer holds all the answers, but only in order to be able to guard them and, where necessary, to be able to throw inquisitive detectives off the scent:

The ego is given the task of a cemetery guard. It stands fast there, keeping an eye on the comings and goings of the members of its immediate family who – for various reasons – might claim access to the tomb. When it lets in some curious or injured parties, or detectives, it takes care to serve them with false leads and fake graves. Those who have visitation rights will be variously manœuvred and manipulated. They too will be kept constantly inside the ego. Clearly, the life of this guard of the tomb – who has to adapt to this varied crowd – is made up of guile, ingenuity, and diplomacy. Its motto is: there is always someone smarter than you.[27]

The cryptophore is cooperative and garrulous, but in order not to be understood. The cryptophore refuses or is unable to speak out the secret; he or she must "disguise the wound because it is unspeakable, for to state it in words would be fatal to the entire topography".[28] The cryptophore does not become the jealous archivist of a loved one's secrets in order to make the details of such secrets available to the diligent historian; the role of the cryptophore is rather to defy any historical investigation which tries naively to excavate "sources". Everything gets in the way of being able to research the sources, to recover the sources and the details. This would be the hermeneutic equivalent of the general principle of the cryptophoric state: "[t]he very thing that provokes the worst suffering must be kept alive" (xxxv). What seems to prompt investigative rigour also defies investigation.

The point of the introduction of historiography into topography is, as I see it, to confuse things irrevocably. Phantom-effects are not harbingers of understanding, but the traces or seals of a comprehensive unintelligibility which may nevertheless provoke all the machinery of an attempt at explanation.

missing a generation

I would now like to return to Shakespeare and Freud. How would it be possible, then, to represent the interimplication of historiography and topography? Something is unsettled in the I which reaches back to the tombs of others; in this place or structure history writhes uncontrollably, poisoning the present. "I have a foreign body in my head"[29], as Derrida says. Or, I have a graveyard in my head which I guard, in which the solidity of the graves and their stones is liable to being breached by the spewing out of zombified forms from another time. Something, then, hardening in and troubling the I; a mote in the (mind's) I:

> A mote it is to trouble the mind's eye.
> In the most high and palmy state of Rome,
> A little ere the mightiest Julius fell,
> The graves stood tenantless and the sheeted dead
> Did squeak and gibber in the Roman streets[30]

On account of the prosthetic intrusion, the graveyard in the head, the dead are not where they should be. The past is improperly alive, not confined to its proper place. Such would be the state of affairs occasioned by the transgenerational transplantation of secrets, of another generation infiltrating the cryptophore; the cryptophore who, I repeat, has a graveyard in the head:

> I then made some short observations upon *the psychological differences between the conscious and the unconscious,* and upon the fact that everything conscious was subject to a process of wearing-away, while what was unconscious was relatively unchangeable; and I illustrated my remarks by pointing to the antiques standing about in my room. They were, in fact, I said, only objects found in a tomb and their burial had been their preservation [*Es seien eigentlich nur Grabfunde, die Verschüttung habe für sie die Erhaltung bedeutet*]: for the destruction of Pompeii was only beginning now that it had been dug up ... Every effort was made to preserve Pompeii, whereas people were anxious to be rid of tormenting ideas like this. (N 176-7; 400)

I will pass over the specificity of Freud's reference to Pompeii – bearing in mind that he devotes a lengthy excavatory treatment to a literary account (or preservation) of Pompeii[31] – and point out that while everyone might like to be free of "obsessional ideas", their internment would be the cryptophore's abiding agony. But the reference to archæology, archæological fantasy, the analogy of psychoanalysis and archæology – even something like the "philosophy" of archæology – would be very much at stake with regard to a description of the cryptophore's mental "landscape". The archæologist sifts through ancient earth, the earth of ancient graves, in order to derive from discovered fragments a historiographical narrative based on unreconstructed artefacts or structures. The only truth available to the archæologist, by and large, is the always already distorted truth of, so to speak, synecdoche. He or she must to some extent imagine a plenitude of meaning, in the definitive absence of meaning. And – crucially – the archæologist is obliged to infer historiography from topographical speculation. He or she – like the psychoanalyst, perhaps, or the literary critic – deals only with the dead, but always with the dream of renovating the remains, transforming them into an impossibly plastic, intelligible or legible form. The archæologist dreams of restoring historical exactitude to the effacement of history, but is finally left with phantoms and graves; he or she aspires to the elegant, intelligible fit of historiography and topography, but ends up grasping only shades. So Freud may uncover the inner graveyard and the troubling displaced history it preserves, but to what end? He too, perhaps, will only be haunted by effects of distortion and secrecy which cannot be willed away.

By saying this, I am not suggesting that Freud is prone to a naive fantasy of digging for the truth of the past and finding it intact (such a fantasy would be reserved for his more deterministic successors). In fact, Freud theorizes the problems and the virtues of the archæological analogy in the most suggestive fashion towards the beginning of *Civilization and its Discontents* (1930 [1929]). In these strange, uncomfortably fitting pages Freud dispenses with his customary hypothesis that the unconscious preserves everything timelessly and indestructibly, and turns his attention – inconclusively, hesitantly, even reluctantly – to "the more general problem of preservation in the sphere of the mind", which despite its importance "has hardly been studied".[32] In order to illustrate how the mind would have to be conceived of if everything were preserved intact, Freud constructs a fantasy of "the high and palmy state of Rome" in which the dead would indeed survive:

> Now let us, by a flight of imagination, suppose that Rome is not a human habitation but a psychical entity with a similarly long and copious past ... This would mean that in Rome the palaces of the Caesars and the Septizonium of Septimius Severus would still be rising to their old height on the Palatine and the castle of S. Angelo would still be carrying on its battlements the beautiful statues which graced it until the siege by the Goths, and so on. But more than this. In the place occupied by the Palazzo Caffarelli would once more stand – without the Palazzo having to be removed – the Temple of Jupiter Capitolinus; and this not only in its latest shape, but also in its earliest one, when it still showed Etruscan forms and was ornamented with terracotta antefixes ... And the observer would perhaps only have to change the direction of his glance or his position in order to call up the one view or the other.
>
> There is clearly no point in spinning our phantasy any further, for it leads to things that are unimaginable and even absurd. If we want to represent historical sequence in spatial terms we can only do it by juxtaposition in space: the same space cannot have two different contents.[33]

Freud summons up a grand fantasy of omniscience. Such a scenario would no doubt expose crypts to the desiring glance, if this were possible. Here would be habitation for squeaking, gibbering phantoms (who else would walk amidst this extraordinary architecture?) The hypothesis of the crypt would necessitate a rethinking of or disabling of certain architectural or archæological suppositions, and any "common sense" notion of topography. The crypt is, after all, "erected by its very ruin, held up by what never stops eating away at its foundation". The same space begins to be capable of having different contents, but it is not possible to claim a view of this space. And this impossible architecture is what testifies to the fact that something has interfered with the temporal integrity of generations. Such paradoxes or aporias represent also, I would say, the ineluctable *difficulty* of the work of Abraham and Torok which succeeds at once in regenerating certain theoretical questions, expanding certain interpretative possibilities, while restraining the possibility of these questions being answered definitively. The fecundity of their work intimates also, and always, the imminent deterioration of an effort to displace paradox in favour of unified understanding. The barely conceivable account of the crypt and the phantom relates also to reading this account; the need for careful reading is enhanced by the "cryptic" nature of Abraham and Torok's work, but this diligent activity fails to dissipate its difficulty. One cannot call up a different view at will without expecting any such "view" to be defaced to the eye, or deformed by textual representation. Perhaps, like Freud, one is condemned only to imagine the opportunity of beholding every aspect of what lurks in the mind.

The phantom, then, abides with or within the cryptophore. They are in a relationship with one another of both temporal and spatial side-by-sideness and intermeshing. This is a very paradoxical relationship. What are incompatible interact. The hypotheses of the secret and its bearer might in this way reveal some repressed historical or historiographical features of (psychoanalytic) interpretation. If interpretation is to be authoritative, if it is to be at all exhaustive, it must insist upon the finality of death. But if a secret does not pass away with death, if a secret can linger scandalously, can endure long after it should have been forgotten, and if this happens precisely because the possibility of a straightforward revelation has long been foreclosed, then history becomes entirely anarchic and out of control. Abraham and Torok suggest that something can be transmitted across generations, but something – some message or secret – that remains undepleted by time, whose weighty undecipherability is neither eroded nor mitigated by its capacity to endure, to live on. To posit the presence of a phantom might offer a promise of its exorcism, its disclosure. In such a case, the vicarious interrogation by which the phantom could be forcefully understood (again assuming that such a procedure were possible) would attempt to exhaust history, to uncover every last detail and leave nothing to linger inexplicably and eerily. However, the work of Abraham and Torok may be directed against the hubristic assumptions underpinning any such attempt. One might begin to consider that there is a possibility that a "phantom-effect" might haunt ostensibly successful acts of communication or interpretation.[34] One would begin to be suspicious about such acts, and perhaps especially when they occurred (or were claimed to occur) in analysis. The confident cessation of interpretative effort – however partial, contingent, momentary – could be just a feint, a cover for the continuing effects of history and secrecy. To put this another way, one would have at least to consider the possibility that a felicitous explanation, the sly nod of those who proclaim themselves mutually understood, might guarantee the continuing consolidation of a secret rather than its disclosure. This possibility would have to be kept in mind.

IV

I would now like to turn to a further implication of the work of Abraham and Torok, what I shall call – with considerable hesitation – its "economic" dimension. I take economy to signify, on the one hand, Freud's use of the term to denote the satisfaction in discharge of a build-up of stimuli. But I also mean something in the order of the efficient settling of debts, and a kind of oral economy, an economy of speech. If some kind of exchange is going on – is ongoing – between, say, Freud and Shakespeare, this exchange would tend not to the diminution of what remains outstanding between their texts, but to a continuing circulation of interpretative possibilities between them. By the same token the resistance of Abraham and Torok's work to being explained away would exacerbate the extent to which their work tends not to be paid off in understanding. These formulas are a little crude but they bear on a problem fundamental to psychoanalysis. Psychoanalysis justifies its practice and its methodology according to the principle of the felicitous and instrumental exchange of speech between analyst and patient. Analytic speech is directed at making something explicit by – eventually – whittling down the profusion of symptomatic production to a compact, highly economical pronouncement. Speech at a certain point exhausts itself in explanation and the dissolution of symptoms. Freud announces the end of his treatment of the Rat Man in this way: "[w]hen we reached the solution that has been described above, the patient's rat delirium disappeared" (N 220). In this regard, one might ask what happens when this instrumental speech only renews itself, or when it cannot be represented except tortuously, textually, uneconomically. The conclusion of this article will be concerned with such a situation.

One could say that a failure of felicitous and economical explanation would be another account of the cryptophore's paradoxical topography. According to Freud, such a failure is what instigates and prolongs mourning.[35] Mourning proceeds or is unaccomplished so long as the individual who mourns fails to explain away the loss of a loved one. In mourning, an effigy of the loved one is preserved within the mental layout, and remains there subject to the restoration of efficient "reality-testing". An entity is preserved in an artificial space and an artificial temporality, and resists being consigned to history and the "outside world". Abraham and Torok have made the distinction between introjection as the mechanism of so-called normal mourning (which succeeds in dispensing with the loved object) and incorporation which characterizes mourning when it cannot dispense with the object (xvi-xix).[36] One cannot be sentimental about the latter process, which Abraham and Torok elsewhere call "endocryptic identification" (thus problematizing the agency of mourning).[37] Mourning which operates – or fails to operate – by incorporation can never be reconciled to the lost object which it is able to preserve. Incorporative mourning keeps the loved object at bay by including it within the ego; which would equally be to say that the loved object is able to be included within the ego only if it is at the same time withheld, held in:

> [I]ncorporation is a kind of theft to reappropriate the pleasure object. But that reappropriation is simultaneously rejected: which leads to the paradox of a foreign body preserved as foreign but by the same token excluded from a self that henceforth deals not with the other, but only with itself. The more the self keeps the foreign element as a foreigner inside itself, the more it excludes it. The self *mimes* introjection. But this mimicry with its redoutable logic depends on clandestinity. Incorporation negotiates clandestinely with a prohibition it neither accepts nor transgresses. (xvii)

Such incorporation ensures that what is perpetually disavowed will always return, even if what perpetually returns continues to be disavowed. It would be the exemplary cryptogenic process: "[c]ryptic incorporation always marks an effect of impossible or refused mourning" (xxi). Mourning which is impossible, refused or unaccomplished represents the failure of or unwillingness to settle debts with the past, to abandon a loved one – the father, say – to the past, to a dead memory. But to stay in touch in this way, to perpetuate an identification by incorporating a loved object, involves never being able to come to terms with a death, never to pay off or despatch the loved one. The cryptophore's endangered topography survives precisely because of the cryptic wound. And it is this intimate topographical anomaly which allows the dead, the secrets of the dead, surreptitiously to persist. This is, incidentally, very close to what Freud describes as being the consequence of the cannibalistic incorporation of the murdered primal father: "[c]annibal savages as they were", Freud writes, "it goes without saying that they [murderous brothers] devoured their victim ... and in the act of devouring him they accomplished their identification with him".[38] The recapitulation of this devouring in the totem meal represented at once a re-enactment of the original deed, and a placatory gesture to the dead father, a display of guilt which kept the father's influence alive: "[t]he dead father became stronger than the living one had been".[39] It will perhaps come as no surprise to those unfamiliar with the work of Abraham and Torok, or Derrida's reading of it, that the orality with which they associate incorporation is organized around a considerable paradox which has topographical or metapsychological implications. Cryptogenic incorporation is, among other things, the means by which a loved one (or the scene associated with the secrets of a loved one, a scene which may implicate the cryptophore) is neither "digested" in the mind nor vomited out. Derrida describes incorporation as "an act of vomiting to the inside"; cryptic incorporation involves a process – neither purely a fantasy, nor the consequence of a "real" event – of "eating the object (through the mouth or otherwise) ... in order to vomit it, in a way, into the inside, into the pocket of a cyst" (xxxviii).[40] The difficulties pertinent to this oral metaphor – not least among them being whether it is a metaphor (xxxvii-viii) – would include the difficulty of how to imagine an orality which both swallowed and vomited, achieving the finality of neither action. In the discussion of the Rat Man's orality which follows, this difficulty would begin to apply to the questions of analytic speech and communication. Could these imply an orality which both withheld and disclosed something (meaning, truth, the details of past events)?

I would like now to take up again the question of *Hamlet* and then return to the Rat Man. First an obvious passage from the former:

> 'Tis sweet and commendable in your nature, Hamlet,
> To give these mourning duties to your father,
> But you must know your father lost a father,
> That father lost, lost his – and the survivor bound
> In filial obligation for some term
> To do obsequious sorrow. But to persever
> In obstinate condolement is a course
> Of impious stubbornness, 'tis unmanly grief,
> It shows a will most incorrect to heaven,
> A heart unfortified, a mind impatient,
> An understanding simple and unschool'd;
> For what we know must be, and is as common
> As any the most vulgar thing to sense –
> Why should we in our peevish opposition
> Take it to heart? Fie, 'tis a fault to heaven,
> A fault against the dead, a fault to nature,
> To reason most absurd, whose common theme
> Is death of fathers, and who still hath cried
> From the first corse till he that died today,
> 'This must be so'.[41]

It is no great insight to invoke Hamlet's passion of mourning or – as some might have it – its "half-heartedness". But Claudius, rationalist that he is, indicates the manner in which to mourn is to intern the dead. To mourn effectively is to dispense with the dead; to mourn unsuccessfully is to remain permeable to the dead. History is repetitious, rhythmic, cyclical and in order to come to terms with or submit to its mechanical quality one must be separated from it dispassionately. With the death of a father, a certain circuit completes itself and recedes from the here and now of existence. "Reason" and "understanding" demand that the dead not be admitted into the heart, taken to heart. To bear the grievances of the dead, to take up another's unsettled scores with "obstinate condolement" is to remain behoven to an improper influence of the past, to what is not one's own; it is to sacrifice temporal – not to mention topological – integrity in favour of being in contact with, custodian of, what is immaterial and proper to a lost generation. And to maintain this generation is to surrender – willingly or otherwise – to indecision, prevarication and a verbal copiousness at odds with instrumental speech. Claudius is undoubtedly correct in his account of mourning: reason is overcome by the act of gathering in the past, not disowning it. "It shows ... /A heart unfortified"; a heart – or a head – that does not keep out an intrusion. And what is unfortified remains permeable, susceptible to being invaded by a parasitic structure, an inner fort capable of generating both subsidiary defensive enclosures and internal breaches: "the Cryptic safe can only maintain in a state of repetition the mortal conflict it is impotent to resolve". Fort. *Da*. To refuse or to be unable either to mourn or to stop mourning is to encourage the admission of a foreign body into oneself which will play havoc with all manner of fortifications, and with concepts of fortification and defence, in an exemplary disruption of understanding.

Such may be the painful consequences of the death of a father, and the preservation of the dead father. Freud quickly identifies that the Rat Man is besieged by ambivalences towards his father which are noticeably intensified after the latter's death. The Rat Man begins to blame himself for his father's death, and is therefore not always prepared to admit to this event. Uncertainty and conflicting loyalties and desires are increasingly fraught after the death of the Rat Man's father. I cannot possibly discuss the many complexities that appear in the case history, and would rather restrict myself to considering some aspects of the identification between the Rat Man and his father, and especially its disguised irresolution.[42] What should be noted is that a mimetic relationship between father and son is pursued and played out between generations, even or especially after the father's death. The prospect of the dissolution of this identification is what seems to invigorate it; the identification is reinforced by the prospect of its not being renewed. Freud reports the following exchange:

> He went on to adduce the fact of his illness having become so enormously intensified since his father's death; and I said I agreed with him in so far as I regarded his sorrow at his father's death as the chief source of the *intensity* of his illness. His sorrow had found, as it were, a pathological expression in his illness. Whereas, I told him, a normal period of mourning would last from one to two years, a pathological one like this would last indefinitely. (N 186)

Such pathological mourning would – if one were to accept Abraham and Torok's metapsychological revision of Freud's theory – be characterized by a secretion in the ego, the inclusion there of a prosthetic sepulchre which allows for a ceaseless identificatory negotiation with the dead to be continued through and beyond the grave.

V

What is so fascinating about this case history is that it exists in a more primitive form. This case has a precedent. This case is not closed. Freud's "original" notes of the first part of the Rat Man's analysis have extraordinarily survived – but, inevitably, as a fragment. It is worth recalling that – like that other fascinating fragment, the "Project for a Scientific Psychology" (1950 [1895]) – the "Original Record" is discovered after Freud's death. It returns from the grave, so to speak.[43] As such, this mutilated and spectral text is capable of triggering a certain phant(om)asmatic reaction on the part of its readers. Such a text holds secrets long thought to have been lost. Or – to put this in terms which I will justify later – it reinvokes or reveals a state of mourning in the published record of the treatment. By rights, the "Original Record" should be out of sight, long gone, dead. It should be the absent progenitor of the case history. And its preservation thus disturbs the integrity of the case history, since between the two texts it becomes possible in an almost unprecedented fashion to observe an instance of the return of the dead. For Patrick Mahony, the most notable scholar of the Rat Man texts, this occasion allows for an examination of what has been left out of the case history: the extent of "Ernst Lanzer"'s anal fixation (and particularly a dream of an anal phallus), his unresolved oedipal tie to his mother. The "Original Record" also provides Mahony with extra material with which to rebuke (it is as forceful as this) the Rat Man for a failure to accomplish mourning.[44] The "Original Record" seems to help to clear things up. In terms of my much more limited concerns what is fascinating is – on the contrary – the extent to which the "Original Record" not only intensifies what is already problematic in the case history but also promotes other difficulties which the case history had perhaps succeeded in effacing. Mahony's researches allow one so see that when Freud wrote up the case (if one can refer to such an event), he emphasized the extent of his patient's identification with his father and the obstruction this posed to the Rat Man's marriage plans. This identification was emphasized to the exclusion of much else. However the "Original Record" does not necessarily clarify the nature of this identification; rather it may indicate how this identification is even more vexatious than it is presented as being in the case history. The "Original Record" seems often to magnify the crisis engaging the Rat Man and his father, to indicate the extent of the Rat Man's failure to mourn effectively. If the survival of the "Original Record" deprives the act of rewriting of its ability to dispatch a precursor text, if this event prevents an exorcism in a kind of expository mourning, it also begins to unsettle the conclusiveness of the treatment described. The identification between father and son begins to seem more obdurate and more impervious to analytic unravelling than the case history would allow.

To settle debts with the dead, this is the stake. The Rat Man's father married advantageously, and could be sure of being able to pay his debts. But the question remains, Freud comments, regarding what previous debts – and one in particular – had not been acquitted. The question of what might still be in circulation is what circulates between father and son, keeps them in contact: "[t]he patient was uncertain whether he [father] had ever succeeded in returning the money" (N 210), "([d]id he ever pay him back?)" (O 290). The father's unpaid debts are transferred to the son as something unresolved, as an unpaid debt; after his father's death, the Rat Man has "phantasies of his father still being in contact with him", and that "his father might suffer because of his phantasies even in the after-life" (O 275). To this might be added that Freud's patient was allegedly in the habit of intellectually accepting the death of his father while acting as if the latter would imminently appear, and: "the prospect of seeing a ghostly apparition [*Geistererscheinung*] of this kind had had no terrors for him; on the contrary, he had greatly desired it" (N 174-5; 399). For in the prospect of the return of the dead, it was possible for the Rat Man to perpetuate his ambivalence towards his father, to keep active what was unresolved between them, facilitating and prolonging transgenerational communion by keeping this ambivalence in circulation.

Moreover the Rat Man had, apparently, two strategies by which he hoped to repossess himself, to recover self-explanatory autonomy: to confide in and be comforted by a male friend, and – at last – to obtain from a doctor a note commanding him to pay his debts indirectly, according to the strictures of his obsessional thinking.[45] The doctor can arbitrate the matter. In the doctor's room, the Rat Man comes across a book of Freud's (N 173) and seeks out its author, commits himself to analytic speech and to Freud's oral sanction. What role is Freud playing here? If it is analogous to that of the male friend, then there is certain cause for concern. For the ostensible assistance that the friend offers disguises a re-enactment of the mimetic relationship between father and son:

> When he had arrived in Vienna, however, he had failed to find his friend at the restaurant at which he had counted on meeting him, and had not reached his friend's house till eleven o'clock at night. He told him the whole story that very night. His friend had held up his hands in amazement to think that he could still be in doubt whether he was suffering from an obsession, and had calmed him down for the night, so that he had slept excellently. Next morning they had gone together to the post office, to dispatch the 3.80 *kronen* to the post office [Z–] at which the packet containing the pince-nez had arrived. (N 172)

The cryptopsychoanalytic function that the friend performs is able to ensure, finally, the payment of the debt that has caused the Rat Man so much trouble. But, the "Original Record" suggests that this is only in order to strengthen another debt; the Rat Man's relationship with his friend is not one simply consisting in the latter's support for the former; what emerges in the "Original Record" is that the Rat Man supports his friend financially, pays his debts, and:

> The way in which the patient secretly supports his friend is an identification with his father who behaved in just the same way to their first lodger, whose rent he used to pay, and to other people, too. (O 294)

Something is wrong here. The circuit that appears to be broken or complete is being secretly renewed. Certain debts remain unpaid.

And thus something unsettled in the I; "I have a foreign body in my head". The Rat Man's self, states Freud, was not his own, internally other, subject to an intrusion which was not recognized: he was able to feel "horror at pleasure of his own of which he himself was unaware" (N 167, emphasis suppressed); and, with regard to his scopophilia:

> [I]f the quality of compulsion was not yet present in the wish, this was because the ego had not yet placed itself in complete opposition to it and did not yet regard it as something foreign to itself. (N 162-3)

A disturbance of the ego of this kind allows for the comprehension of a crypt, for something to be hidden within the ego, not repressed away but repressed within. In the

missing a generation

"Original Record", what does the Rat Man relate his father having said to him? You will get ideas in your head. The Rat Man has had a dream:

> He fell into a violent state of emotion and knocked his head against the bed-post. He felt there was a lump of blood in his head. On similar occasions he had already had the idea of making a funnel-shaped hole in his head to let what was diseased in his brain come out; the loss would somehow be made up... [H]is father used often to say 'you'll get things into your head some day'.
> (O 271-2)

This extraordinary, suppressed, passage could be read in a number of ways. But it would certainly be conducive to being read in the light of the theory of the crypt. The Rat Man has something diseased, like a lump of blood, in the head, which is associated with a delayed memory of his father speaking. The father returns in some sense to prompt the pressure of something in the head. Moreover, this inclusion in the head is disruptive of any straightforward mechanics of orality. Not only can the "lump of blood" not be ejected out of the mouth, but it also would enter in so forceful a manner as to disable the body's vocal, glottal defence mechanism. The Rat Man makes reference to a particular device for torture, the so-called "Nuremberg Funnel" which was used to force water down or past an individual's throat, straight into the body, a device "which in fact his father used often to talk about" (O 272).

This, to my mind, gestures towards a very considerable problem with regard to Freud's work at large, a problem which I will be able to treat only cursorily in the present context. Simply, this problem arises from the question of the kind of disclosure to which psychoanalysis is committed. Abraham and Torok, despite always insisting on the possibility of the therapeutic and explanatory efficiency of psychoanalysis, have raised the possibility that analysis could be complicit in keeping secrets, could be haunted:

> Does the analyst have an ear for *all* 'poems' and for all 'poets'? Surely not. But those whose message he failed to hear, those whose deficient, mutilated text he listened to time after time – the riddles with no key – those who left him without yielding up to him the distinctive *œuvre* of their lives, these come back forever as phantoms of their unaccomplished destiny, haunting ghosts of the analyst's own deficiency.[46]

I take the textual or bibliographical metaphor to be of the greatest significance, and will return to it in a moment. But if analysis were to be haunted in this way, one could imagine its "deficiency" being described in the following ways: as a failure to pay off what is traumatically unresolved in the patient; and as a failure of speech, a failure to "speak the truth" (assuming that this would imply a failure of disclosive, explanatory speech which holds nothing back, vomits out the truth). What if something always prevented analytic speech from "saying" everything it knew or comprehended? This is a loaded question, for reasons which will become apparent.

The question arises, then, concerning what debts psychoanalysis can acquit. What is Freud's patient's choice of currency? Rats. When the Rat Man says, with regard to his payments to Freud, "'[s]o many florins, so many rats'", Freud comments that "he had coined himself a regular rat currency" (N 213). "This shows us that rats are something which is payable" (O 296-7). But – bizarre as the question may seem – what would it mean in this case to pay with rats? For all its gestures toward anality, the rat represents a powerful oral figure, and is bound to the Rat Man's father. The rat symbolizes the Rat Man's childhood orality, his propensity to bite, to incorporate:

> The notion of a rat is inseparably bound up with the fact that it has sharp teeth with which it gnaws and bites. But rats cannot be sharp-toothed, greedy and dirty with impunity: they are cruelly persecuted and mercilessly put to death by man, as the patient had often observed with horror. He had often pitied the poor creatures. But he himself had been just such a nasty, dirty little wretch, who was apt to bite people when he was in a rage, and had been fearfully punished for doing so. (N 215-6)

To incorporate, thus, the father('s secret):

> On one occasion, before he fell ill, while he was visiting his father's grave, he saw a beast like a rat gliding past it. ... He assumed – as might seem very likely – that the creature had just been having a meal off his father. (O 297; see also N 215)

Moreover, the Rat Man is disgusted at the thought of eating rats – like his cousin and his uncle who had found a rat's tail in a sausage (causing them to vomit). But the rat is also a notorious carrier of disease – syphilis for instance; rats represent the possibility of transgenerational infection via the father (O 288-9; N 214). The rat is a carrier of infection and a devouring agent, a symbol of mimesis and an overdetermined trope. In the light of the complexity of this symbol, one could at least suggest that, according to some facet of its logic, it represents not something which can be exhausted or explained away, but stands for everything which tends not to be resolved in the Rat Man texts. The rat seems to take in what passes between generations and survives across generations, as well as the paradox of

robert white

orality in which vomiting and eating, effectively communicating and speaking in order to avoid letting anything important slip, begin to be bound up inextricably.[47] I am in no position to pass a judgement on Freud's treatment of the Rat Man, but believe that to read this case history – and the other texts with which it is more or less overtly in affinity – is to be struck by all kinds of uncertainties, inconsistencies and disturbances which are to some extent exemplary of Freud's work. A speculation, then: to pay with rats is not to settle debts but to renew them, to infect analytic speech with secrecy, not to promote meaning but to keep the circuit open.[48] In Renaissance thought, the rat was believed to bring about its own death by drawing attention to itself.[49] But the rat may still be alive, undisclosed, after the Rat Man's treatment. Freud may not have ratted on him.

VI

This problem might be otherwise described in terms of the question raised earlier concerning whether haunting, or an unrepealed mourning, might infect textuality; could either of these states be proper to textuality, its vocation or calling? Could there be a calling between texts which would never speak openly, but would nevertheless transmit something – a secret, perhaps – in a highly efficient manner. Could textuality be cryptophoric? In the present context, the question can only be posed. But I would like to suggest that such a description would be particularly appropriate to psychoanalytic textuality, and above all to the case histories of Freud. The case histories appear more or less to be the record of the revelation in speech of the repressed secrets of a patient. In analysis – supposedly – a disclosive orality prevails, eventually tending to utter reve-

missing a generation

lation. But the record of this event or process supplements the assumed efficiency of revelatory speech in the most paradoxical manner. In the case history, psychoanalysis becomes other than itself. The case history memorializes unhindered speech by encrypting again what is apparently divulged, according to an exemplary principal of textual "distortion". For analysis is inseparable from a contract of secrecy, of confidentiality. The analyst is bound not to reveal the personal details of the patient. And thus, when it comes to textual presentation of an analysis, psychoanalysis becomes haunted by what it is *unable to "say"*. The disclosure proclaimed in the case history – like the cryptophore's dream of vomiting out the crypt once and for all, of emptying the head – is never realized; disclosure withdraws into the layers of secrecy which the text patrols. This would be built into the "architecture" of psychoanalysis insofar as the work of Freud is not accessible in any conceivable sense except through the text. Although I make no claims for the foregoing readings of Freud and Shakespeare, they might participate in a similar logic of secrecy. Such readings could never reveal anything except the inextricability of textual interlodging. Such readings could only engender the process whereby "phantom-effects" are multiplied and reinforced in reading, reading being an activity which perhaps never tends to the dissipation of phantoms. I will quote from the introduction to the Rat Man case the simplest instance of this in Freud's work:

> I should gladly have communicated more if it had been right or possible for me to do so. I cannot give a complete history of the treatment, because that would involve my entering in detail into the circumstances of my patient's life. The importunate interest of a capital city, focused with particular attention upon my medical activities, forbids my giving a faithful picture of the case. On the other hand I have come more to regard the distortions [*Entstellungen*] usually resorted to in such circumstances as useless and objectionable. If the distortions are slight, they fail in their object of protecting the patient from indiscreet curiosity; while if they go beyond this they require too great a sacrifice, for they destroy the intelligibility of the material, which depends for its coherence precisely upon the small details of real life. (N 155-6; 381-2)

This paradox seems rather innocuous, but it is as much as to say that psychoanalytic communication is necessarily incomplete, that it cannot help but find itself remaking what it claims to undo. Analysis distinguishes itself as a therapeutic procedure in being a mode of communication that circumvents or transgresses the obstacles that the patient throws up to block the analyst's investigation and explanation. But the record of such a therapeutic explanation depends on the restitution of these obstacles.

The typical and slightly desperate protestation of self-imposed censorship cannot mitigate the fact that Freud is thus inscribing himself in the same order of repetitious prevarication which psychoanalytic speech is designed to dispel. So long as psychoanalysis consigns itself to textual representation, it will of necessity become contaminated by secrecy and an encrypting urgency:

> I have already asserted that obsessional thoughts have undergone a distortion [*Entstellung*] similar to that undergone by dream-thoughts before they become the manifest content of a dream. The technique of this distortion may therefore be of interest to us, and there should be nothing to prevent our exhibiting its various modes by means of a series of obsessions which have been translated and made clear. But here

again the conditions governing the publication of this case make it impossible for me to give more than a few specimens.
(N 225-6; 443)

Freud's elliptical textuality commits speech into an order of greater or lesser unintelligibility which becomes essentially indistinguishable from, in this case, obsessional constructions. Distortion is characteristic both of obsessional constructions and of Freud's text. The exigencies of publication, of textuality, upset everything. But this is not by any means to suggest that one can discredit the psychoanalytic search for meaning. It is just that at a crucial point this search begins to impose upon itself an injunction not to reveal certain secrets. Freud's texts become secret-bearing. This, I think, has implications which I would like to sketch very briefly. What may be most notable is that the Freudian text is not cryptophoric in any exact sense; an account of this textuality would invoke all the methodological or hermeneutic uncertainties and confusions which, I have argued, make the work of Abraham and Torok so provocative but so disconcertingly resistant to being unpacked definitively. One consequence of this might be to disrupt any notional topography of psychoanalysis or psychoanalytic textuality. Derrida has hesitantly made the indispensable suggestion that there may be "a crypt or phantom within the Ego of psychoanalysis"[50], but this is not to say that it would be clear where one could locate such an entity. Something somewhere is lodged, engraved or engrafted like a foreign body; something continues to circulate and be renewed, fails finally to be paid off in explanation. But part of the phantom-effect to which texts are subject, to which they necessarily submit, or which they generate, would consist in the disguising of the very location of the crypt or the phantom. The crypt produces effects, that is to say, *in order not to be located* (xxxviii). So, if it was possible to read between some texts, to suggest their mutual uncanniness, I cannot see that such an activity would not necessarily confuse or confound the topography – or the attempt to construe a topography – of intertextuality. How could such readings be anything other than, in some sense, a collaboration with some more fundamental principle of secrecy? Such readings would not, I venture to suggest, to any extent elucidate what is paranormal or uncanny about texts or reading. If anything, such readings, this activity of "ghost-reading", could only generate further uncertainty.

Before returning to the questions with which this article began, I would like to quote a famous passage from *Moses and Monotheism* (1939 [1934-8]), the other Freudian text concerned with the endurance of the father from beyond the grave, and a text about which its author remarks: "it tormented me like an unlaid ghost".[51] Could a text mourn, incorporate its loss, intern the dead within and thus never relieve its own distress? Freud is discussing the texts relating to the life (and alleged murder) of Moses, the "history of King David", regarding which it is impossible to determine "how far reports about former times go back to early records or to oral tradition". In the absence of historical and bibliographical evidence, the Mosaic text is fragmented, distorted:

> Two mutually opposed treatments have left their traces on it. On the one hand it has been subjected to revisions which have falsified it in the sense of their secret aims, have mutilated and amplified it and have even changed it into its reverse; on the other hand a solicitous piety has presided over it and has sought to preserve everything as it was, no matter whether it was consistent or

missing a generation

contradicted itself. Thus almost everywhere noticeable gaps, disturbing repetitions and obvious contradictions have come about — indications which reveal things to us which it was not intended to communicate. In its implications the distortion of a text represents a murder: the difficulty is not in perpetrating the deed, but in getting rid of its traces. We might well lend the word '*Entstellung*' the double meaning to which it has a claim but of which to-day it makes no use. It should mean not only 'to change the appearance of something' but also 'to put something in another place, to displace'. Accordingly, in many instances of textual distortion, we may nevertheless count upon finding what has been suppressed and disavowed hidden away somewhere else, though changed and torn from its context. Only it will not always be easy to recognize it.52

Such a text conceals, according to Freud, but also represents a murder; and a murder of a father, let it be said, subject to the return of the dead, to perpetual mourning. The text also mourns. It participates in a continuing process of distortion, unable to express itself utterly and irrevocably, always resilient in the face of an effort at definitive understanding. But the text always displays its distorting function, cannot cover over the traces of its failure to be completely transparent or to hide its secrets unobtrusively. It mourns the passing of meaning, but its distressed state generates and encourages attempts to repair its damaged body. Either that, or the distorted text generates the attempts made by energetic readers to evacuate it entirely, to reduce it to nothing by divesting it of what it nurtures at its heart – its inconsistencies, gaps, contradictions. These traces are cryptic enough, but they nevertheless offer a spectral intimation of other, deeper secrets. But these will be even more elusive, and subject increasingly to the vicissitudes of textual distortion. Such a textuality seems to promise the possibility of recovering an entire, ideal, fully readable text — but who can say whether distortion is ever susceptible to being breached or overcome? The strange, elegiac familiarity of this passage with notions of crypts, secrets, phantoms even would, I think, gesture again to the discomforting possibility that the processes which have been analysed by Abraham and Torok are just that — processes which lead not to the discovery of secret meaning, but to the keeping of meaning out of reach. Textuality, one might say, is synonymous with secrecy. The text, its secrets, always haunt and are haunted. The crypt is not accessible to being exploded in definitive explanation, its truth is absent, other; it wards off intruders, even if it always leaves a trail or a track to entice them.

According to this account, one might be able to describe the text not as bearing an isolated secret, but being always in the middle of generations, harbouring phantoms which in turn give rise to other hauntings. Could the text raise the dead? Again, would it not be the text's vocation? According to the various accounts of the return of the dead discussed in this article, the dead father must be interred, lost sight of, must suffer some kind of degenerative transformation in order to be regenerated ("[f]ull fathoms five thy father lies/ ... Those are pearls that were his eyes"). So, could one not speculate that the text might be undergoing regeneration and degeneration, to the extent that the two processes would intermingle? Might the text not only be haunted, but at the same time haunt, always missing a generation and generating again? Could the text — the book — not be impossibly and magically both cryptophore and

56

robert white

phantom? In other words, how else could the dead be raised?

[G]raves at my command
Have waked their sleepers, oped, and let 'em forth
By my so potent art. But this rough magic
I here abjure; and when I have required
Some heavenly music (which even now I do)
To work mine end upon their senses that
This airy charm is for, I'll break my staff,
Bury it certain fathoms in the earth,
And deeper than did ever plummet sound
I'll drown my book.[53]

notes

I am grateful for the detailed comments of Sarah Wood during the composition of this article, and for the encouragement of Robert Smith. The final stages of composition were enlivened after reading the article by Nicholas Royle which appears in this issue of *Angelaki*.

1 *The Correspondence of Sigmund Freud and Sándor Ferenczi*, vol. I (1908-14) eds Eva Brabant, Ernst Falzeder and Patrizia Giampieri-Deutsch, tr. Peter T. Hoffer (London and Cambridge, Mass.: The Belknap Press of Harvard University Press, 1993) p305.

2 Ibid. p306.

3 *The Standard Edition of the Complete Psychological Works of Sigmund Freud*, tr. and ed. James Strachey (London: The Hogarth Press and the Institute of Psycho-Analysis, 1953-74) vol. X, p303; hereafter abbreviated *SE*. I will give references to this volume in the text. The "Original Record" will be abbreviated "O", "Notes upon a Case of Obsessional Neurosis" (1909) – the case history of the Rat Man – will be abbreviated "N". Where I have included parts of the German text of the case history, a second page number will be given, taken from the *Gesammelte Werke*, eds Marie Bonaparte and Anna Freud (London: Imago, 1940-52) vol. VII.

4 *SE* XIII, p155.

5 Ibid. p155n2; I. ii. 399-404, *The Complete Signet Classic Shakespeare*, ed. Sylvan Barnet et al. (London: Harcourt Brace Jovanovich, 1972) p1549.

6 I. ii. 408, ibid.

7 From the 1908 preface to *The Interpretation of Dreams*; *SE* IV, pxxvi.

8 Ibid. p265. See Mark Edmundson, *Towards Reading Freud: Self-Creation in Milton, Wordsworth, Emerson, and Sigmund Freud* (Princeton: Princeton University Press, 1990) p41-3; Nicholas Royle, "The Distraction of 'Freud': Literature, Psychoanalysis and the Bacon-Shakespeare Controversy", *Oxford Literary Review* 12:1-2 (1990) p109.

9 I. i. 70-2; quoted from the edition of *Hamlet* in *The Arden Edition of the Works of William Shakespeare*, ed. Harold Jenkins (London: Methuen, 1982) p170, hereafter referred to as *Arden*.

10 I. v. 13-16; *Arden* p216; see Royle, "The Distraction of 'Freud'" p114: "[s]trange *occupatio* – saying without saying, saying by not saying, remaining by disappearing".

11 I. v. 97-104; *Arden* p221-2.

12 See *Totem and Taboo*, *SE* XIII, p157-8.

13 Abraham, "Notes on the Phantom: A Complement to Freud's Metapsychology", tr. Nicholas Rand, *Critical Inquiry* 13:2 (winter 1987) p287-92.

14 Derrida, "Fors: The Anglish Words of Nicolas Abraham and Maria Torok", tr. Barbara Johnson, "Foreword" to Abraham and Torok, *The Wolf Man's Magic Word: A Cryptonymy*, tr. Nicholas Rand (Minneapolis: University of Minnesota Press, 1986); where Roman numerals appear in the text, they refer to this essay.

15 Abraham and Torok, "The Topography of Reality: Sketching a Metapsychology of Secrets", tr. Nicholas Rand, *Oxford Literary Review* 12:1-2

(1990) p65; "A Poetics of Psychoanalysis: 'The Lost Object – Me'", tr. Nicholas Rand, SubS-tance 43 (fall 1984) p4.

16 See Derrida, "Me – Psychoanalysis: An Introduction to the Translation of 'The Shell and the Kernel' by Nicolas Abraham", tr. Richard Klein, Diacritics 9:1 (spring 1979) p12; The Wolf Man's Magic Word, p76, 80; compare Abraham, "The Phantom of Hamlet or the Sixth Act: Preceded by the Intermission of 'Truth'", tr. Nicholas Rand, Diacritics 18:4 (winter 1988) p3.

17 See also "Notes on the Phantom" p290.

18 "The Topography of Reality" p64.

19 "Me – Psychoanalysis" p12.

20 "'The Lost Object – Me'" p5.

21 "The Topography of Reality" p65.

22 "Me – Psychoanalysis" p12.

23 See, for instance, "'The Lost Object – Me'" p9-10.

24 "Notes on the Phantom" p287, 288.

25 "The Intermission of 'Truth'" p3.

26 Ibid.

27 "The Topography of Reality" p65.

28 "'The Lost Object – Me'" p6.

29 Derrida, "Telepathy", tr. Nicholas Royle, Oxford Literary Review 10:1-2 (1988) p35.

30 Horatio, I. i. 115-19; Arden p173.

31 Delusions and Dreams in Jensen's Gradiva (1907 [1906]), SE IX.

32 SE XXI, p68; see Malcolm Bowie's important reading of this passage and others dealing with archaeology in Freud, Proust and Lacan: Theory as Fiction (Cambridge: Cambridge University Press, 1987) ch. 1.

33 SE XXI, p69-70.

34 See Nicholas Royle, Telepathy and Literature: Essays on the Reading Mind (Oxford: Basil Blackwell, 1991) p43-4, p24-5.

35 See "Mourning and Melancholia", SE XVII, p245-7 and passim.

36 See Telepathy and Literature p29.

37 "'The Lost Object – Me'" p5.

38 Totem and Taboo, SE XIII, p142.

39 Ibid. p143.

40 A similar confusion of orality is very marked in the figural logic of Hamlet. All the deformations which happen to the face, the scarring and liquefaction, the filming over of the flesh or its metamorphosis into bark or mildew, Hamlet's grotesque verbal productions (which are, to dredge up a cliché, only prevarications, blocks to understanding and instrumental speech), are juxtaposed (or otherwise deployed) with an equally unsettling image of the *oral grave*:

> I'll speak to it though hell itself should gape
> And bid me hold my peace.
>
> King, father, royal Dane. O answer me.
> Let me not burst in ignorance, but tell
> Why thy canoniz'd bones, hearsed in death,
> Have burst their cerements, why the sepulchre
> Wherein we saw thee quietly inurn'd
> Hath op'd his ponderous and marble jaws
> To cast thee up again.
>
> 'Tis now the very witching time of night
> When churchyards yawn and hell itself breathes out
> Contagion to this world.
> (I. iii. 244-61, I. iv. 45-51, III. ii. 379-81; Arden p196, 212, 310.)

The dead speak out, or are vomited out, of sepulchres, cerements, crypts. Speech is encrypted; that is, incorporated. This primordial speech might be absolutely allergic to the excessive, self-renewing communication of the cryptophore. The latter it might be said, prevaricates as it seems to offer disclosure – precisely in order not to speak out the most inner truth. The cryptophore's garrulous speech must feign sincerity to conceal the prohibition of the posibility of vomiting out once and for all the secret that is inside, in response perhaps to the efficacy of whatever process transmits the dead into the living. See also Claudius' remark, III. i. 166-9, *Arden* p285: "[t]here's something in his soul/ O'er which his melancholy sits on brood,/ And I do doubt the hatch and the disclose/ Will be some danger".

41 I. ii. 87-106; *Arden* p184-5.

42 I would refer the reader to the case history and the "Original Record" which, in my opinion, generously repay any amount of attention paid to them, and to Patrick Mahony's very stimulating and extensive commentary on the case, *Freud and the Rat Man* (expanded edition; New Haven and London: Yale University Press, 1987). Mahony reveals a great deal of extra material about the Rat Man's life.

43 Strachey comments on the posthumously published metapsychological manuscript: "in fact the *Project*, or rather its invisible ghost, haunts the whole series of Freud's theoretical writings to the very end" (*SE* I, p290).

44 See, for instance, *Freud and the Rat Man* p39, 42, 215. But for pressure of space, I would liked to have provided a reading of Mahony's book, mentioning for instance the analogy between his normative, teleological account of mourning and his desire for explanatory, factual, and bibliographical exhaustion. Mahony often corrects Freud on matters of detail or interpretation and – more often – is critical of Strachey's translation of Freud. Mahony also describes psychoanalysis as "pre-eminently the most oral" contemporary discipline (Mahony 135). Referring to a complete, bilingual (German-French) edition of the "Original Record", Mahony asserts emphatically that it is "*the only bibliographically competent publication that we have of Freud's writings at large and the case histories in particular*" (22). If such bibliographical competence were prevalent or possible this would, one assumes, prevent any effects of textual "mourning".

45 I am referring here to the incident which is described at the beginning of the case history (N 47ff). The Rat Man is unable to pay off a fellow-soldier who has settled an account on his behalf at a post office. I must again refer the reader to the text itself for the details of this incident.

46 "'The Lost Object – Me'" p4.

47 See "The Topography of Reality" p64:

> It would seem that, when the secret is too heavy to bear, it suffices to accept the exquisite defeat of unburdening. The tension having become unbearable, you would simply go to the police and give yourself up. 'To spill the beans and come clean', what a relief! the dream of all cryptophores. In point of fact, do they not go to see the analyst in order to give themselves up? Once they are there, they will have no alternative but to recognize that even this desperate relief is denied to them. From the first attempt on, they cannot carry out their endeavour. How indeed could one put the unnamable into words? If they were to do so, they would die of it, thunderstruck, the whole world would be swallowed up in this cataclysm, the police and the analyst's couch included. If they were tempted to speak, it was surely not to destroy the universe, but the better to protect it, even at the risk of turning it into a prison. So, after some hesitation, cryptophores will make a different choice, the only one open to them: they will turn the policeman-analyst into an analyst-accomplice and will relive with him or her between the words that which has no place in words.

48 Again – suppressed in the case history – is the coincidence of the name of the Rat Man's lady with that of a childhood sweetheart of Freud (O 280).

49 See a note to the *Arden* edition of *Hamlet* p319-20.

50 "Me – Psychoanalysis" p12.

missing a generation

51 *SE* XXIII, p103.

52 Ibid. p43. See Jean Laplanche and J.-B. Pontalis, *The Language of Psychoanalysis*, tr. Donald Nicholson-Smith (London: Karnac Books and the Institute of Psycho-Analysis, 1988) p124; the article on "distortion" is, as far as I can tell, about the shortest in this volume.

53 Prospero, *The Tempest*, V. i. 48-37; *Signet* p1564-5.

select bibliography

Abraham, N., "The Phantom of Hamlet or the Sixth Act Preceded by the Intermission of 'Truth'", tr. N. Rand, *Diacritics* 18:4 (winter 1988) p2-19.

Abraham, N., "Notes on the Phantom: A Complement to Freud's Metapsychology", tr. N. Rand, *Critical Inquiry* 13:2 (winter 1987) p287-92.

Abraham, N., "The Shell and the Kernel", tr. N. Rand, *Diacritics* 9:1 (spring 1979) p16-28.

Abraham, N. and M. Torok, "The Topography of Reality: Sketching a Metapsychology of Secrets", tr. N. Rand, *Oxford Literary Review* 12:1-2 (1990) p63-8.

Abraham, N. and M. Torok, *The Wolf Man's Magic Word: A Cryptonymy*, tr. N. Rand (Minneapolis: University of Minnesota Press, 1986).

Abraham, N. and M. Torok, "A Poetics of Psychoanalysis: 'The Lost Object – Me'", tr. N. Rand, *SubStance* 43 (fall 1984) p3-18.

Bowie, M., *Freud, Proust and Lacan: Theory as Fiction* (Cambridge: Cambridge Universiy Press, 1987).

Derrida, J., "Telepathy", tr. N. Royle, *Oxford Literary Review* 10:1-2 (1988) p2-41.

Derrida, J., "*Fors:* The Anglish Words of Nicolas Abraham and Maria Torok", tr. B. Johnson, "Foreword" to Abraham and Torok, *The Wolf Man's Magic Word*.

Derrida, J., "Me – Psychoanalysis: An Introduction to the Translation of 'The Shell and the Kernel' by Nicolas Abraham", tr. R. Klein, *Diacritics* 9:1 (spring 1979) p4-12.

Edmundson, M., *Towards Reading Freud: Self-Creation in Milton, Wordsworth, Emerson and Sigmund Freud* (Princeton: Princeton University Press, 1990).

Freud, S., *Gesammelte Werke: chronologisch geordnet*, eds M. Bonaparte and A. Freud, 17 vols (London: Imago, 1940-52).

Freud, S., *The Standard Edition of the Complete Psychological Works of Sigmund Freud*, ed. and tr. J. Strachey et al., 24 vols (London: Hogarth Press, 1953-74).

Freud, S. and S. Ferenczi, *The Correspondence of Sigmund Freud and Sandor Ferenczi*, vol. I (1908-14) eds E. Brabant, E. Falzeder and P. Giampieri-Deutsch, tr. P.T. Hoffer (London and Cambridge, Mass.: The Belknap Press of Harvard University Press, 1993).

Mahony, P., *Freud and the Rat Man*, expanded edition (New Haven and London: Yale University Press, 1987).

Rand, N., "Translator's Introduction: Toward a Cryptonymy of Literature" in Abraham and Torok, *The Wolf Man's Magic Word: A Cryptonymy*.

Rand, N., "Psychoanalysis with Literature: An Abstract of Nicolas Abraham and Maria Torok's *The Shell and the Kernel*", *Oxford Literary Review* 12:1-2 (1990) p57-62.

Rand, N. and M. Torok, "Questions to Freudian Psychoanalysis: Dream Interpretation, Reality, Fantasy", tr. N. Rand, *Critical Inquiry* 19:3 (spring 1993) p567-94.

Rand, N. and M. Torok, "The Secret of Psychoanalysis: History Reads Theory", *Critical Inquiry* 13:2 (winter 1987) p278-86.

Royle, N., *Telepathy and Literature: Essays on the Reading Mind* (Oxford: Basil Blackwell, 1991).

Royle, N., "The Distraction of 'Freud': Literature, Psychoanalysis and the Freud/Bacon Controversy", *Oxford Literary Review* 12:1-2 (1990) p101-38.

Shakespeare, W., *Hamlet*, ed. H. Jenkins (London: Methuen, 1982).

Shakespeare, W., *The Complete Signet Classic Shakespeare*, ed. S. Barnet et al. (London: Harcourt Brace Jovanovitch, 1972).

Torok, M., "Unpublished from Freud to Fliess: Restoring an Oscillation", tr. N. Rand, *Critical Inquiry* 12:2 (winter 1986) p391-8.

Torok, M., "What is Occult in Occultism? Between Sigmund Freud and Sergei Pankeiev Wolf Man", tr. N. Rand, "Afterword" to Abraham and Torok, *The Wolf Man's Magic Word*.

> Indeed, till I reached a very mature age I always ate badly.
> *Friedrich Nietzsche,* Ecce Homo

> I have a taste only for that taste.
> *Jacques Derrida, "Dialanguages"*

Between Abraham and Thyestes, between sacrifice and cannibalism, God and dinner, there is the question of the ethical and the good. Could Atreus's vice ever be understood as generosity and could Abraham's willingness to sacrifice his son to the Absolute come to resonate in a register of obligations that determines the Good? Can murdering and eating another uncover a conception of relation and even a model ethics? Of course not. And yet what if the object of sacrifice is sacrifice itself and what if dining is really a symbolic act of mourning? In an attempt to understand the exchange between ethics and eating, incorporation and introjection, experience and communication, *oikos* and mourning, nutrition and the Good, it is time we came to terms with the aporetic and rhetorically slippery ethics of "Eating Well".

Expounding on why he is so clever, Nietzsche, in *Ecce Homo*, insists upon his diet – he knows "a question on which the 'salvation of humanity' depends far more than on any theologian's curio: the question of *nutrition*" (*Ecce Homo* 237 (further refs. will be abbreviated *EH*)). To eat – to eat well – is to be and become virtuous. If this is a treatise on the body, and Nietzsche's own ailing body in particular, it is also the inscription of a menu and the rigorous imposition of a diet – "*Une nouvelle diététique*", Sarah Kofman names it. Ingestion becomes a moral act when Nietzsche rhetorically conflates national cuisines with national "spirit", rendering "[t]he German spirit ... an indigestion", because "it does not finish with anything" (238). The Germans are what they

sara guyer

ALBEIT EATING
towards an ethics of cannibalism

eat, and the poorly cooked meats and vegetables Nietzsche so despises never leave the body once ingested. They are unassimilable. Indigestion, indeed incorporation, at once defines "German-ness" and identifies it as always in excess of itself, perpetually failing to swallow itself.

Eating badly, Nietzsche therefore explains, is to eat without regard for the self and with an indifference for one's own needs. This altruism is impersonality, whereby one eats to please one's hosts or to bolster the nation – "for the benefit of cooks and other fellow Christians" (237). For Nietzsche, then, eating can never be a task of obligation to another (this evades the Good), but is rather always a dedicatory ingestion of things that are good to eat. No coffee or alcohol ("just like Richard Wagner, who converted me" (239)), soup after the meal, tea in the morning, and plenty of water throughout the day. And one should

albeit eating

also eat meat: Nietzsche is "an opponent of vegetarianism from experience" (239). Anti-vegetarianism for Nietzsche exudes a certain virility in the face of his insistence upon abstention from alcohol. Derrida too questions vegetarianism and so renders eating an ethico-philosophical issue.[1] Clearly differentiating himself from unproblematised vegetarianism in "'Eating Well' or the Calculation of the Subject", an interview conducted by Jean-Luc Nancy, Derrida rather suggests an economy of ingestion where "eating well" is eating all. Negotiating between the possibility of the subject and the exclusion of the animal from even the most original conceptions of subjectivity, Derrida nevertheless reassures his readers that he is "not recalling this [the status of animal in Heidegger] to start a support group for vegetarianism" ("Eating Well" 112 (further refs. will be abbreviated EW)). In fact, the radical reversal of the situation of the animal coupled with certain rhetorical strategies leave Derrida an eater not only of animal flesh in particular, but also of flesh in general. And so this founding of a subject beyond humanism comes to resonate as an ethics of cannibalism: *Il faut bien manger*.

Is the question of "Eating Well" (*Bien Manger*) an inquiry into "eating" (*manger*) or into "the Good" (*Bien*)? *Bien* at once announces the proper and the moral, the restricted economy and the absolute spirit. It is the "good" of *Beyond Good and Evil* and remarks the commonwealth (emphasis on wealth) in *le bien public*. And yet, *un homme de bien* is not merely a good man, but a man of property as well. *Le Bien* has a part in real estate and in charity work. *Bien* is in fact *oikos* itself, when *oikos* is "... the home, ... the proper, ... the private, ... the love and affection of one's kin" (Derrida 1995a, 95). Following this definition, *le Bien* is therefore the scene of woman's impossible place and her necessary displacement, a point that can hardly be overlooked when "having once become committed to the path of this topography [of woman's place, but also of place generally], we would inevitably find ourselves back 'at home' or 'in the kitchen'" (Derrida 1982, 93). Of course it is the kitchen, and the work of the kitchen that is uniquely human[2], that announces a certain economy of the Good and that also reinscribes another economy, one of sacrifice and so of eating.

If *manger* is less ambiguous than *bien* in its translation, it is also less determinate in its meaning and demands to be read other than literally. This double movement – towards a definition on the one hand and away from it, into symbolization on the other – already situates the predicament of eating well. Moreover, it is the simultaneity of an idiom where eating well is not only about "eating" and "well", but about "eating well" that implies eating until one is full, eating with grace, and satisfaction. As Nietzsche articulates this association:

> A few more hints from my morality. A hearty meal is easier to digest than one that is too small. That the stomach as a whole becomes active is the first presupposition of a good digestion. (*EH* 239)

Nietzsche's private morality, Nietzsche's body, becomes a public domain with this assimilation and digestion. The instruction is not "Bon Appetit!" or "Have a good meal!" This is a different good, as it is a different kind of dining. And one must eat.

"Eating Well" is an interview – perhaps a dialogue – between two about one, between friends, about the subject. And it is the very situation of this exchange – a spoken one, born of the scarcity of time (i.e. "Jacques Derrida was unable to write a text in time" (Derrida 1995b, 473n)) and the sound of the

sara guyer

voice – which already raises the question of mouth-work at the heart of this ethic. As Derrida explains in another interview undertaken some years earlier:

> ... [W]hat I like to do, for example, is to give courses in my own manner: to let be heard in what I write a certain position of the voice, when the voice and the body can no longer be distinguished – and obviously this passes by way of the mouth. I have a taste only for that taste, for what is written by tongues/languages, from mouth to ear, from mouth to mouth, or from mouth to lips ... (Derrida 1983a, 141)

The presupposition of an indistinguishable relationship between the body and the voice in speaking announces exactly what is at stake in Derrida's later interview with Nancy. That the body might pass through the orifices – mouth, ear, etc. – to be swallowed, savoured, rejected, returned, but most of all affirmed in every exchange of voices renders the interview format exemplary for (and of) coming to terms with this ethic of ingestion and the eerie specificity of "a taste only for that taste". Moreover, Derrida's own translation of this mode of communication – "*entrevoir*" – explained in yet another interview, and suggestively one about sexual difference, further articulates the stakes of "Eating Well". *Entrevoir*, to inter-view, is "[i]n French, to take a glimpse, to look into the space between things" (Derrida 1982, 90). A thought of the subject as a relation of "eating well" therefore takes place in witnessing the silences, gaps, and spaces that already pocket essences in question.[3] And we might remember that here "the feminine is understood as spacing" (Wigley 137).

The interview – undertaken in response to the question (posed to twenty French philosophers) "Who comes after the subject?" – thrives on an engagement with Heidegger and attempts to render a sufficient relation to the other as the grounds for subjectivity. This shared conception of the self and other arrives with the subtle and unnamed presence of psychoanalysis, and particularly of Nicolas Abraham and Maria Torok. Working under their sign, I want to render apparent the implications of incorporation and introjection for Derrida's conception of "eating". When the source and scene of *oikos* is mourning, the presupposition of eating the other, even if always only a metonymy, demands that we recognise the stakes of this ingestion.

Derrida offers a relation of "eating well". If "eating well" is an ethics, it is also a cannibalism. That the one could be the other seems not only the height of paradox, but also the place of a devastation so radical that it defies any possibility of reconciliation. The aporia of these questions is the intersection of the paradigmatic and the "real". This is a century of concentration camps as it is the time of a nostalgic and radical privileging of blood relations.[4] So too is this an epoch where metaphysics, according to Derrida, has critically failed to "*sacrifice sacrifice*" (EW 113).[5] The consequence of this conservation for disruptive "[d]iscourses as original as those of Heidegger and Levinas" is that they "nonetheless remain profound humanisms" (113). The sacrificial valence of philosophy in the West is met by Derrida's cannibalism. While the paradox is apparent, its implications for an ethics have yet to be thought. "Eating well" imposes an economy of strange reserve, where every generosity becomes another instrument of salvation. Calling the very possibility of the Good (*du Bien*) into question, while at the same time insisting upon its necessity, an ethics of cannibalism recognises the status of the other and then compels us to eat him.[6]

albeit eating

The question of eating itself does not surface until the end of the interview and is preceded by a discussion of animality and of the other, of *Dasein* and subjectivity. What is in question is the difference between "Thou shalt not kill" and "Thou shalt not put to death the living in general" (113). The former is taken to refer only to the virile subject – always man, *Dasein*, the other who is the same as the only one for whom this prohibition holds.[7] If on the one hand the stakes of problematising the prohibition against killing are the return of a repressed humanism in the work of both Heidegger and Levinas, the alternative to this general edict seems a situation where every relation takes place between mourning *or* melancholia. Here, the body becomes a building, a house, and the locus of the internalised structure of *oikos*. Because Derrida has already articulated the slippage (metonymy) between body and voice, the body as the reworked scene of the proper, in this (interview) context, also recalls the "secret of the mother tongue" (Derrida 1995a, 88). This body, this home, becomes the scene of a language, "the *Geheimnis* of language that ties it to the home, to the motherland, to the birthplace, to the economy, to the law of the *oikos*, in short to the family and to the family of words derived from *heim* – home, *heimlich*, *unheimlich*, *Geheimnis*, etc." (88). And it is in this space of the maternal, of the proper in its becoming *atopic* that the secret of sacrifice – that Isaac's sacrifice, but also the more quotidian sacrifices incurred by the hungry and the diseased – takes place.[8]

Arguing that in the work of Heidegger and Levinas "there is a place left open in the very structures of these discourses (which are also 'cultures') for a noncriminal putting to death" (EW 112), Derrida shifts the status of these deaths (animal and human) – all of which are rendered equal violences, for, as Jonathan Swift reminds us, the ingredients for a ragout are various – to a rhetorical register. This move blurs any heretofore apparent notion of the good or the proper (*bien* and *oikos*). In citing the Napoleonic code as the inscription of "the concept of subject we are talking about" (114), Derrida acknowledges an historical situation where like animals or children, women too were the property of men and belonged to an economy of exchange between fathers and husbands. When imposed deaths are treated differently, when some are criminal and others are "legal" (because one is a woman) or "necessary" (because one is of a certain race), there is always a structure of sacrifice.[9] Indeed, there is a structural contingency between heads of state and heads of households – both of them *chefs* of a carnivorous kind. The former is murderous because he must be (willing to go to war, willing to divide and conquer – to devour). Heading the household remains ingestive, because the household is always ingested. This head ("father, husband, or brother" (114)) – a subject – "does not want just to master and possess nature actively. In our cultures, he accepts sacrifice and eats flesh" (114). He demands to "eat well". In this, the conservation of sacrifice becomes emblematic of the situation of mourning at the very core of Western metaphysics. The legal putting to death of another, when that other is neither virile nor male are "the executions of ingestion, incorporation, or introjection of the *corpse*" (112, my italics). Not only is this ontologico-ethically not murder, but, in fact, the decentering of the subject names it dinner. With this move, in addition to promising an "ethics of cannibalism", Derrida replaces the "real" with the "symbolic", the living body with the dead corpse, eating with anthropophagy, and in moving from outside to inside, finds himself

sara guyer

so deep within the body that real deaths and sufferings – social and political abuses – belong only to mourning and to symbolic ingestion.[10] This risky loss of loss will become more apparent in a closer consideration of eating well.[11]

Derrida explains the ingestion of the "animal" corpse is "as real as it is symbolic", while it is "a symbolic operation when the corpse is 'human'" (112). This further move recognises that the "symbolic" devouring of the human corpse imposes the structure of cannibalism without its actual enactment. One always eats another; even if one eats a "human" that human is always eaten as other than human (his language is different, she is feminine, one only eats the dead ...), so that – as with the animal – the human is first situated outside legality and prohibition before he is served for dinner.[12] The terms of appropriation suggested here – incorporation, and so eating, but also their tenors in political, sexual, and friendly relations – are all moments of mourning. As Derrida will argue, it is not that this sacrificial structure should be entirely withdrawn, but rather that it should arrive with even greater responsibilities and stronger discretions.[13] It is "eating well", as opposed to merely eating. This economy and sense of the proper resonates in Abraham and Torok's analysis of the work of mourning. In fact, it is from this "theory" of mourning, where the other remains "non-subjectivable" (107), that Derrida derives his own conception of eating.

Following the initial work on introjection set out by Sándor Ferenczi, Abraham and Torok in an essay titled "Mourning *or* Melancholia: Introjection *versus* Incorporation" recognise mourning as taking place between two consistently related poles: incorporation and introjection.[14] The former cannot accommodate loss and so instead warrants and imposes a silence (a story and a crypt) that shields the one who should suffer from both the source of the pain incurred in loss and the strange, even magical, contrivances that have allowed for its disappearance. Incorporation then is the situation of a secret lodged in the unconscious (a false unconscious) as a monument to the dead, which at the same time keeps the dead alive. This secret – which is always illegal, and always circulates deep within the body of the living (even if it is the surreptitious (written) body of the dead) – is perpetually disclosed, albeit secretly.[15] The confusion of the *atopic* with the *hypertopic* introduces a corporeal economy where outside and inside, self and other, become substitutive, because unlocatable, terms. In this, the crypt is a monument so excessive that it tarnishes and interrupts one's sentences, even if this occurs in only the most obscure and almost indiscernible ways. This symptom of incorporation is demetaphorisation or antimetaphor, which is "the active destruction of representation", where words' "very capacity for figurative representation is destroyed" (*The Shell and the Kernel* 132 (further refs. will be abbreviated as *SK*)). Incorporation itself is a situation of antimetaphor.[16]

With the rejection of representation, words become things and these objects (as undisclosed memories, secrets, siblings, parents, etc.) are swallowed and eaten. According to Abraham and Torok, the source of this devouring is shame, a shared guilt between the dead and the living: "the cryptophoric subject's solution, then, is to annul the humiliation by secretly or openly adopting the literal meaning of the words caused by humiliation" (131). Incorporation is consequently always "false incorporation", it suffers an inability to accommodate language and representation and so utters a perpetual demand for food: "[t]he desperate

albeit eating

ploy of filling the mouth with illusory nourishment" (129). Antimetaphor can be understood then as ingestion rather than representation, and so as the incorporation of a secret (whose locus is a thing) rather than its sharing in language. This is what Abraham and Torok call "one mouth-work in place of another" (128).

Introjection – as "true" incorporation – on the other hand establishes a "community of empty mouths", whereby ingesting the other takes place at the level of representation and so of language. The formal identity of incorporation and introjection in the shared image of the open mouth nevertheless suggests the profound difference of melancholia and mourning, of retention as total censorship versus recognition in sharing. If the former, incorporation, is always about the literalisation of the situation, the latter, introjection, is the repetition of the very first loss and the first moment of grief in the necessary shift away from the mother's breast and towards the articulation of absence and desire. The mouth filled with food and with the body, becomes the mouth filled with words, and so introjection – in its ability to utter a demand and recognise contiguity – communicates metonymically. The mouth filled with words is always the empty mouth, but that very emptiness involves the sharing of a secret – both a parcelling of the self out into the world and an unwavering sense of representation and communication.[17]

Abraham and Torok outline the relationship between incorporation and introjection by explaining that

> the literal ingestion of food becomes introjection when viewed figuratively. The passage from food to language in the mouth presupposes the successful replacement of the object's presence with the self's cognizance of its absence. (128)

What is most interesting here, and what will lead us back to a reading of Derrida is the deliberation (and de-liberation) that takes place at the orifices. In this, it is the shift from literal to figurative – at the site of eating – that determines introjection. This hermeneutic recognises an act as symbolic and representative rather than identical to itself. What is the vehicle and what is the tenor; what is literal and what is figurative? The risk is that eating is never just eating and, moreover, that if ingestion always takes on a figurative status, its real situation – in a sacrificial scene of the so-called West, for instance – will never have any more than symbolic value. And so what is required is an important differentiation between the symbolic and the representative.

The underlying importance of a conception of mourning to Derrida's figuration of the ethical, emphasises the necessity of distinguishing between symbolic and representative ingestions. In this, the import of representation affirms that eating *qua* eating is not at all what is at stake in Derrida's remarks. At the same time, and, as Nietzsche explains, in the most maniacally literal prescriptions, one must eat nutritiously. When the animal and the human are simultaneously in question, which is to say, when it is the viability of the subject that is in question – and when differentiation between these terms is said to lead back to a certain humanism (of which both Heidegger and Levinas are the purveyors) – it would seem that Derrida chances an already incorporated reading of Abraham and Torok in proposing that we eat the other. As if repeating the symptomatic movement Abraham and Torok delineate, Derrida literalises the figurative strategy of mourning which in the psychoanalytic schema always maintains a syntactic and semantic valence. Because voice and body in Derrida's work are indistinguishable, and because the voice always traces language even in writing, incorporation comes to be understood under the aegis of the body and is therefore described as literal eating.[18] The interview consequently seethes with an ambiguity – or incalculability – which, although self-aware, needs to be further drawn out.[19]

In shifting the conception of activity at orifices from the breast (Abraham and Torok) to the phallus, from the other to the self, Derrida attempts to explicate the sense in which ingestion is always ingestion of the same and so is the establishment of the (*carno-*)phallogocentric self-identicality of the subject (EW 113). Because this festering virility has come to find its devastation, a new relation that might emblematise subjectivity is posited here. If the term of introjection is sharing, it is the "metonymy of 'eating well' (*bien manger*) that would always be the rule" (114). In establishing this exchange, the relationship between animal and human, dead and living, self and other, and the overall sense of the "good" are re-conceptualised. Eating well is a metonymy; it is the introjective situation of representation, communication, and community.[20] Moreover, Derrida's strategy involves inscribing ethico-moral determinations on the most everyday of occurrences.[21] As he explains:

> The moral question is thus not, nor has it ever been: should one eat or not eat, eat this and not that, the living or the nonliving, man or animal, but since *one must* eat in any case and since it is and tastes good to eat, and since there's no other definition of the good (*du bien*), *how* for goodness sake should one *eat well* (*bien manger*)? (115)

It is in this first explication of "eating well" that Derrida links the good – *du bien* – in its ethical situation (but also resonating with all of the implications of taste and of distinction) with eating. The simultaneously "symbolic" and "real" instances of eating at play in this formulation disrupt any sense of calm dining, or for that matter calm mourning. In at once addressing incorporation and introjection, anthropophagy and nonanthropophagy within the context of the Good [*du Bien*], not only is every other ethics and every other humanism called into question, but the sheer ambiguity or incalculability of the situation always threatens (and reveals the threat of) sharing as well.

If this is an affront to historical conceptions of the Good, it at the same time interrupts Nietzsche's sense of self in *Ecce Homo*. In fact, dining in Nietzsche's exposition always emblematises a national taste and hence a national/cultural instinct, need, and desire in addition to a moral framework that identifies what is and is not good to eat. Eating becomes a question of the individual, of differentiating oneself from the other (oftentimes abominable) national cuisine in order to "eat to attain your maximum strength" (*EH* 237). The literality of this ingestion replaces "questions that are none" (236), theological questions. And this preoccupation with "what to eat" leads Nietzsche to illuminate himself – because neither ascetic nor theologically interested when it comes to ethics – as "too *questionable*, too exuberant" (236) to substitute God for "real" salvation. And it is eating as salvation – as the appropriation (and partial assimilation) of the other, the corpse – that determines the symbolic as well as the real status of "eating well". Moreover, because incorporation and introjection always overlap, and because "true incorporation" or "pure introjection" is consequently impossible, Derrida explains:

> The infinitely metonymical question on the subject of 'one must eat well' must be nour-

albeit eating

ishing not only for me, for a 'self', which, given its limits, would thus eat badly, it must be *shared*, as you might put it, and not only in language. 'One must eat well' does not mean above all taking in and grasping in itself, but *learning* and *giving* to eat, learning-to-give-the-other-to-eat ... It is a rule of offering infinite hospitality. (EW 115)

The subject of "One must eat well" is the question at once of what eating is (speaking, sharing, mourning, eating *for real* ...) and consequently of who or what is eaten (our words or our neighbors or our enemies or our farm animals ...). Moreover, the very possibility of a self, and a conception of *sharing* "as you might put it", when you is obviously Jean-Luc Nancy who has already written about sharing, voice, and community, emphasises the sense in which eating (like relation) always involves becoming plural with the introduction of a foreign body, and even affirms what Blanchot might call *rapport sans rapport*.

The insistence upon metonymy here seems to rearticulate the sense in which introjection and eating are in this context perpetually identified as metonymic functions.[22] If metonymy is literally understood as a "change of name" (from the Greek) and rhetorically deployed as the replacement of the literal with "another term with which it is closely associated, because of contiguity in common experience" (Abrams 69), this current understanding of metonymy works doubly. On the one hand, the metonymy of "eating well" or of "introjection" identifies the psychoanalytic usage of these terms, which is still figurative, with their literal meaning, while on the other, the literal meaning is associated with actual eating in the world, and so "true" cannibalism. The slippage between this double conception of the literal seems always to defer an arrested sense of what "eating well" might be, and consequently, in its multiplicity, exemplifies what this notion of subjectivity entails.

While introjection introduces metonymy (in representation and in replacing the lost object with a demand for it and/or acknowledgment of its loss), incorporation can be said to be a metonymy of introjection: it shares the image, but is always the failure of introjection.[23] It is in this sense that the "infinitely metonymical question" (EW 115) is the question of both introjection and its failure in incorporation. Moreover, metonymy is itself a rhetorical term of relation and always implies more than a singularity. Abraham and Torok's description of their relation and mutual failures is instructive here:

> As the empty mouth calls out in vain to be filled with introjective speech, it reverts to being the food-craving mouth it was prior to the acquisition of speech. Failing to feed itself on words to be exchanged with others, the mouth absorbs in fantasy all or part of a person – the genuine depository of what is now nameless. (*SK* 128)

When language is no longer sufficient (and often it is not, being too painful, too indicative), introjective metonymies fall flat in the infant mouth, the mouth that hence must devour the other because it can no longer name him or call out to him.[24] Because introjection can always become incorporation, because orificial relations can slip from conversation to digestion, the situation can become "carnivorous" (EW 115). But is the carnivore a cannibal, and isn't this equation at stake in the ambiguities of eating well?

The evidence here becomes a little confusing. Abraham and Torok insist that "*the crucial aspect of these fantasies of incorporation is not their reference to a cannibalistic stage of development, but rather their annulment of figurative language*" (*SK*

132). For Abraham and Torok cannibalism is not the issue; language always comes first. This is an almost strange indifference. Although the reference to cannibalism is maintained and virtually addressed, it is only a secondary concern. Abraham and Torok's suspicious dismissiveness seems to overlook that in the language of eating and ingestion, the real necessarily accompanies the symbolic. It is the residual demand for an ethics that will always leave the ethical – or the Good – incalculable. The ease with which Abraham and Torok phrase the cannibal as apparently "real" implies that it no longer inhabits a transgressive place. Cannibalism has become carnivorous.

Nietzsche incidentally also assumes this equation, arguing that "the *English* diet, too – which is, compared to the German and even to the French, a kind of 'return to nature', meaning to cannibalism – is profoundly at odds with my instincts" (*EH* 238). Again, Nietzsche's sense of the Good – and what is good to eat – evades a seemingly unmediated equivalence between the body and its desires. In this, the one who eats badly, nostalgically and "naturally" eats in a way that so disagrees with Nietzsche that it would inevitably make him vomit. But more than just everyday regurgitation whereby the inside becomes outside, the very question of inside and outside, self and other within an ethical context is raised. In her reading of *Ecce Homo*, Sarah Kofman introduces this situation:

> ... [L]e diététique anglaise est rejetée, non en elle-même mais comme antinomique à l'instinct nietzschéen le plus profond: elle ne pourrait que le faire vomir, car son aspect – naturaliste – n'est que le retour, sous une forme plus ou moins déguisée, du cannibalisme: celui-ci n'est pas condamné parce qu'il transgresserait un des interdits majeurs fondateur du social comme tel, mais à cause de ses effets sur l'esprit: une nourriture 'bestiale' ne peut qu'enlever à l'esprit toute sa spiritualité, toute sa légèreté et sa grâce.[25] (Kofman 282-283)

"Back to nature" introduces the more primitive stage of a cannibalism that is at once transgressive and antithetical to the spiritual life Nietzsche is attempting to illustrate. Kofman recognises that Nietzsche rejects cannibalism *only* because of its bad nutritional effects. In a move not unlike the one in "Eating Well", cannibalism then evades prohibition. This can be read either as a mere dismissal of cannibalism in its equation with English cuisine or as a resitutation of prohibition whereby it is the self and spirit rather than traditional social and moral relations that determine an ethics.

Moreover what Kofman so provocatively suggests (a point not so explicit in Nietzsche's own text) is that vomiting and cannibalism are in some sense substitutive terms. English cuisine can only make Nietzsche vomit; English cuisine is a "more or less disguised" cannibalism. Kofman reinscribes the ambiguous relationship between incorporation and introjection, but within a different literality, in that introjection becomes the literal "casting aside" (*SK* 127) which always succeeds incorporation rather than the prior substitution of language.

The proximity between vomiting and cannibalism can be rephrased within the more explicitly psychoanalytic context of mourning and incorporation. In "*Fors*", Derrida cites Abraham and Torok and explains that:

> ... The fantasy [of incorporation] involves eating the subject (through the mouth or otherwise) in order *not* to introject it, in order to vomit it, in a way, into the inside, into the pocket of a cyst ... If, on the one hand, incorporation could be said to resemble, paradoxically enough, an act of vomit-

ing to the inside, then on the other hand, a successful necrophagy in which the dead would be assimilated, and in which there would be 'alimentary communion among the survivors', would be a 'preventative measure of anti-incorporation'. (*Fors* xxxviii (further refs. will be abbreviated as *F*))

As Kofman seems to imply, vomiting can represent cannibalism (as eating badly) in that it is the (moral) response to it. But in the confusion of literal and figurative cannibalisms, there is also a confusion of actual and representative vomiting.[26] Vomiting to the inside remarks the redoubling of the relationship between inside and outside, and while apparently like eating, nevertheless only allows that the other remain a part of the self. In refusing to recognise the other as other, vomiting to the inside cannot recognise the other at all. The assimilation of the other, is at once the ingestion of the indigestible and the situation of a body for which there can be no outside. Eating badly then becomes eating well, in that the other becomes the self-same, when the self becomes other. But here the question of necrophagy repeats the situation of a humane cannibalism, for as Montaigne argues: "I consider it more barbarous to eat a man alive than to eat him dead" (Montaigne 113). Although it might be said that the disintegration of the ethical binary is here inaugurated, the difference between the living and the dead is finally lost within a strategy of eating well. Vomiting, and especially to the inside, therefore raises the question of place, of the foreign and so of the feminine. This *atopia* is a becoming plural. While "[n]o one will ever have asked the dead person how he would have preferred to be eaten" (*F* xxxviii), the one who might have asked is already no one in that there is no (longer) one within the ethical relation. In this, "[e]verything is organized in order that he *remain* a missing person in both cases, having vanished as *other*, from the operation, whether it be mourning *or* melancholy. Departed, nowhere to be found, *atopique*" (xxxviii). But the missing person, the missing subject, is the subject in excess. Eating the other in the duplication of the self and also the inhabitation of the self by another is also the return to a sometimes authoritative pedigogico-rhetorical strategy: the saying of a "we".

In eating without asking – eating because one cannot ask – one replaces one mouthwork with another, what Derrida, in "Eating Well", calls a relation of the "eat-speak-interiorize" (EW 114). Asking is taking the other to eat, allowing the answer to become one's own: it is already "symbolic anthropophagy" (114).[27] The dead then disappear, because there is no longer a place for them, because they are no place, foreign to every place, while nevertheless everywhere. Doubly excessive – with their missing bodies and perpetual punctuations of every sentence – the dead ("when the limit between the living and the non-living now seems to be as unsure, at least as an oppositional limit, as that between 'man' and 'animal'" (114)) become the living dead in their incorporation. And so when one eats – even if one eats the animal, even if one eats the dead – one always risks eating otherwise.[28] In the disintegration of these rigorous limits, each meal chances an impossible anthropophagy as it demands the thinking of ethical ingestion.

William Arens's extensive anthropological study of cannibalism is suggestive here. Arguing that historically cannibalism was far less prevalent than the fictions of it and that it was submitted to far greater prohibitions than both academic and folk culture would like to believe, Arens seems to offer a precedent for the incorporative reading of cannibalism. In this, he explains that "[t]he most certain thing to be said is that all cultures, subcultures, religious sects, secret societies and every other possible human association have been labeled anthropophagic by someone" (Arens 139). And so it is clear that nothing at all is certain when it comes to the situation and accusation of cannibalism, a positing always coincident with denying "the accused their humanity" (140). This traditional linking of the cannibal and the inhuman only reaffirms Derrida's gestures in reconceiving an ethics beyond humanism. Arens continues this argument by identifying the discourse of the "cannibal complex" (161), furthermore asserting that:

> Anthropology and anthropophagy, as views of the external world, have had a comfortable and supportive relationship. It is possible that in their present form one could not exist without the other. (162)

The myth of anthropophagy (as well as the myth of anthropology), as Arens names it, therefore functions as the foundation of one of the most traditional humanisms. In rendering the hypothetical a basic truth, anthropologists have historically attempted to marginalise the other by rendering him a cannibal.[29] Moreover, as Arens argues, that cannibalism has tended more often to be a fiction intent upon precluding the subject status of cultures under evaluation. The point interestingly reflects upon the local indifference to "real" cannibalism I have attempted to identify. Is cannibalism merely what the reading public desires (to read and to become), as Gananath Obeyesekere argues? If this is the case, we might understand it as an introjective situation whereby the absence of the event is witnessed by its newly figurative status. Is an ethics of cannibalism then merely an ethics for reading and representation (always introjective rather than incorpo-rative)? But again, this imposes nothing beyond cannibalism-as-speech. The question then remains: "What is eating?"

In a gesture towards answering his own question, Derrida explains:

> This [maxim – 'One must eat well'] evokes a law of need *or* desire, ... orexis, hunger, and thirst ('one must', 'one must [eat] well'), respect for the other at the very moment when, in experience (I am speaking here of metonymical 'eating' as well as the very concept of experience), one must begin to identify with the other, who is to be assimilated, interiorized, understood ideally, ... speak to him in words that also pass through the mouth, the ear, and sight, and respect the law that is at once a voice and a court (it hears itself, it is *in us* who are *before it*). (EW 115)

Whereas earlier Derrida seemed to insist upon eating as a metonymic strategy, here he recognises that a term always suggests more and less than its metonymical function and moreover, he admits to understanding its doubled status very specifically. And yet this is by no means clear. Rather, the law of hunger becomes at the same time a law of respect. At the moment when the other is rendered distant enough to be edible, one must identify with him, in an acknowledgment that eating the other is always synonymous with eating the self, that eating is always cannibalistic, and cannibalism is carnivorous.

Nevertheless, Derrida's earlier insistence that this is not only a linguistic issue still needs to be addressed. Despite the shift from "cannibal" to "carnivore", an understanding of ethical ingestion cannot sound a "primitive" return to non-metonymic eating, to anthropophagy and its prohibition, and to the spectacular feast – not unlike the glorious dinner scene in Peter Greenaway's *The*

albeit eating

Cook, The Thief, His Wife, and Her Lover (where the last word, a last insult, is "Cannibal!"). To share the question beyond language is then to incorporate it, to swallow and protect it, to defer language, and to eat in ways symbolic and real. We eat the dead. One forgets that. But we also bury them. And so to share this is to continue to eat, to continue to serve up meals that are good and that introduce the good into our bodies. It is also to maintain the memory of the dead (feminine, other) and to visit their marked graves. This involves the perpetual recognition of our non-self-identity (especially subsequent to a meal or a conversation) but also the acknowledgment that we "put to death the living" (114) – symbolically and really. And so what happens to the subject? Who comes after the subject?

In *Totem and Taboo*, Freud also raises the question of who comes before (a reversal Nancy accuses Derrida of committing (107)), in an attempt to trace psychoanalytically the relation between totemic ritual and modern religious practice. Attempting to elucidate the economy of sacrifice, and particularly to follow the complex emotional and psychical movement from the initial totemic sacrifice to the subsequent mourning and final celebration of that sacrifice – each of which demand the participation of the entire clan – Freud introduces Darwin's primal horde, and posits it as the origin of the totemic system. Freud's explanation comes in the form of a story, perhaps a parable:

> One day the brothers who had been driven out came together, killed and devoured their father and so made an end of the patriarchal horde. United, they had the courage to do and succeeded in doing what would have been impossible for them individually. (Some cultural advance, perhaps command over some new weapon, had given them a sense of superior strength.) Cannibal savages as they were, it goes without saying that they devoured their victim as well as killing him. The violent primal father had doubtless been the feared and envied model of each one of the company of brothers: and in the act of devouring him they accomplished their identification with him, and each of them acquired a portion of his strength. (Freud 141-142)

This cannibalism so original that it precludes the need for subsequent actual cannibalisms, while at the same time introducing a cannibalistic relation, is the accomplishment and distribution of an identity. In sharing responsibility as the sharing of a meal, the authority of the one (primal father), in its ingestion, becomes the invisible tie of a community. Responsibility, while both instrumental to a classical definition of the subject, is also a requirement for "nonclassical motifs" such as "eating well" (EW 100). Here, eating – the anthropophagic devouring of the father and the lost *topos* of authority – is possible only as sharing whereby, as Derrida explains: "The singularity of the 'who' is not the individuality of a thing that would be identical to itself" (100). Not only is the shared and equal participation of the community demanded by the occasion, but moreover, subsequent to it, in the ingestion of another, these partners are no longer even self identical, as the body of another fills their own. But this feast need only take place once. Likewise, the project of a shared signature might come to repeat another incision in the violent authority of the father – disseminating "the virile strength of the adult male ... that dominates the concept of the subject" (114). Might the question "Who comes after the subject?" also ask "Who signs here?" (*F* xlviii).

It is only together that the brothers could eat the father. It is only in the sharing of voices and signatures, in the opening of our

74

sara guyer

bodies that the subject unravels and that the precarious work of mourning and celebration remarks the perpetual taking place of these shared ingestions. Derrida locates this exchange in the *atopia* of an instance of the "who" –

> besieged by the problematic of the trace and of *différance*, of affirmation, of the signature, and of the so-called 'proper' name, of the *je[c]t* (above all subject, object, project), as *destinerring* of missive. (EW 100)

The double situation of address and errancy that takes place in the doubly signed and doubly affirmed "missive" comes to stand, when coupled with responsibility, both as a "*metonymy* of 'eating well'" – itself never singular or self-identical – and also a metonymy of "'Eating Well', or the Calculation of the Subject: An Interview with Jacques Derrida". It is the *destinerring* of missive, that is the confusion of address and signature, reader and writer, subject and object in the necessary and necessarily shared project that perhaps becomes an ingestion, or at least a vomiting to the inside, which is to say, following the logic of the *je[c]t*, the metonymy of intro*ject*ion, and its confusing double: incorporation

That new weapon – "an abandoned stone instrument, like a tombstone burning in the grass, the double-edged stare of a two-faced Medusa" (*F* xlviii) – that marks the end of the father's rule, might also be

> the crack in a symbol, the upright column of a name, for example or the blank voice of a scruple, [that] always extends out on the other side, beyond the self. (lviii)

Already there is a confusion between the instrument and the crime/crack it enacts. The double signature – Nicolas Abraham and Maria Torok – a joining of names in the deciphering of a crypt that marks the task of Derrida's *Fors*. To live in one's own name but also to sign in and with the name of another is to introduce another relation – in the name of friendship and in the name of the reader.[30] This is also the double signature of Jacques Derrida and Jean-Luc Nancy (someone who often signs with another). In the united project of an interview, they together "devoured their victim [the subject] as well as killing him" (Freud 141). The giving and swallowing of words – sacrifice, mourning, affirmation – becomes a loss of self and other in eating and eating well, which always demands that there be more than one: living or dead, animal or human, woman or man. And so it is within the *atopia* of the proper name having become double – the already uncertain site between inside and outside – that the annunciation of a speaking subject who is always "we" is shared. In the sharing of mouth-work, the subject can be eaten in the mutual obligation of eating well. What might be a repetition of the original anthropophagic feast, the introduction of cannibalism into ethical life, at the same time remarks its impossibility. For us readers, and so us writers, the Good is always carnivorous.

notes

This paper is indebted to Forbes Morlock's careful reading and could not have been thought without Sarah Wood's initial instruction.

1 It is interesting to note that even before Nietzsche and Derrida, Kant recognises the import of these ethico-culinary questions, but his work lies mainly in the realm of "tasteful" party-planning, dinner conversation, and "pleas[ing] the ladies present" (Kant 146). Moreover, these musings are relegated to the space of his *Anthropology*. For Kant, it is not so much *what* we eat, but *how* we eat:

> Insofar as they intend not merely to have a

albeit eating

meal in common but to enjoy one another's company (this is why their number must not greatly exceed that of the graces), a small dinner party of this sort must have as its primary purpose not physical satisfaction – each could have that by himself – but companionable enjoyment for which physical satisfaction must seem to be the only instrument. (144)

This of course is "eating well".

2 Cf. Robert G. Hamerton-Kelly, ed., *Violent Origins: Ritual Killing and Cultural Formation* and Michel de Montaigne "On Cannibals" in *Essays*.

3 "Witness" is interesting here, for it maintains the optic metaphor of knowledge within Western thought. In a certain sense, this understanding of the interview remains suspicious, for it re-encodes the privileged panoramic whole that only seeing (rather than speaking) can afford. Following Blanchot, "speaking is not seeing" (Blanchot 1993, 25). Speaking is the giving and taking, swallowing and ingesting of another, whereas seeing asserts the priority of light, the appropriation of an undifferentiated whole, and cannot accommodate affirmation. Incidentally, Blanchot's own inquiry into the partition between speaking and seeing takes place within a conversation, a veritable interview, with Martin Heidegger ("Speaking is not Seeing"). Nevertheless, at risk in Derrida's definition of the interview is the substitution of eye-work for mouth-work.

4 Hannah Arendt explains that Himmler selected "the members of the elite according to 'good blood'" (Arendt 385). The ideological strategy of privileging "good blood" seems to emphasise the stakes of an ethical situation (and so a situation of subjectivity) that uses ingestion as its metonymy.

5 In *The Gift of Death*, Derrida further explains what it would mean to "sacrifice sacrifice" within a Christian ethico-theological context and the consequent logic of inner light: an economy of sacrifice and absolute subjectivity that comes to resemble Bataille's general economy (Derrida 1995a, 101-102).

6 At stake in rendering this relation is the question of sex and gender, and so of the grammatical subject. As Derrida says, "I would not want to see the 'who' restricted to the grammar of what we call Western language" (EW 111). If this interview attempts to locate traditional humanisms within a Heideggerian (and Levinasian) thinking of Being, it necessarily recalls Derrida's other project of uncovering Heidegger's thought on *Geschlecht*, and so sexual difference amongst other things (race, nation, etc). This too, even if not actually, is a thought of *entrevoir*, or interview. The question here – and a question that traces questions of cannibalism, incorporation, and this ethics generally – is one of sexual difference. Who eats and who is eaten? When *oikos* becomes a term in this thinking, the question of sexuality is again phrased in that it is *woman* (whose place is in the home) who is traditionally inhabited by man. But for woman there is only an *atopia*. *Dasein's* sexuality is before the mark. The *chef* is always a man. If the traditional subject is a man, the subject of "eating well" is a relation, and so an always plural subject. And yet the other still has some mark, and demands some arresting term as grammatical subject. Who comes after the subject? On this, and more out of ease than agreement, I will follow Derrida's own direction and render a masculine grammatical subject (i.e. "One eats *him* regardless and lets oneself be eaten by *him*" (114, my italics)). This necessarily remains inadequate, and yet perhaps frames the masculine-as-other in ways more interesting than the traditional marks of sexual difference would otherwise permit.

7 Cf.

> On the other hand, the smooth functioning of such a society [that would try and prosecute Abraham as a murderer], the monotonous complacency of its discourses on morality, politics, and the law, and the exercise of its rights (whether public, private, national or international), are in no way impaired by the fact that, because of the

structure of the laws of the market that society has instituted and controls, because of the mechanisms of external debt and other similar inequities, that same 'society' *puts to* death or (but failing to help someone in distress accounts for only a minor difference) *allows* to die of hunger and disease tens of millions of children (those neighbors or fellow humans that ethics or the discourse of rights refers to) without any moral or legal tribunal ever being considered competent to judge such a sacrifice, the sacrifice of others to avoid being sacrificed oneself. (Derrida 1995a, 86)

8 On the relationship between the maternal and proper, one might note that in *Totem and Taboo*, Freud explains that "the introduction of agriculture" allowed the son to reorient his "incestuous libido, which found symbolic satisfaction in his cultivation of Mother Earth" (Freud 152). This shift – from (totemic) sacrifice and mourning, guilt and rebelliousness – nevertheless exemplifies "[t]he son's efforts to put himself in the place of the father-god" (152). The eroticised relationship to place, *topos*, raises the predicament of the displacement here in question.

9 As Jean-Luc Nancy argues elsewhere, communion in death insists upon an immanence that is inevitably fascist. Cf. *The Inoperative Community*. Blanchot also repeats these statements in his *The Unavowable Community*.

10 This use of symbolic/real does not follow a Lacanian structure, which it might seem to resemble, but rather is an attempt at following the interview's own terms for the representative and the actual. Nevertheless, recent anthropological studies arguing that anthropophagy is more mythic than it is actual, might place cannibalism in the realm of the Lacanian "real".

11 Moreover, in the interview, Nancy's final interjections refer to Derrida's failure to recognise political abuses and their historical situation, even if Nancy's tack repeats too familiar questions about Heidegger's silence, rather than interrogating the relationship between "responsibility" and "eating well". While this might be a product of the inherently ingestive interview format, one would have to approach Derrida's more recent work – namely, *Specters of Marx* and *The Gift of Death* – in order to find a response to more traditional political and social concerns.

12 In an attempted psychoanalytic reading of Maori cannibalism, Gananath Obeyeskere argues that cannibalism was a term by which the British colonisers could name the other as other. In fact, Obeyeskere attempts to implicate the British in the very practice of cannibalism (the title of his article is "British Cannibals"), and insists both that "Cannibalism is what the English reading public wanted to hear" (Obeyeskere 635) and that "those who sacrifice humans [i.e. the British colonialists] carry with them an unconscious wish to partake of that substance" (635). Despite all this psychologising, Obeyeskere does not address the psychic and political relationship between prohibition, difference and similarity that seems to be the basis of cannibalism.

13 In fact, he explains his task as "a matter of *discerning* a place left open ..." (EW 112, my italics), rather than the enactment of the sacrifice of sacrifice. Within a grammar homonymous with taste (i.e. discernment), Derrida acknowledges this recognition, and the caution that accompanies it as the basis of "eating well". This exposure of the other might be understood within Blanchot's register of reading. Cf. "The Limit-Experience" in *The Infinite Conversation*.

14 This essay can be found in the recently translated first volume of Abraham and Torok's major work entitled *The Shell and the Kernel: Renewals of Psychoanalysis*.

15 Joseph Litvak, in an essay on the svelte politics of *Pride and Prejudice*, valorises this notion of incorporation and associates it "with an admirably perverse resistance to the normalising (i.e. heterosexualising) pressures of the marriage plot" (Litvak 45). This insistence on a kind of glorious transgression tends

albeit eating

to overlook the very nature of incorporation as symptom (of mourning). In my discussion of Derrida's use of "incorporation", I am intent upon offering a more conservative – retentive? too literal? incorporative? – reading of Abraham and Torok, and offer this example as the reason for my insistence.

16 Simply, incorporation can be understood as taking the figurative literally and mistaking it for an original narrative (i.e. incorporation is imagined to be prior to all representations). The reason for this again, is to destroy the devastating event by "outwriting" it, without acknowledging that writing *as* writing.

17 Cf. "Chaos refers precisely to the abyss or the *open mouth*, that which speaks as well as that which signifies hunger" (Derrida 1995a, 84, my italics). This more recent work affirms the open mouth and introjecting body as communicative, but introduces a sense of desire (in hunger) somewhat in excess of Abraham and Torok's formulation. Moreover, this becomes a *chaotic* situation (presumably in that the emptiness presupposes words and things passing through the body and remaining in circulation). This chaos might be the chaos of metonymies generally, in the confusion of words and food, that no doubt seethes in the thought of "eating well".

18 This is a slippage specific to "Eating Well", and is reworked in *The Gift of Death*, see especially p84-85.

19 If it is the animal who is in question, the animal, that is, who does not have language, in what sense can introjection – which thrives on sharing in language – take place? For further insight into the ethical import of the animal as other in Levinas's work – a point that will not be taken up here – see Simon Critchley, *The Ethics of Deconstruction: Derrida and Levinas*: "The ambiguity of ethical selfhood is that it is only as an animal, as a being that eats and is capable of giving its food to the other, that I can be for the Other" (Critchley 81). Also see John Llewelyn, "Am I Obsessed by Bobby? (Humanism of the Other Animal)" p234-246.

20 It is perhaps important to point out that in "Eating Well", Derrida does not specify the actual image of the "community of empty mouths". I think this is the product of a two-fold gesture. On the one hand, the literal grafting of Abraham and Torok, including their very term (i.e. "the metonymy of introjection" (EW 115)), onto his own schema, would render this *always* a situation of mourning rather than the ethics he is attempting to describe. Moreover, Abraham and Torok alternate between calling this "communion" and "community", and after the attention both Jean-Luc Nancy and Maurice Blanchot have brought to the question of "communion" (a potentially fascist singularity) and "community", their term requires rethinking – unfortunately a task beyond the scope of this paper. Cf. Nancy, *The Inoperative Community*. Nevertheless, as mentioned above, the empty mouth becomes an important term in identifying the abyss in *The Gift of Death*.

21 Suggesting the similarities between the Jewish dietary laws of Kashrut here indicates the most literal example of the figurative practice Derrida is inventing. Again, Nietzsche's insistence upon diet in *Ecce Homo* is relevant as well.

22 Cf. "the *metonymy* of 'eating well'" (EW 114, my italics); "this *metonymy* of introjection" (115, my italics).

23 "Certainly the image [between incorporation and introjection] is identical, but for reasons that will soon be apparent, it is important to differentiate between them, as we would distinguish between metaphoric and photographic images, between the acquisition of language as opposed to buying a dictionary ..." (SK 127).

24 And so it is between incorporation and introjection that the animal can be accommodated, because the animal is always only an incorporating being, just as occasionally the human, becoming speechless, becomes just an eater too.

25

... [T]he English diet is rejected, not in itself,

but as antinomical to the most profound Nietzschean instinct: it can only make one vomit, because its 'naturalistic' aspect is only the return to cannibalism in a more or less disguised form: this is not condemned because it would transgress one of the major prohibitions founding the social as such, but because of its effects on the spirit: a 'bestial' nutrition can only remove from the spirit all its spirituality, all its lightness and its grace.

26 In this, the very idea of cannibalism might make one vomit on a moral basis, whereas the mediocrity of British cuisine might make one vomit on a physical basis. These two poles form a chiasm, whereby eating, and so vomiting, which is to say the economy of the body, become moral structures. The similarity of response implies the interchangeability of deed. And so all eating (speaking, mourning) risks and repeats anthropophagic eating.

27 It is worthwhile to compare this conception of eating and speaking to Blanchot's notion of affirmation, especially as it is thought in the many *entretiens* that punctuate *The Infinite Conversation*.

28 One might again compare this to Montaigne's argument that cannibalism – "to roast and eat a man after he is dead" – is morally superior to "tortur[ing] a body still full of feeling" (Montaigne 113).

29 It should be pointed out that while groundbreaking, Arens's study is hardly accepted by all anthropologists. Renato Rosaldo, for instance explains that "Despite lurid over reporting, there is in fact cannibalism in the world" (Hamerton-Kelly 220). Rosaldo substantiates this claim by citing: "The thing that's absolutely decisive is that in New Guinea there is a disease that's only transmitted through human flesh. It results from the custom of eating the human brain" (240). Less convincingly though, Walter Burkert, in the same volume, explains that: "The force of such a tradition [of cannibalism] might still be seen in the fact that on the secret market of video, as can be read in our newspapers, cannibalism is a very big hit now" (176). It is clear that Burkert uses the term cannibalism in order to differentiate himself from a greater "tradition" – of violence? of video? of pornography? of Peter Greenaway? – which once named, he can be dissociated from.

30 Derrida signs "*Fors*" in the reader's name – "In you, anonymous reader in this much sealed case" (*F* xlviii). The sharing – of reading and friendship – in question also resonates with Blanchot's understanding of an "accompanying discourse" whereby reading introduces community. Cf. "The Limit-Experience".

sara guyer

bibliography

Abraham, N. and M. Torok, *The Shell and The Kernel: Renewals of Psychoanalysis*, ed. N.T. Rand (Chicago: University of Chicago Press, 1994).

Abraham, N. and M. Torok, *The Wolf Man's Magic Word: A Cryptonymy*, tr. N. Rand (Minneapolis: University of Minnesota Press, 1986).

Abrams, M.H., *A Glossary of Literary Terms*, 6th ed. (Fort Worth: Harcourt Brace College Publishers, 1993).

Arendt, H., *The Origins of Totalitarianism* (New York: Harcourt Brace, 1979).

Arens, W., *The Man-Eating Myth: Anthropology and Anthropophagy* (New York: Oxford University Press, 1979).

Blanchot, M., *The Infinite Conversation*, tr. S. Hanson (Minneapolis: University of Minnesota Press, 1993).

Blanchot, M., *The Unavowable Community*, tr. P. Joris (Barrytown, NY: Station Hill Press, 1988).

Critchley, S., *The Ethics of Deconstruction: Derrida and Levinas* (Oxford: Blackwell, 1992).

Derrida, J., "Choreographies" (1982) in *Points ...* , p89-108.

Derrida, J., "Dialanguages" (1983a) in *Points ...* p132-155.

Derrida, J., "'Eating Well', or the Calculation of the Subject: An Interview with Jacques Derrida" in *Who Comes After the Subject?*, ed. E. Cadava, P. Connor and J.-L. Nancy (New York: Routledge, 1991) p96-119.

Derrida, J., "Fors: The Anglish Words of Nicolas Abraham and Maria Torok", tr. Barbara Johnson in *The Wolf Man's Magic Word: A Cryptonymy*, pxi-xiviii.

Derrida, J., "Geschlecht: sexual difference, ontological difference", *Research in Phenomenology* XIII (1983b) p65-83.

Derrida, J., *The Gift of Death*, tr. D. Wills (Chicago: University of Chicago Press, 1995a).

Derrida, J., *Points ...* , ed. E. Weber (Stanford: Stanford UP, 1995b).

Derrida, J., *Spectres of Marx: The State of the Debt, the Work of Mourning, and the New International*, tr. P. Kamuf (New York: Routledge, 1994).

Freud, S., *Totem and Taboo* in *The Standard Edition of the Complete Psychological Works of Sigmund Freud*, vol. XIII (London: The Hogarth Press, 1953) p1-162.

Hamerton-Kelly, R.G., ed., *Violent Origins: Ritual Killing and Cultural Formation* (Stanford: Stanford UP, 1987).

Kant, I., *Anthropology from a Pragmatic Point of View*, tr. M.J. Gregor (The Hague: Martinus Nijhoff, 1974).

Kofman, S., *Explosion I: De l' Ecce Homo de Nietzsche* (Paris: Galilée, 1992).

Litvak, J., "Delicacy and Disgust, Mourning and Melancholia, Privilege and Perversity: *Pride and Prejudice*", *Qui Parle* 6:1 (fall/winter 1992) p35-51.

Llewelyn, J., "Am I Obsessed with Bobby? (Humanism and the Other Animal)" in *Re-Reading Levinas*, ed. R. Bernasconi and S. Critchley (Bloomington: Indiana UP, 1991) p234-246.

Montaigne, M. de, *Essays*, tr. J.M. Cohen (London: Penguin Books, 1958).

Nancy, J.-L., *The Inoperative Community*, tr. P. Connor et al. (Minneapolis: University of Minnesota Press, 1991).

Nietzsche, F., *On the Genealogy of Morals and Ecce Homo*, tr. W. Kaufmann (New York: Vintage, 1967).

Obeyeskere, G., "'British Cannibals': Contemplation of an Event in the Death and Resurrection of James Cook, Explorer", *Critical Inquiry* 18 (summer 1992) p630-654.

Wigley, M., *The Architecture of Deconstruction: Derrida's Haunt* (Cambridge, MA: The MIT Press, 1993).

stephen keane

IMAGINARY HOMELANDS
notes on heimat and heimlich

This essay borders the theoretical and the political in the form of a speculation. I hope to define the two terms, "*Heimat*" and "*heimlich*", with one suggestion, that there are common linguistic and conceptual properties to be found between them, with implications beyond already apparent notions of "homeliness". On an elementary level, my aim is to introduce the terms. On a comparative level, I suggest cause to merge them. On neither level is my aim specialist or dogmatic. The following episodes are proposals towards a critical orientation.

imagined community

Heimat is both geographical place and mythic space, the locus of national dispute and collective identity. Geographically, historically, the original *Heimat* existed as the Pfalz, a province bordering the Rhine in South-West Germany which was created out of Bavarian compromise in 1815 but which was to develop its own marginal yet significant identity in Bismarck's Reich by 1871.[1] But, the semantic notion of *Heimat* has far outstripped "rooted place", and it is that which has most clearly entered into the discourse of German identity, through moral and political significations. Beyond the centralised, colonising *language* of the German state (that ensured by terms such as "sovereignty" and "Germanness"), *Heimat* offered a sense of diversification, its own – their own, for there were many *Heimat*s – sense of identity. It created its own ideal of community irrespective of the enforced nationalising language of community-writ-large that was surrounding it. What I would like to argue is that, ultimately, *Heimat* is able to resist the official language of nationalism through unique (political) feeling. Instead of being told how to feel, how to belong, the *Heimat* community itself felt.

The emotional capacity of *Heimat* begins with its very specific linguistic being. As Celia Applegate maintains, the term remains wholly alien to the English language. The translations, "homeland" or "hometown", inadequately convey its emotional depths, and the only time that an English equivalent has come close to it was during World War One, when "*Heimat*" and "home front" shared resonances of longing. There is a clue as to the cultural significance of *Heimat* when Applegate likens it to a Raymond Williams-type "keyword". Although Applegate does not go on to follow this allusion through, what *Heimat* represents is that sense of wholesome village nostalgia which Williams has located in the English literary scene as the cosy, countryful "knowable community".[2] In the German context, Ferdinand Tönnies had already addressed the issue with his distinction between *Gemeinschaft* and

imaginary homelands

Gesellschaft (broadly "community" and "civilisation") (Applegate 4-6).

As such debates suggest, what is at stake in the notion of *Heimat* is an ongoing cultural discourse, one which extends far beyond immediate political effect. For example, in its most overtly political beginnings, *Heimat* retains a linguistic symbolisation beyond existing legislative necessities. Certainly, it is self-avowedly this linguistic aspect of *Heimat* which Applegate is trying to trace. So when she writes that

> [t]he ... confrontation between the reforming, centralizing, rationalizing representatives of the so-called General Estate and the community-bound people of the hometowns is the proper context in which to understand the evolution of the term *Heimat*,

it is the "term" which becomes the important correlative of a primary political context. What we might ask in this instance is, need linguistic symbolisation *continue* to be bound by "proper context"? In itself, the term, *Heimat*, remains the same. That is in its very character. Whilst modernity progresses, *Heimat* stays the same. But, its extrinsic significance, if not its intrinsic meaning, has been necessarily altered by changing context. *Heimat* cannot continue to define itself, it must enter into relations within language. Thus, within the language of German nationalism, as Applegate maintains, *Heimat* became as important, in "the vocabulary of German public, bourgeois life", as terms like *Nation, Staat, Volk,* and *Vaterland* (7-8). Despite attempting a certain independence, *Heimat*, as concept, was bound to enter nationalistic discourse. But on whose terms?

Under Prussian leadership after 1871, *Heimat* was pulled into social and economic service, literally through railway connections and technical developments in communication. Although Applegate concedes these as material facts, she correctly defends the idealist position to *Heimat*. There is "material existence" and there is "interpretation" of that material existence (12). If *Heimat* can be tied down to a nationalist vocabulary, in relation to other terms, then that is where resistance begins. It is, strictly, the "idea" of nation which is being rehearsed in the *Heimat*'s relationship to the whole. It is, strictly, a dialogue which is occurring between regionalism and nationalism. Certainly, "Nationalism" and "Germanness" are the larger terms – "Nationalism could embrace their smaller worlds; Germanness could encompass their diversity" (13) – but, far from remaining supplementary, *Heimat* becomes central to this vocabulary, in a more properly reciprocal grammar of federalist identity. From 1870 onwards, Germany has needed the myth of *Heimat*, the *illusion* of unity, to disguise its own material disparities: "the abstraction of the nation must be experienced through one's appreciation of a locality, a *Heimat*" (15).

history and memory

Released from geography into the conceptual, *Heimat* also allows a revisiting of historical time through subjective memory. It is always past. Even within linear progressive historical time, *Heimat* existed as *gemeinschaft*, barely at home in the rapid social changes of the nineteenth century and seemingly wholly anachronistic in the twentieth. As place, *Heimat* exists as village community; in time, it exists as tradition. *Heimat* is the parochial in history. But, as I have argued, *Heimat*-as-concept has far outstripped *Heimat*-as-place, and the same is true of the historicist in history: "[i]t represents the modern imagining and, consequently, re-making of the hometown, not the stephen keane

hometown's own deeply rooted historical reality" (8). *Heimat* now exists as "a myth about the possibility of a community in the face of fragmentation and alienation" (19). Such a remaking of (the myth of) *Heimat* is the method of Edgar Reitz's nine-part film, Heimat. First shown in West Germany in 1984 and then enthusiastically received internationally, Reitz's Heimat has renewed debates surrounding *Heimat*'s place in history.[3] For many, the film Heimat has replaced that history. Anton Kaes, for example, has argued that actual memories and experiences of German history have been superseded by the popular screened memories of post-war German cinema. Likewise, "'*Heimat*' can exist only, some would argue, as memory evoked in a film".[4] It is this return of history as film, this recoding of *Heimat* as cinematographic memory, which shapes Kaes's thesis, as well as Reitz's method. Constantly, Reitz emphasises the personal, subjective experience of *Heimat*:

> The word is always linked to strong feeling, mostly remembrances and longing. '*Heimat*' always evokes in me the feeling of something lost or very far away, something which one cannot easily find or find again ... '*Heimat*' is such that if one would go closer and closer to it, one would discover that at the moment of arrival it is gone, it has dissolved into nothingness. It seems to me that one has a more precise idea of '*Heimat*' the further one is away from it. (Kaes 163)

Throughout Heimat, the fictional village community of Shabbach evolves from 1919-80, untouched by the catastrophic historical events which shape the German political scene. Located in the Hunsrück, in the west of the Federal Republic, Shabbach remains relatively insular. Family is on the margins of country, and history is historicised at the level of the parochial and the private. In this sense, Heimat is wholly characteristic of the New German Cinema that emerged prominently in the 1970s. Thomas Elsaesser, for example, has argued that, after 1968, German culture could only come to terms with its past indirectly. Thus, the political past was approached at the level of the private, "history in the home and Fascism in the family unit".[5] That is, individual and personal memories were cinematised to compete with the publicly sanctioned memory that was German history. This new revisionist cinema was concerned with re-presenting the past, in films like Hans Jürgen Syberberg's *Our Hitler* (1976), Rainer Werner Fassbinder's *The Marriage of Maria Braun* (1978), Helma Sanders-Brahms's *Germany, Pale Mother* and Alexander Kluge's *The Patriot* (1979). Elsaesser finds a psychoanalytic complement to this privatisation in Alexander and Margarete Mitscherlich's 1967 *The Inability to Mourn*. In the Mitscherlich scenario, the formation of the state is realised in Oedipal terms. From a pre-Oedipal attachment to the mother, the individual subject must turn to larger love objects in order to become part of the mass, hence nation, race, state and ultimately, *Führer*. With the loss of the ego-ideal of the *Führer*, post-war Germany became a "fatherless society". Before coming to terms with their warring and defeated past, therefore, Germans first had to mourn the loss of this primary narcissistic attachment. What New German Cinema of the 1970s offered was such an examination, through representation, of this lost self (Elsaesser 239-43). Of course, this is a convenient psychoanalytic scenario. Possibly too convenient. But, as Elsaesser concedes, its importance lies in its *symbolic*, rather than necessarily actual, effects. After all, metaphor can express indirectly that which is too painful to openly address. The *literal*

imaginary homelands

truth beneath this metaphor is that Germany did, indeed, become a fatherless society, as many present and potential fathers were killed in the war (241-2).[6] But, the recoding nature of New German Cinema is such that (psychological) metaphors are required to express a view, hence the family becomes a central micronational concern. A cinematic retreat into family and the subjective becomes an expansion into collective, national psychology.

no place like *heimlich*

Freud's *unheimlich* is an unsettling experience because of an unsettled semantic effect. Its fundamental quakes take place at the level of meaning, merging at its borders into *heimlich*. What is presently new and terrible becomes old and familiar. And it is at this level of crossover, of mutation, that we can truly say there is, literally, no place like it. Pure *unheimlich* doesn't exist. Its *doppelgänger* effect is a cause of its own predicate.

Like "*Heimat*", "*un/heimlich*" suffers in English translation. At the furthest level of reduction, the English "un/canny" is merely "un/homely". But, Freud's strategy of displacing the familiar takes place around these very terms of reduction. Conventional definitions of fright, dread and horror are insufficient to encompass that "special core of feeling" which makes *unheimlich* such a particular conceptual term.[7] Nor can conventional binary structures contain its duplicities. So, when Freud begins through oppositional deductions it is with the forethought of imminent collapse. Versus homely "*heimlich*" and native "*heimisch*", the known and the familiar, "*unheimlich*" would logically be that which is frightening because new and unfamiliar (Freud 341). In order to distort this picture, Freud excavates another definition of *heimlich*, which *unheimlich* might doubly oppose. Certainly, *heimlich* can be seen as the familiar, the tame, intimacy, friendliness and comfort, belonging to the house or family. But, the second significant meaning of *heimlich* becomes that of concealment. In this more customary sense, *heimlich* contains *unheimlich* because to conceal is the exact opposite of making familiar, the first definition (342-7). Thus, *unheimlich* is the hidden core of *heimlich*:

> *[H]eimlich* is a word the meaning of which develops in the direction of ambivalence, until it finally coincides with its opposite, *unheimlich*. *Unheimlich* is in some way or other a sub-species of *heimlich*. (347)

Freud's exposition of Hoffmann's "The Sand-Man" is well known, but it is worth briefly following through his offshoot treatment of regression. *Unheimlich* begins with the past. Prefiguring Lacanian terms, the "double" is a pre-mirror entity, original contact with pre-dissociated self. It represents a "harking back" to "self-regarding feeling", a "regression to a time when the ego had not yet marked itself off sharply from the external world and from other people" (358). As Freud's essay progresses, so does regression. We move from *Innenwelt* to mother's body to womb. Fear at the Medusa's Head is given particular attention. In male neurotics, for example, the female genital organs appear uncanny because they are the entrance to "the former *Heim* of all human beings ... the place where each one of us lived once upon a time and in the beginning" (368). The fear of being buried alive may be the ultimate uncanny feeling because our end lies in our beginning. This is a "lasciviousness" made "terrifying", death as a panic transformation of the desire for "intra-uterine existence" (366-7). So, it is regression which marks out the distinctiveness of *unheimlich* as opposed to the complacent

stephen keane

presentism of *heimlich*. Or, more correctly, it is *repression*, the attempt to forget, which makes *unheimlich* so alienating. We are strangers only to ourselves. We have the Other within:

> There is a joke saying that 'Love is homesickness'; and whenever a man dreams of a place or a country and says to himself, while he is still dreaming: 'this place is familiar to me, I've been there before', we may interpret this place as being his mother's genitals or her body. In this case too, then, the *unheimlich* is what was once *heimisch*, familiar; the prefix 'un' is the token of repression. (368)

from repression to remembrance

Belonging is a political feeling. When Freud turned from case studies to later group psychologies, the transition was that from individual need to "political love". "Political love" is Mikkel Borch-Jacobsen's term for what Freud himself should have expressly addressed, the more concretely *political* effects of mass psychology. In his reading of *Group Psychology and the Analysis of the Ego*, Borch-Jacobsen follows through Freud's extrapolation of "love relationships" (erotic *qua* emotional reunions) from the individual couple to the whole, into the "collective desire of the individual".[8] Through the bond/link of the *Bindung*, self coheres to other and a "social organism" is formed. As Borch-Jacobsen develops Freud's thesis, this expanding metaphor of the bodily organism encompasses a multitude of sins. At its most obese, the social organism becomes a "cellular super-State". And, as references to a "primal band" might suggest, we are here entering the discourse of totalitarianism. The extreme of the organicist whole is a complete giving up of the self to suggestion and control (Borch-Jacobsen 155-6). The Leader becomes so successful because he is like you and me. He (for it is always a he, a *Vaterersatz*, a father substitute) is a narcissistic projection of our ego-ideal (157-8).

But, Love must prevail, in every sentimental sense available. What prevents Borch-Jacobsen's account from being that of a fascistic Freud is exactly love, a mutual projection of a love which must first arise from love of self. For a close harmony of subject with object, ego with other, all friction must be overcome: "[t]he movement of *Bindung* ... is precisely a movement of reducing opposition in general", "[i]f suggestibility is involved ... it must be because subjects allow themselves to be open to suggestion, out of love" (159-60). Ultimately, the love for a leader (who must surely be a democratic equal, but the best democratic equal) becomes necessary for group constitutions. The leader (whether he or she is good mother or good father) must bind individuals together and prevent destruction of those bonds, and bonds with others (163).

The political opposite of belonging is fear of regression and origin. For at the end of origins is the primal bond which needs to be repressed. It is the distinct lack of object relations which characterise the nightmare illustrations in Klaus Theweleit's *Male Fantasies*. Here, the "fascist imaginary" is depicted in *unheimlich* terms, because, for Theweleit, the mother's body as place and the maternal origin in time are the two psychoanalytic determinants of the right-wing character. In extreme paranoid fantasies, the mother's body exists as mass, flowing and gushing in its inconsistencies, threatening to engulf the fascist male back into the symbiosis from which it never escaped.[9] Solid nationalistic and imperialistic boundaries are thus constructed to protect everybody from

imaginary homelands

individual vicissitudes and irresolutions — the mass becomes the people (*Das Volk*) becomes the nation becomes Empire (*Reich*).[10] When imperialism attempts to force itself forwards, all that is "behind" (*hinten*) is disregarded. On the Front, where that *putsch* occurs, *Heimat* actually carries negative repercussions (Theweleit I, 395). The womb and the home are the centres of memory and origin which the fascist male soldier tries to forsake.

What Theweleit's study offers is a gendered reading of the original bond, primally that between mother and child. But in order to offset the deadly negativity of this fascist imaginary (at once demonising and destructive) I would like to propose a benevolent imaginary, in distinctly canny terms. In order to approach a canny view, I would suggest, that which was once the extreme projected *un*canny needs to be exorcised of its dreaded prefix through the positive regressive feelings of *Heimat*. It is, finally, the fantasy of the mother's body which links both *heimlich* and *Heimat*. *Heimlich* is the psychoanalytic symptom of *Heimat*. Celia Applegate, for example, depicts the relationship to *Heimat* in wholly masculine terms, *Heimatliebe* on the level of *amor matris* (Applegate 3). As well as home/land, the more personal, interpersonal, aspects of the term can now be registered. In a conflation of the motherly and the homely, *Heimat* also means "birthplace", "shelter", "identity", "a sense of belonging" (Geisler 26); "native soil", "motherland", "place of origin and belonging" (Santner 57). However much the Fatherland has attempted to steep its Mother Earth in the rhetoric of "blood and soil", it is the Motherland which promises psychoanalytic complements to ontogenesis and phylogenesis. At the centre of Reitz's Heimat, Maria Wiegand, as daughter, wife then mother, never leaves the *Heimat*. She is always *at home*. But more than that, as Anton Kaes suggests, she comes to define *Heimat*: "Maria embodies security, safety, and permanence. The film's secret message is: wherever she is, there is *Heimat*" (Kaes 168). Wherever she may be (mobile beyond the traditional confines of the house), the mother herself is always *home*. This is the male fantasy of belonging, an antidote to internalised fear and projected abjection.

As I have tried to hint throughout this essay, there is more to *Heimat*, and, indeed, *heimlich*, than place. Time is also of the essence. If repression denies regression for the fascist male, remembrance offers the potential for a breakthrough. The answer to a politics of hate caused through *unheimlich* must be a politics of love caused through *heimlich*. And such a modified politics, I would suggest, can be found in the work of Ernst Bloch. *Male Fantasies* contains its own critique of Bloch, typical of many, but also highlights ways in which Bloch can be usefully considered. Bloch's idealism is, of course, wholly in contrast to Theweleit's more rigorous, "scientific" psychoanalysis. This idealism takes itself into the content of Bloch's writing. In particular, Theweleit seizes on Bloch's derealisation of women, his reduction of them to the mythical expansiveness of Venus and Mary:

> Behold: it is women who contribute so much of the raw material for the concept of 'hope'. This may be the most benign way of disembodying them, but that is nonetheless what [he] does to them. (Theweleit I, 168-9)

It is due to Bloch's seemingly hopeless idealism that he is often disregarded as politically viable. But, it is such idealism which makes him ideal for the crossover of politics and psychoanalysis. Bloch's political hope for the future, the spirit of Utopia, is ultimately derived from the psychoanalytic lessons of the past.

Previously, Bloch has only had an epigrammised relation to *Heimat* and Reitz's Heimat.[11] He ends his epic *The Principle of Hope* with typical evocation:

> *True genesis is not at the beginning but at the end*, and it starts to begin only when society and existence become radical, i.e. grasp their roots. But the root of history is the working, creating human being who reshapes and overhauls the given facts. Once he has grasped himself and established what is his, without expropriation and alienation, in real democracy, there arises in the world something which shines into the childhood of all and to which no one has yet been: homeland.[12]

The backward looking nature of Bloch's prose is also something which has led to his displacement from political theory. His is a sentimental Marxism, nostalgic and anti-modern. These properties of his conveyed thought have led to a certain obsolescence. He is old-fashioned. I would like to counter this by stating that Bloch's is a politics of origin and *destination* rather than solely of origin. Whilst we must begin by grasping our roots, "[t]rue genesis is not at the beginning but at the end". It is the anticipatory "Forward Dawning" of Bloch's thesis which holds out for a politics of hope.

In *The Principle of Hope Vol. 1*, Bloch criticises psychoanalysis for its persistent backwardness. Specifically, Freud and Jung go back to origins but do not bring anything back from them. They have no concern for the future. Hence, we remain "Not-Yet-Conscious" – in "The Uncanny", for example, there is no solution; we are always afraid. For Bloch, if repression denies regression then we can only overcome the former by excavating unrealised meaning from the past and putting it to future use. The buried past is revealed by memory and expectation gives it futurity. Hope comes from remembering the past (Bloch 114-78). If it is solely the (past) return to homeland which has been the dominant critical relation of Bloch to Reitz's Heimat, this is due to ignorance of Bloch's presentism and futurity. For Bloch, the present remembering of the good old past and its further forward extrapolation into a potential good new future are the principles of hope. Hope is always a future aspect from a present perspective. We hope something *will* happen. From the intersection of the present, we look forward to regaining something precious that we have lost. But, when does the present become the future? Surely, when hope is attained it becomes something else, fulfilment, and we must find new hopes to defer that end. We must always have something to live forward to. It is in this sense that we can see futurity as being as elusive as the past. Just as memory is the present phantom of the past, hope is the present fiction of the future. The conundrums of time are endless, timeless. I would like to suggest that we are only, actually present. It is exactly as an *intersection* that the present remains the best of both worlds.

For Reitz, it is also the presentism of *Heimat* which makes it relevant. His terms for *Heimat* are recognisably nostalgic, "'closeness, childhood, security, warmth, grandmotherliness'", but he also acknowledges that they can "'only exist as memory, as longing'" (Kaes 168). That is, they exist, now, as memory. The *futurity* of *Heimat*, the present-to-be, was taken up by Reitz seven years later, in his 13-part sequel, *Die Zweite Heimat*. This *Second Heimat* is the extrapolated destination of origin, learning from the past. Reitz explicitly addresses the forward looking aspect of his sequel:

> It's the story of a twenty-year-old who breaks away from his past and sets out with

a belief in freedom and a vision of his own future. That's my story too. It's where my other roots lie. This film uses my own memories, just as *Heimat* did, but nevertheless it is a totally different film. It reflects the other side of my nature.[13]

In the film's opening narration, Maria's son, Hermann, tells of his hopes on leaving for Munich, and he refuses to look back: "I would be born a second time. Not from my mother's body but from my own mind. I would seek my own – a second home". The fact that Hermann returns home by the end of the film shows that history can never be escaped because it always exists, at present, as memory. This may signal defeat, that the only lesson of the present is that the past is always better. But, to put it more promisingly, more hopefully, if there is a *wish* to return to community, then the *unheimlich* fear of the past can be overcome. Only through an acceptance of the past – the good old imagined past, certainly, but also a coming to terms with the bad old (actual?) past – can present, and future, belongings and communities be reached.

notes

I am grateful to Sarah Wood for helping this project find its way home. My thanks, also, to Barry Stocker for final pointers.

1 Celia Applegate, *A Nation of Provincials: The German Idea of Heimat* (Berkeley, Los Angeles, Oxford: University of California Press, 1990) p1-3. See also Chapter 2, "Taming the Revolution".

2 Of course, this is a particular literary scene. For Williams, the ideal Victorian fiction is that which negates the alienating effects of the Industrial Revolution (e.g. George Eliot's *Middlemarch*). The ideal Modernist fiction is that which harks back to an age before Monopoly Capitalism (e.g. D.H. Lawrence's *The Rainbow*). See, in particular, Williams's *The English Novel from Dickens to Lawrence* (London: Chatto & Windus, 1970).

3 For a census of reactions to *Heimat* see the "Special Issue on *Heimat*", *New German Critique* 36 (fall 1985). Especially useful are Miriam Hansen's "Dossier on *Heimat*" and Michael E. Geisler's "*Heimat* and the German New Left: The Anamnesis of a Trauma".

4 Anton Kaes, *From Hitler to Heimat: The Return of History as Film* (Cambridge, Massachusetts, London: Harvard University Press, 1989) pix-xi.

5 Thomas Elsaesser, *New German Cinema: A History* (London: MacMillan, 1989) p239.

6 For an interesting theoretical equivalent to this debate see Eric L. Santner's *Stranded Objects: Mourning, Memory, and Film in Postwar Germany* (Ithaca and London: Cornell University Press, 1990). Through post-structuralist terminologies, Santner argues that primary narcissistic injuries can only be worked through by a "semantic supplement", the ability to "say 'we' non-narcissistically". This involves "the integration of the *unheimlich* into the first person plural". That is, we must welcome back into ourselves the Other (the Enemy) we have created (32-3). For Santner, whereas the Imaginary realm is *heimlich*, part of the nature of the Symbolic is to create and project a demon *unheimlich*, to divide "good" self from "bad" other (160-1).

For a feminist reading of the national mourning debate see Susan E. Linville's "The Mother-Daughter Plot in History: Helma Sanders-Brahms's *Germany, Pale Mother*", *New German Critique* 55 (winter 1992). Here, Linville argues the case for a pre-Oedipal Motherland, as opposed to the enforced Oedipal scenario of the Fatherland. Clearly, there are ways in which Linville can be joined with Santner. The Imaginary is where we all belong.

7 Sigmund Freud, "The Uncanny" (1919), in *The Pelican Freud Library*, vol.14, tr. James Strachey, ed.

Albert Dickson (Harmondsworth: Penguin, 1985) p339.

8 Mikkel Borch-Jacobsen, *The Freudian Subject* (1982), tr. Catherine Porter (London: Macmillan, 1989) p153-4.

9 Klaus Theweleit, *Male Fantasies vol. I: Women, Floods, Bodies, History* (1977), trs Stephen Conway, Erica Carter and Chris Turner (Cambridge: Polity Press, 1987). See, in particular, Theweleit's use of Margaret Mahler, and Deleuze and Guattari's *Anti-Oedipus* (206-13). Whilst I am not wholly convinced by Theweleit's broad synthesis of psychoanalytic methodologies, I believe that, like the Mitscherlich scenario, the illustrative value of his study lies in precisely its preference for fantasy. In this case, due to their paranoid character (and as endemic to the uncanny), these male soldier fantasies take on particularly extreme manifestations.

10 *Male Fantasies vol. II: Male Bodies: Psychoanalyzing the White Terror* (1978) (Cambridge: Polity Press, 1989) p94.

11 See, for example, Applegate, *A Nation of Provincials* (246) and Kaes, *From Hitler to Heimat* (165).

12 Ernst Bloch, *The Principle of Hope*, vol. 3 (1959), trs Neville Plaice, Stephen Plaice and Paul Knight (Oxford: Basil Blackwell, 1986) p1375-6.

13 This quotation was taken from an *Arena* programme entitled "Edgar Reitz: Return to *Heimat*", shown on BBC2 on 12/4/93. This documentary coincided with the first transmission of *Die Zweite Heimat* on British television, shown as *The Second Heimat: A New Generation*.

bibliography

Applegate, C., *A Nation of Provincials: The German Idea of* Heimat (Berkeley, Los Angeles: University of California Press, 1990).

Bloch, E., *The Principle of Hope*, vol. 3 (1959) trs N. Plaice, S. Plaice and P. Knight (Oxford: Basil Blackwell, 1986).

stephen keane

Borch-Jacobsen, M., *The Freudian Subject* (1982) tr. C. Porter (London: Macmillan, 1989).

"Edgar Reitz: Return to *Heimat*", Arena (BBC2, 12 April 1993).

Elsaesser, T., *New German Cinema: A History* (London: Macmillan, 1989).

Freud, S., "The Uncanny" (1919) in *The Penguin Freud Library*, vol. 14 (Harmondsworth: Penguin, 1985) p335-376.

Kaes, A., *From Hitler to Heimat: The Return of History as Film* (Cambridge, Mass.: Harvard University Press, 1989).

Linville, S.E., "The Mother-Daughter Plot in History: Helma Sanders-Brahms's *Germany, Pale Mother*", New German Critique 55 (winter 1992) p57-70.

Santner, E.L., *Stranded Objects: Mourning, Memory and Film in Postwar Germany* (Ithaca: Cornell University Press, 1990).

"Special Issue on *Heimat*", New German Critique 36 (fall 1985).

Theweleit, K., *Male Fantasies vol. I: Women, Floods, Bodies, History* (1977), trs S. Conway, E. Carter and C. Turner (Cambridge: Polity Press, 1987).

Theweleit, K., *Male Fantasies vol. II: Psychoanalyzing the White Terror* (1978), trs as vol. I (Cambridge: Polity Press, 1989).

Williams, R., *The English Novel from Dickens to Lawrence* (London: Chatto & Windus, 1970).

> I have always regarded card houses as the only dwellings worthy of mankind.
>
> *Günter Grass*

It should be easy to attack the concept of *Heimat*. After its service in the name of Nazism, not merely its usage, but the very notion, conjuring up images of stiflingly kitschy, rustic *Eintopf* ("one pot") dinners and sun-drenched cornfields, seems to confirm the bitter accusations levelled against Hitler in Syberberg's *Hitler – A Film From Germany*:

> You occupied everything and corrupted it with your actions, – everything, honour, loyalty, country life, hard work, movies, dignity, fatherland, pride, faith ... Nothing more will grow here. An entire nation stopped existing.[1]

And yet, only forty years after the end of the apparently *Heimat*-destroying war (both figuratively and literally, for the Germans from the east), Chancellor Kohl deemed it not inappropriate to talk at a convention of *Heimatvertriebene* (exiles), under the unequivocal slogan, "Silesia Remains Ours".[2] And, even more unnerving, since not publicly acknowledged, the German government, as a leaked copy of the top secret CDU *Fuchsbriefe* of 19th March, 1992, reveals, is once again seeking to re-establish that "lost" *Heimat* in the east; to this end it is funding the "return" of "ethnic Germans" from the Volga region to Kaliningrad (Königsberg).[3] It is in this context that Richard von Weizsäcker's seemingly innocent assertion that "[t]he peoples of Europe love their homelands. The Germans are no different"[4] must be read.

Has the word not been stripped of all credibility already? Do these unsavoury goings-on not simply confirm Kaes's assessment that any "nostalgia for a *Heimat*" can only be "revisionist" in character?[5] Do we

dan stone

HOMES WITHOUT HEIMATS?
jean améry
at the limits

need to be told once again what Adorno told us in 1959, that the *Wirtschaftswunder* (economic miracle) was not a substitute for "*aufarbeiten die Vergangenheit*" (coming to terms with the past)?[6] that the silence in Germany after 1945 was not, as Hermann Lübbe would have us believe, a "silent mastery over the past"?[7] Why does Syberberg's intention of "find[ing] some redemptive way back to the spiritual *Heimat*" of the Germans, which he believes has been lost to both fascism and postwar materialism"[8] not chill us to the bone?

It is the intention of this essay to show that the continued hankering after a *Heimat* is part of a wider European tradition of nationalism, one that rests on a fundamental confusion – the need for a home is, with varying degrees of intention, elided with the desire for a mythical homeland/fatherland, be it village, free port or country. Home becomes a common homeland, one's roots

homes without *heimats?*

grow into life-governing principles. Of course, the specifically German context that is the *Heimat* carries more frightening resonances than most; as Gustav Heinemann commented: "[t]here are troublesome fatherlands. One of them is Germany".[9] But the rise of nationalist revanchism is not confined to Germany, and the circumstances peculiar to this (extreme) case are not without basic similarities with other countries. Using the concept of *Heimat* as paradigmatic, then, I hope to demonstrate this confusion via an examination of a short piece by Jean Améry, respecting its attack on the sentimental attachments to the notion of the homeland, with their accompanying "regional foolery of all kinds"[10], but also not ignoring its fundamental dependence on a conception of home which leaves it susceptible to traditionalist arrogation. Why, that is, the piece is ultimately incapable of solving the problem of having a home without the typical concomitant, described by Jean-Luc Nancy, of the mythic community, in which "nothing is more *common* to the members of a community than a myth, or a group of myths".[11]

Dislocation is one of the defining experiences of the twentieth century. Its obbligato is homesickness. No one has described this with such trenchant resentment as Améry, in the section of his seminal work, *At the Mind's Limits* (1966), entitled "How Much Home Does a Man Need?". His experience, whilst in exile in Belgium and fighting for the resistance, of attempting to come to terms with this "nasty, gnawing sickness ... which one cannot speak of in the Eichendorff [i.e. romantic] tone", left him only with a homesickness which equated with an "alienation from the self" (Améry 43).

It was this inner feeling of loss, the knowledge of being rejected from one's childhood land merely because of *what* one was born, that allowed Améry to distinguish his homesickness not only from that of "those emigrants who fled the Third Reich exclusively because of their ideology", but also from "those who were expelled from their homelands in the East" (42). After all, the latter, who lost the combination of life-experiences ("possessions, homesteads, business ... land, meadows and hills, a forest, a silhouette of a city, the church in which they had been confirmed") that permit "traditional homesickness" (50), did not also lose the people and the language, as Améry did (42). This meant that unlike the expellees from the east, Améry's experience of homesickness was synonymous with "self-destruction", the process of "dismantling our past piece by piece, which could not be done without self-contempt and hatred for the lost self" (51). Like his later experience of torture at the hands of the Gestapo, this dispossession of origin contributed to his loss of what he calls "trust in the world" (28).

No wonder then, that earlier on, in the eponymous first chapter, Améry dismisses Heidegger ("that disquieting magus from Alemmanic regions" (18)) and his attempt to think Being apart from beings, by asserting instead the primacy of existence, particularly as it was manifested in the concentration camps:

> [I]n the camp it was more convincingly apparent than on the outside that beings and the light of Being get you nowhere. You could *be* hungry, *be* tired, *be* sick. To say that one purely and simply *is*, made no sense ... To reach out beyond concrete reality with words became before our very eyes a game that was not only worthless and an impermissible luxury but also mocking and evil. (18-19)

This finds contemporary resonances in the work of Andrew Benjamin, who, in questioning the presupposed connection between a "plurality of modes of being" and "a conception of being as without exception singular", writes that:

> There is no singular question of 'the meaning of Being' that can be posed independently of modes of being ... There is therefore no question of Being *qua* Being, there is simply the plurality of questions pertaining to the plurality of ways in which things are.[12]

Heidegger, who of course knew little about leaving home, was free to formulate his notion of "Being-in-the-world" at the same time as Améry was losing trust in it.

In fact, Améry's "loss of trust in the world" provides a substantial counterweight to Heidegger's more famous concept of "Being-in-the-world". For example, when talking about "bad moods", Heidegger writes that it is because:

> States-of-mind are so far from being reflected upon, that precisely what they do is to assail *Dasein* in its unreflecting devotion to the 'world' with which it is concerned and on which it expends itself. A mood assails us. It comes neither from 'outside' nor from 'inside', but arises out of Being-in-the-world, as a way of such Being.[13]

If only Améry had not allowed his "State-of-mind" to "assail" his *Dasein* in its unreflecting devotion to the 'world'", perhaps he might have transcended his situation (he may surely be forgiven, in his plight, for not interpreting Heidegger's Being as itself differential). Heidegger, unable to conceive of modes of being which strictly precluded thinking Being, such as Auschwitz, where merely continuing to be able to devote oneself to the "world" was an achievement of the highest order, surely failed to appreciate the freedom that his own fortunate mode of being gave him to devote himself to anything but the "world".[14]

It is all the more surprising, then, that Améry is unable to release himself from certain romanticised ideals of the home. His traumatic experiences, whilst they bred in him an ineradicable cynicism, if anything only strengthened his convictions where the homely ideal was concerned. Améry's writing is that of a man of profound feeling, and its genuineness is beyond doubt. Nevertheless, I do not believe it is an insult to his achievements, or his importance as a witness to the Holocaust, to examine more closely some of his conclusions. Améry was certainly a man of much bitterness, who knew more than most the awful truth of Gregor von Rezzori's claim that:

> [Y]ou are likely to lose faith in yourself and in mankind when you see the survivors of the cataclysm trying to build up a new world by building into it all the same structures that led to the decomposition of the old.[15]

(He confirmed this with his suicide in 1978, in the light of the *Tendenzwende*, the rise of neo-conservatism in Germany.) So it is all the more surprising that he should anchor his desire for security in a reality entirely reminiscent of the world which had only recently expelled him from its midst. Such is the power of the myth of the *Heimat* that even those who have seen at first hand its barbaric side cannot always remove themselves from its range of affectivity. As in Bataille's theory of fascism, in which the release of "revolutionary effervescence" that the mass movement constitutes is "fundamentally negated" by "the imperative presence of the leader", once more returning the affective life to a false unity[16], Améry's outburst of energy actually ties him all the more strongly to what he denounces. (It should be stressed at this point, lest misunderstandings

homes without *heimats?*

arise, that I am in no way proposing the outrageous hypothesis that Améry was a subtle, or even unwitting advocate of fascism.)

He is undoubtedly correct to assert that "[r]educed to the positive-psychological basic content of the idea, home is *security*" (46). It follows quite satisfactorily that "[i]f one has no home, however, one becomes subject to disorder, confusion, desultoriness" (47). And one is only too happy to acquiesce when he says that "[o]ne would like to dispel the embarrassingly sweet tones that are associated with the word home" (48). But here, however, Améry cannot make the necessary leap of faith: [t]hat reactionary indolence has taken over the entire complex of ideas associated with home does not obligate us to ignore it (48). Why not? Somehow, although his former homeland has become "hostile" and "enemy country" (50), it remains his homeland. Améry cannot distinguish between *home* and *homeland*.

In fact, he abandons any such distinction, and concentrates instead on levelling it, by talking in terms of *homeland* and *fatherland*. He objects to the fact that:

> [A] widespread attitude claims to accept the idea of homeland in its regional, folkloristic limits at least as something of picturesque value, while fatherland is extremely suspicious to it as a demagogic catchword and a characteristic of reactionary obstinacy. (54)

And he claims that whoever has no fatherland has no homeland either. This is backed up by his opinion that his own experience proves "with sufficient clarity how home ceases to be home as soon as it is not at the same time fatherland" (55). Irrespective of his prediction (remarkably similar, incidentally, to Salman Rushdie's use of "the migrant" as a paradigm for the postmodern condition) of a cosmopolitan, rootless future which

will certainly expel the homeland and possibly the mother tongue and will let them exist peripherally as a subject of specialized historical research only... (57)

Améry chooses to celebrate the necessity of having a homeland. This is a curious position indeed, when one considers the fact that, according to Alvin Rosenfeld:

> What Améry feared most but expected to occur eventually was a normalization of Nazism, a process of historical revision that would have the inevitable effect of blurring and ultimately denying the reality of his own experience.[17]

His suicide made it clear, for those who ever doubted it, that these were genuine sentiments. Nevertheless, Améry's need for "a house of which we know who lived in it before us" (57) is blurred, in his mind, with the "homeland" in which the house is (supposedly) to be found.

At the end of the essay, then, Améry has taken us from expulsion, through homesickness, through recognition of never being able to return, to a desire for a renewed sense of home, equated with homeland/fatherland. Our surprise at such an outcome is somewhat mitigated by the fact that Améry's experiences are remote indeed from those of present generations of most Europeans, for it is indubitably the case that when all is said and done, "[w]hat remains is the matter-of-fact observation: it is not good to have no home" (61).

Yet the very emotional response which this last line is designed to create is also that which is exploited by "the pedagogues who are always waiting in the wings".[18] It is indeed not good to have no home, but Améry's description of what that means is akin to George Orwell's peculiarly "patriotic" form of socialism, one of old maids on bicycles, warm beer and hedgerows, one that he did not intentionally conceive for the purpose of furnishing Tory speeches – but for such it proved apposite, at least for those, waiting in the wings, who applauded it.

How could it be that someone who really knew about Weber's *"Entzauberung der Welt"* ("disenchantment of the world") could remain attached to such an integral component of that "old world"? The answer may (partly) be found in a passage from an essay by Horst Ehmke, entitled *What is the Germans' Fatherland?* It is worth quoting at length:

> The word 'fatherland' denotes two things: the region a nation settles and inhabits, and its homeland in a spiritual-political sense. As a rule the word designates the country in which one is born and raised. It is at once more and less than the state. It has no organs or powers, but as the area in which a nation lives it must also not be restricted to the territory of a sovereign state ... One's homeland can be taken away. Over the centuries German governments have forced German patriots to emigrate. Millions of refugees have been driven from their homeland through outside forces. It is impossible, however, to strip anyone of his fatherland as a spiritual homeland.[19]

Such writing, exactly what one would expect from one of Grass's pedagogues, is in fact written by a man who concludes his essay by stating that:

> Just as the past of socialism is not to be separated from the development of Germany, so the future of the German nation is not to be separated from the development of socialism.[20]

The notion of the homeland in its spiritual sense (although very much bound to the memory of a particular place) is exactly what Améry strove to retain, without yielding to sentimentality. As Ehmke's ridiculous nostalgia makes abundantly clear, this is an impossible dream, for it is always open to being overthrown by its own constituents.[21] The lure of the *Heimat* has proved irresistible even to those whose own experience, whose own supposedly ultramontane ideologies, should have rendered them unsusceptible to its call.

It has become clear that the concept of *Heimat* is not as open to opprobrium as may at first have been assumed. Those who berate a "loss of community" are to be found across the political spectrum. As Winkler has shown, nationalism was originally a slogan of the liberal *Bürgertum* before it was taken over as an instrument of the right, so it is perhaps not surprising that it still maintains its hold in initially unexpected quarters.[22] It is obvious that we are not automatically left cold by Syberberg's intentions because they are, in fact, ones that are easy to empathise with – after all, it is not good to have no home.

The trouble lies in the conjunction of "homeland" with "identity", as if the loss of the former necessarily entails the loss of the latter. This is not simply to agree with Benedict Anderson's famous heuristic of the "imagined community", for his formulation applies only to industrial and post-industrial societies.[23] Rather, if we are really to conceive of homes without *Heimat*s in a way that Améry was unable to do (and that this is necessary has, I hope, become evident), then the very concept of the community in which the home is located itself needs to be rethought – and not just the community of the "age of nationalism" as it is understood by Anderson.

It is telling that the need for a home has been conflated, etymologically, with the desire for a homeland: *Heim* becomes

homes without *heimats?*

Heimat. But as Freud explained, what is homely, *heimlich*, is not only the cosy, the languid, the domestic, but also the sinister, the secret, the concealed.[24] The *Heimat* revels in comfort on the one hand, and hypocrisy on the other. Thus what Nancy has to say about the obsession with the "lost community", which began with Rousseau, should not surprise us:

> [A]t every moment in its history, the Occident has given itself over to the nostalgia for a more archaic community that has disappeared, and to deploring a loss of *familiarity, fraternity and conviviality*.[25]

In other words, what Anderson fails to recognise is that it is the *theorising* of community, as lost community, that is modern – which does not mean that pre-modern communities were not also "imagined", even if not explicitly. As Nancy suggests, community thus conceived has not existed, not for the Guayaqui Indians, nor for our ancestral hut-dwellers, nor for the age of the Hegelian "spirit" (Nancy 11). Since it never existed in the first place, but was a construct of "society" (*Gesellschaft*), "community" (*Gemeinschaft*) was never lost. Only we are lost, for "we have wrung for ourselves the phantasms of the lost community" (12).

It is clear where these phantasms lead. It was in the era of McCarthyism that Robert Nisbet noted:

> The dread spectacle of totalitarianism as an organised movement in every western country at the present time cannot be divorced from its proffer of community to individuals for whom sensations of dissolution and alienation have become intolerable ... The almost eager acceptance of the fantastic doctrines of the Nazis by millions of otherwise intelligent Germans would be inexplicable were it not for the accompanying proffer of moral community to the disenchanted and alienated German worker, peasant, and intellectual.[26]

Yet as Nancy demonstrates, the very idea of community, based on the immanence of communion, is itself destructive of community as it has traditionally been desired. No doctrine more clearly proves this than Nazism, in which the drive to absolute immanence can lead only to death:

> Immanence, communal fusion, contains no other logic than that of the suicide of the community that is governed by it. Thus the logic of Nazi Germany was not only that of the extermination of the other, of the sub-human deemed exterior to the communion of blood and soil, but also, effectively, the logic of sacrifice aimed at all those in the "Aryan" community who did not satisfy the criteria of *pure* immanence ... (12)

But, it may be objected, Nazism represents a limit case. Certainly, fascism "was the grotesque or abject resurgence of an obsession with communion" (17). But does this knowledge of immanence-as-death threaten the wider application of *community*?

Lyotard notes that: "Nazism requires nothing of what is not 'Aryan', except for the cessation of its appearing to exist".[27] Herein lies the reason why Nazism represents not an exception, but simply the logic of community *in extremis*. It is the role of the *name* that is vital, for the name of the community legitimates it and its practices, as in the name "Aryan". It alleges "proper names and proper social bodies".[28] It constructs the "others" who cannot be part of that community, and, in certain circumstances, demands their extermination in order to maintain the purity of the dominant group. Lest this be doubted, it is enough to recall the memory of Freud's eldest son Martin of walking with his aunt Dolfi in Vienna:

96

> [W]hen we passed an ordinary kind of man, probably a gentile, who, as far as I knew, had taken no notice of us, I put it down to a pathological phobia, or Dolfi's stupidity, when she gripped my arm in terror and whispered: 'Did you hear what that man said? He called me a dirty stinking Jewess and said it was time we were all killed'.[29]

Jean Améry's reinstated homeland cannot but suffer from the same problem of exclusivity (though of course he does not propose such a closed system, nor did he desire one), for it is on the basis of whom it excludes that any community acquires its self-identity.

But what are the possibilities of achieving homes without *Heimats*? Such a likelihood certainly seems as remote as ever, for the myth of the homeland is enjoying a renaissance in Europe not seen since 1945. But since we stated above that the mythic notion of community has never actually been realised, and that the thinking of community had attained particular strength in the modern age with the imagined community being articulated in terms of extreme nationalism, the nature of any given society in which such mythic conceptions can take root must be examined. Homes have always existed; *Heimats* never have. Only in a society in which celebrating the security which the home offers is not expanded to encompass a mythic conception of community is the possibility for non-nationalist thinking embodied. Such a "community" would be, in Nancy's words, "the sacred stripped of the sacred":

> [C]ommunity is transcendence: but "transcendence," which no longer has any "sacred" meaning, signifying precisely a resistance to immanence (resistance to the communion of everyone or to the exclusive passion of one or several: to all the forms and all the violences of subjectivity). (35)

The *Heimat* with which we began, then, cannot be dismissed lightly, for it is obvious that a community will, in some form or another, be with us; it "is given to us with being" (35). Where "home" and the necessary security that it connotes is indistinguishable from "homeland", the question of community, however, enters the mythic realm, in which community can never be attained, for it is imbued with nostalgia and a destructive drive for immanence. Community, on this reading, must be "a matter of incompleting its sharing" (ibid.), for determining who shares in the community is necessarily a statement of who lies outside it. We all feel a need for community, and this is why the advance, once again, of nationalism, spreads its insidious message with such ease – its appeal lies primarily in the ease with which it channels our desires. It is this confusion of community with the nation, the homeland, the modern version of the imagined community, that contains the danger.[30] The home *per se* can be shared (unshared); it does not, as even Améry thought, have to be eulogised in the shape of a homeland. In fact, the home must be (un)shared if such a confusion is to be avoided.

The need for a home is inescapable; on this score, Améry is undoubtedly correct. The need for a *Heimat*, however, is a result of a certain organisation of society in which the desire for an unobtainable pristine community becomes the form of reality-production for which people are willing to strive. In the modern age, the greater the problems, the more outrageous the myth, to the point at which, in the fascist production of reality, the equation of the home with the mother becomes something to be escaped at all costs, with the celebration of the monolithic fatherland the only refuge for what Theweleit calls the "soldier male" who typifies fascism.[31] Only once those who benefit from the chan-

homes without *heimats*?

nelling of the desire of the masses in such a direction are shown to be other than the masses themselves will the grip of such myths diminish. Unfortunately, Améry appears to have been correct in his assessment of the continued hold of the idea of the homeland, for the conflation of home and *Heimat* shows no sign of weakening. The desire for a *Heimat* is indeed revisionist in its implications; only when the vision of a non-exclusive community – a community open to the plurality of modes of being – gains acceptance will the dangers of nationalism recede, and will we be able to live an alternative to Améry's reintegration of the "new world" into the "old". Until such time, we can only take heed of the words of George Steiner: "though the ideal of a non- national society seems mockingly remote, there is in the last analysis no other alternative to self-destruction".[32]

notes

1 Cited in Anton Kaes, "Holocaust and the End of History: Postmodern Historiography in Cinema" in *Probing the Limits of Representation: Nazism and the "Final Solution"*, ed. Saul Friedlander (Cambridge, Mass.: Harvard University Press, 1992) p219.

2 Cited in Anson Rabinbach, "The Jewish Question in the German Question", *New German Critique* 44 (spring/summer 1988) p181.

3 See *Searchlight* 216 (June 1993) p18.

4 Richard von Weizsäcker, "Speech by Richard von Weizsäcker, President of the Federal Republic of Germany, in the Bundestag during the Ceremony Commemorating the 40th Anniversary of the End of the War in Europe and of National Socialist Tyranny, May 8, 1945" in *Bitburg in Moral and Political Perspective*, ed. Geoffrey Hartman (Bloomington: Indiana University Press, 1986) p269.

5 Kaes, op. cit. p217.

6 T.W. Adorno, "What Does Coming to Terms with the Past Mean" in Hartman, op. cit. p114-129.

7 Cited in Rabinbach, op. cit. p161.

8 Kaes, op. cit. p221.

9 Cited in Günter Grass, "Germany – Two States, One Nation?" in *Two States – One Nation? The Case Against German Reunification*, trs Krishna Winston and A.S. Wensinger (London: Secker and Warburg, 1991) p55.

10 Jean Améry, *At the Mind's Limits: Contemplations by a Survivor on Auschwitz and its Realities*, trs Sidney Rosenfeld and Stella P. Rosenfeld (New York: Schocken, 1986) p48. Further references will appear in the text.

11 Jean-Luc Nancy, *The Inoperative Community*, ed. Peter Connor, trs Peter Connor et al. (Minneapolis: University of Minnesota Press, 1991) p42.

12 Andrew Benjamin, *Art, Mimesis and the Avant-Garde* (London: Routledge, 1991) p11-12.

13 Martin Heidegger, *Being and Time*, trs John Macquarrie and Edward Robinson (Oxford: Basil Blackwell, 1962) p175-176.

14 Cf. Levinas's statement: "[w]e were subhuman, a gang of apes. A small inner murmur, the strength and wretchedness of persecuted people, reminded us of our essence as thinking creatures, but we were no longer part of the world". Emmanuel Levinas, "The Name of a Dog, or Natural Rights" in *Difficult Freedom*, tr. Seán Hand (London: Athlone Press, 1990) p153.

15 Gregor von Rezzori, *Memoirs of an Anti-Semite* (London: Picador, 1983) p251.

16 Georges Bataille, "The Psychological Structure of Fascism" in *Visions of Excess: Selected Writings 1927-1939*, ed. Allan Stoekl, trs Allan Stoekl, Carl R. Lovitt and Donald M. Leslie, Jr. (Minneapolis: University of Minnesota Press, 1985) p153.

17 Alvin Rosenfeld, "Jean Améry as Witness" in *Holocaust Remembrance: The Shapes of Memory*, ed.

Geoffrey H. Hartman (Oxford: Basil Blackwell, 1994) p67.

18 Grass, op. cit. p58.

19 Horst Ehmke, "What is the Germans' Fatherland?" in *Observations on "The Spiritual Situation of the Age"*, ed. Jürgen Habermas, tr. Andrew Buchwalter (Cambridge: MIT Press, 1985) p325-326.

20 Ibid. p332.

21 Cf. Renan's definition of the nation as "a soul, a spiritual principle". His eulogising over the "cult of the ancestors" with its "heroic past", however, is more suited to a politics of exclusion and the typical nationalist devotion to chimera. Ernst Renan, "What is a Nation" in *Nation and Narration*, ed. Homi Bhabha (London: Routledge, 1990) p19.

22 Heinrich August Winkler, "Nationalism and Nation-State in Germany" in *The National Question in Europe*, eds Mikulás Teich and Roy Porter (Cambridge: Cambridge University Press, 1993) p186.

23 Benedict Anderson, *Imagined Communities: Reflections on the Origin and Spread of Nationalism* (London: Verso, 1983). Cf. Hobsbawm's comment on Anderson which rests on the same mistake: "the question still remains why, having lost *real* communities, people should wish to imagine this type of replacement". Eric Hobsbawm, *Nations and Nationalism Since 1780* (Cambridge: Cambridge University Press, 1990) p46 (my italics).

2 Sigmund Freud, "The Uncanny" in The Penguin Freud Library, vol. 14, ed. A. Dickson, tr. J. Strachey (Harmondsworth: Penguin, 1985) p355-376.

25 Nancy, op. cit. p10 (my italics). Further references will appear in the text.

26 Robert A. Nisbet, *Community and Power* (New York: Oxford University Press, 1962) p33-34. (Originally published as *The Quest for Community* in 1953.)

27 Jean-François Lyotard, *The Differend: Phrases in*

dan stone

Dispute, tr. Georges Van Den Abbeele (Manchester: Manchester University Press, 1988) p103.

28 Cecile Lindsay, "Lyotard and the Postmodern Body", *L'Esprit Créateur*, vol. XXXI, no. 1 (spring 1991) p42.

29 Cited in Sander Gilman, *The Jew's Body* (New York: Routledge, 1991) p236.

30 I am not unmindful of criticisms of Nancy, such as Boyarin and Boyarin's, who claim that "within the thought of philosophers such as Nancy lies a blindness to the particularity of Jewish difference that is itself part of a relentless penchant for allegorising all 'difference' into a univocal discourse". I am applying Nancy's thought specifically to the community conceived in national terms; its application to other communities is admittedly problematic, since they embody a different sort of myth, or, as is emphasised here, an exhortation to "create forms of community that do not rely on one of the most potent and dangerous myths – the myth of autochthony". Furthermore, Nancy's insistence on the word "community" can itself be construed as an unnecessary nostalgia. See Daniel Boyarin and Jonathan Boyarin, "Diaspora: Generation and the Ground of Jewish Identity", *Critical Inquiry* 19 (summer 1993) p693-725, here at p699.

31 Klaus Theweleit, *Male Fantasies, vol. 1: Women, Floods, Bodies, History*, tr. Stephen Conway (Minneapolis: University of Minnesota Press, 1987), e.g. p432: "what fascism allows the masses to express are suppressed drives, imprisoned desires... The success of fascism demonstrates that masses who become fascist suffer more from their internal states of being than from hunger or employment".

32 George Steiner, "A Kind of Survivor" in *Language and Silence* (Harmondsworth: Penguin, 1969) p134.

bibliography

Adorno, T.W., "What Does Coming to Terms with the Past Mean?" in *Bitburg in Moral and Political*

homes without *heimats?*

Perspective, ed. G. Hartman (Bloomington: Indiana University Press, 1986) p114-29.

Améry, J., *At the Mind's Limits: Contemplations by a Survivor on Auschwitz and Its Realities*, trs S. Rosenfeld and S.P. Rosenfeld (New York: Schocken, 1986).

Anderson, B., *Imagined Communities: Reflections on the Origin and Spread of Nationalism* (London: Verso, 1991).

Bataille, G., *Visions of Excess: Selected Writings 1927-1939*, ed. and tr. A. Stoekl (Minneapolis: Minnesota University Press, 1985).

Benjamin, A., *Art, Mimesis and the Avant-Garde* (London: Routledge, 1991).

Boyarin, D. and J. Boyarin, "Diaspora: Generation and the Ground of Jewish Identity", *Critical Inquiry* 19 (summer 1993) p693-725.

Ehmke, H., "What is the German's Fatherland?" in *Observations on "The Spiritual Situation of the Age"*, ed. J. Habermas, tr. A. Buchwalter (Cambridge, Mass.: MIT Press, 1985) p309-32.

Freud, S., "The Uncanny" (1919) in The Penguin Freud Library, vol. 14 (Harmondsworth: Penguin, 1985) p335-376.

Gilman, S., *The Jew's Body* (New York: Routledge, 1991).

Grass, G., *Two States – One Nation? The Case Against German Reunification*, trs K. Winston and A.S. Wensinger (London: Secker and Warburg, 1991).

Heidegger, M., *Being and Time*, trs J. Macquarrie and E. Robinson (Oxford: Blackwell, 1962).

Hobsbawm, E., *Nations and Nationalism Since 1780* (Cambridge: Cambridge University Press, 1990).

Kaes, A., "Holocaust and the End of History: Postmodern Historiography in Cinema" in *Probing the Limits of Representation: Nazism and the "Final Solution"*, ed. S. Friedlander (Cambridge, Mass.: Harvard University Press, 1992) p206-22.

Levinas, E., *Difficult Freedom*, tr. S. Hand (London: Athlone Press, 1990).

Lindsay, C., "Lyotard and the Postmodern Body", *L'Esprit Créateur* 31.1 (spring 1991) p33-47.

Lyotard, J.-F., *The Differend: Phrases in Dispute*, tr. G. Van Den Abbeele (Manchester: Manchester University Press, 1988).

Nancy, J.-L., *The Inoperative Community*, tr. P. Connor et al. (Minneapolis: University of Minnesota Press, 1991).

Nisbet, R.A., *Community and Power* (New York: Oxford University Press, 1962).

Rabinbach, A., "The Jewish Question in the German Question", *New German Critique* 44 (spring/summer 1988) p159-92.

Renan, E., "What is a Nation?" in *Nation and Narration*, ed. H. Bhaba (London: Routledge, 1990) p8-22.

Rosenfeld, A., "Jean Améry as Witness" in *Holocaust Remembrance: The Shapes of Memory*, ed. G. Hartman (Oxford: Blackwell, 1994) p59-69.

Searchlight 216 (June 1993).

Steiner, G., *Language and Silence* (Harmondsworth: Penguin, 1969).

Theweleit, K., *Male Fantasies, vol. 1: Women, Floods, Bodies, History*, trs S. Conway, E. Carter and C. Turner (Minneapolis: University of Minnesota Press, 1987).

von Rezzori, G., *Memoirs of an Anti-Semite* (London: Picador, 1983).

von Weizsäcker, R., "Speech, May 8, 1985" in *Bitburg in Moral and Political Perspective*, ed. G. Hartman (Bloomington: Indiana University Press, 1986) p262-73.

Winkler, H.A., "Nationalism and Nation-State in Germany" in *The National Question in Europe in Historical Context*, eds M. Teich and R. Porter (Cambridge: Cambridge University Press, 1993) p181-95.

roger bromley

TRAVERSING IDENTITY
home movies and road movies in paris, texas

Writing in 1983 about Nicholas Ray's films, Wim Wenders describes the ways in which the English and American use of the word "home" covered much of what in German there are many words for: "building", "house", "family house", "home town", etc. (Wenders 1989). A year later discussing the American dream, the director most closely identified with "road movies" locates what for him is the contradictory expression "mobile homes". The expression fascinates Wenders because it suggests somewhere you could be at home yet on the road at the same time; a mobile "belonging", not fixed anywhere.

Paris, Texas is a home movie and it is a road movie. Scene 60 features Super-8 footage of a holiday the five principal characters had three years prior to the diegetic time of the narrative.[1] The roads in the film are the old Route 66, the transcontinental freeway, and other, abandoned roads. The abandoned roads are sites of decay, wrecked cars, and memories absorbed by the desert: sites of loss. At one point early on, Travis leaves the highway and his brother finds him seated on a 1950s pick-up wreck. Initially, Travis is seen to lack directionality as he wanders off the main road or disappears from the motel, at this stage still straying on *excluded ground*. This straying on excluded ground can be linked with Julia Kristeva's theory of the abject, where what has to be excluded is the unclean and the improper. However, in the search for the clean and the proper (Travis cleans a large number of shoes at his brother's house later in the film), the abject from which he is ceaselessly separating himself is, also, what Kristeva calls, a *land of oblivion* that he can never finally forget:

> [f]or the space that engrosses the deject, the excluded, is never *one*, nor *homogeneous*, nor *totalizable*, but essentially divisible, foldable and catastrophic. A deviser of territories, languages, works, the deject never stops demarcating his universe whose fluid confines – for they are constituted of a non-object, the abject – constantly question his solidity and impel him to start afresh. A tireless builder, the deject is in short a *stray*.[2]

Home is conventionally the location of family – homogeneous and totalizable; in the film only one actual home is shown. Significantly omitted from the final cut is what in the shooting script is the final scene. This scene has Travis in Paris, Texas building a house on the plot of land he had purchased when he and his wife, Jane, and son, Hunter, were together: a home for his now "broken" family. He receives a mail delivery which contains Super-8 film of his son and his estranged wife. The footage has images of Hunter and Jane travelling across the country, passing the camera back and forth to each other. What we do not know is whether

traversing identity

they are travelling towards or away from Travis. The use of the footage is one of many distancing motifs used throughout the film, part of the dialogue of fluidity and solidity. As I shall show, the final screen version has a very different ending – on the road with Travis, the *stray* and *deject* impelled to start afresh, but with no home in sight.

The home of Travis's brother, Walt, and his wife, Anne, is situated in Burbank – a suburb of Los Angeles, close to Hollywood – and imaged in a way which suggests an "ideal" movie home. Even Anne and Walt's performance styles are studiedly restricted to the conventions of cinema discourse. Theirs is the only home and family in the primary narration. The trailer home of Travis and Jane is extra-diegetic. Only the child, Hunter, has lived in both spaces, although Travis stays for a while in the Burbank home. Walt (the name needs no comment) works in billboard advertising which confirms his home and family as being constructed from, and financed by, *images*. I stress these points at this stage because my discussion will focus on *home* and *family* in relation to the Symbolic Order and in gendered terms. The film works with a series of binary oppositions, although these are also commutable as many of the borders in the film are traversed.

Burbank is the space of the literal (over-literal) home and the literal family – the place which the shot composition, editing, lighting and acting style suggest is delivered from all depth. Throughout the film there is also a focus on the figurative home and family – sites of dream and gendered fantasy.

My principal theoretical source for this analysis of *Paris, Texas* is Julia Kristeva's concept of *abjection* which is most fully articulated in *Powers of Horror*. The concept is described in a number of ways, but for my purposes I want to focus upon those definitions which refer to the way in which "the abject eludes the binary oppositions that structure the symbolic order" (Taylor 1987, 159); such systems as "home" and "family" are constructed to exclude the heterogeneous abject which manifests itself in transgressive *positions*, on the borders of the binaries of Symbolic codings. The abject cannot be "integrated with a given system of signs" (*PH* 14). In Scene 106 Travis, speaking of himself in the third person to Jane in the Keyhole Club, says "[he] just ran. He ran until the sun came up and he couldn't run any further... For five days, he ran like this until *every sign of man* had disappeared" (Script 180, my emphasis). The figure of Travis/traverse cannot himself be integrated with a system of signs, despite efforts to become the father and to restore the symbiosis of mother and child in the last scenes of the film. The whole film is overcoded, overloaded with "signs of man", the realm of the Symbolic Order. Kristeva argues that the social contract is based on an essentially sacrificial relationship of separation and articulation of differences which produce communicable meaning. This relationship is offered as "natural" but it is a structure obscured in a socio-historical context of Christian/Western culture. The "West" in the film is not simply topographical, or generic, but refers also to a European/American system of discursive power – hence the ambiguity of Paris, Texas. In *Powers of Horror*, Kristeva argues that Discourse is substituted for maternal care, along with a fatherhood – representative of the paternal function – that belongs to the realm of the Symbolic. A rejection of the Symbolic – for example, Travis's flight afetr the trailer fire from "every sign of man" – leads to a rejection of the paternal function and, ultimately, generates psychosis (Travis's "look" and his movements in the initial stages of the film suggest this). Abjection resists the intelligibility and signification of "home" and "family".

102

roger bromley

For Kristeva, abjection is very much concerned with boundary and border, the margin or limen which is "a void that is not nothing but indicates ... a defiance or challenge to symbolization" (*PH* 51). The border is the site of the binary, the locus of gender dichotomy with its links to forms of sexual violence. Ambivalence is the prevailing characteristic of the film and of abjection itself, "[t]he abject is, by definition, the sign of an impossible ob-ject, boundary and limit" (*PH* 154). The title of the film announces boundary and division, a seemingly contradictory state, an *entre-deux* – never reducible to the differences it joins and separates (bonding and separation are themes which recur throughout). Travis tells Walt that their father used to introduce his wife as the girl he met in Paris, then pause for the punchline, "Texas". Later he tells Hunter that his father would look at his mother and he wouldn't see her, just an *idea* of her, that she came from Paris, France. Walt, by marrying a French woman, replicates this "idea". Travis is adamant, however, that his mother was not a "fancy woman", implying that Hunter's is, "[m]y mother, not *your* mother – my mother was not a fancy woman" (Script 168).

Linked with Kristeva's concept of the abject (invariably identified with the feminine – the improper and unclean "refuse" thrown away in the proper and clean family home) and abjection, elaborated through a failure to recognize its kin (Travis's situation when Walt first encounters him after a four year absence) is the notion of "home" as defined by Biddy Martin and Chandra Mohanty. They develop their idea of home as containing at least

> two specific modalities: being home and not being home. "Being home" refers to the place where one lives within familiar, safe, protected boundaries; "not being home" is a matter of realizing that home was an illusion of coherence and safety based on the exclusion of specific histories of oppression and resistance, the repression of differences even within oneself. Because these locations acquire meaning and function as sites of personal and historical struggles, they work against the notion of an unproblematic geographic location of home. (Martin and Mohanty 169)

Apart from the European/American division signified by the film's title, Paris, Texas is also a polaroid photograph, a vacant lot, and, for Travis, the idea that it is his place of conception – the place where his parents first were lovers. Except for the original shooting script, it has no geographic location in the narration of the film. For both Travis and Jane, but for differently gendered reasons, "not being home" is a refuge, an escape, a flight from illusions shaped by specific ideologies of oppression which neither of them can articulate abstractly but only existentially. In the Keyhole club sequences, however, Travis does, at least, begin the discursive tracing of the reasons for his flight.

For Travis Paris, Texas is the site prior to the *inaugural loss* which founds his socio-symbolic being. The abject is constituted as the "object" of primal repression anterior to, but within the breaches of, secondary repression – the entry into the Symbolic order, the Word of the Father, language itself. Before this "entry" was the separation from the Mother – the space of the imprecise, uncertain and transgressive borders of the semiotic *chora*. For Kristeva the *speaking* subject is structured in the Symbolic Order by the separation from the Mother through the paternal agency which "introduces the symbolic division between 'subject' (child) and 'object' (mother)" (*PH* 44). The proper name, in psychoanalytic discourse, is always the name of the father. For Travis, this iden-

traversing identity

tification is compounded by sharing both first name and surname with his father. This is tied in with the linking of the father and death which I will refer to later.

The film begins, in the desert, by tracing the stages of birth in a space marked by the uncertainty of its borders, the "remaindered" wasteland of the abject. Throughout the film, Nature is seen as an opponent. All spaces are colonized by roads, cars, freeways, bridges, railroads, power lines, aeroplanes; there are few signs of earth or water as productive sites of fertility, but only of desertification and abandonment.

As the camera glides over a vast, empty landscape, Travis (unnamed and unknown at this point) is gradually pinpointed, "his lips are cracked and swollen and his tongue moves from side to side as though searching for moisture in the air" (Script 1). As if to underscore the significance of the landscape generically, he discards the empty water bottle of the male Western convention. More importantly, when he arrives at a gas station on a remote highway, he goes directly to the water pipe, as if to suckle a breast, but it is dry. In the gas station store, he opens the fridge and, ignoring the six-packs of beer (because inscribed as an "infant" at this stage), grabs a handful of ice-cubes and starts eating the ice as he collapses. Later, when he enters into Language and becomes again a speaking subject, he tells Walt that when he was a baby his mother gave him ice-cubes to suck on when he was teething. What I am describing is a fairly obvious re-enactment of the birth and nursing process – his body extricates itself, as being alive, from that border.

The collapse on the border (the doctor who is summoned asks him "[y]ou know which side a' the border yer on?") repeats the inaugural loss and separation. This occurs in the Terlingua (third language – neither America or Europe?; language of the earth? – Travis's middle name is Clay) Medical Clinic on the Mexican border. The script describes Travis as "marooned between some tragic event in his past and the helplessness of his present situation"; literally, the reference is to the flight from Jane four years ago and the present car crash; figuratively, it is to the process of expulsion or abjection. For all of the film, Travis remains "marooned between", *entre-deux*. His bruised, unclean body dressed in an ambiguous class and ethnic mix of cheap Mexican suit and sun-bleached baseball cap has, ultimately, to be left behind by Travis as he rehearses his childhood stages in abbreviated, synoptic form. Initially, he is without language (pre-symbolic) and when his brother, Walt, fetches him in a hired car, he sits in the back like a small child, rather than in the passenger's seat. He cries at one point, refuses to fly, and when Walt returns to the car-hire lot, insists on having the same car. The attachment to the safe and the familiar, the vertiginous fear of the loss of boundaries, are all recognisable symptoms of abjection. His movements are robotic, psychotic even, a chiasmic figure still – Walt calls him a "spoiled child" at one point, which, metaphorically, of course he is because of abjection.

In Kristeva's analysis, the abject is caused to exist by the logic of *exclusion*, the jettisoning of defilement (linked to the feminine) from the "Symbolic system". That Travis is unable to live with Jane, takes flight across the Mexican border (his mother's maiden name was Spanish – Sequine), and disappears for four years is the result of a conflict between an imperfect belonging in the Symbolic Order and, what Kristeva calls, the weakness of prohibition which does not succeed in differentiating itself sufficiently from the *(m)other* but allows it to threaten one's own and clean self (we see Travis washed and shaved in the motel on another stage of his return to the Symbolic). Travis's body language, his gentle, uninflected voice, and his relationship to his son (who, when describing space theories to him in Houston, and in his behaviour in the "buddy" sequences in the Broadway bar and in the laundromat, "fathers" him) all suggest an incompletely "masculinized" figure; almost a third gender, or third genre. The tearing of the child from the mother seems, in Travis's case, unfinished. Later, he says to Jane "it was me who tore you apart", as if to re-enact, or revenge even, his own inaugural loss and abjection.

Each stage of the film re-introduces Travis to the Symbolic Order. For example, initially he avoids the mirror in the motel room in his "silent" phase (presumably, he used it while shaving, but this is off-screen) but later he speeds up his growth, eats solid food at the diner, drives Walt's car, engages in conversation, watches the aircraft from his brother's home, walks past a van with an "Airborne" sign on it, and, finally, leaves the ground when he joins Walt on one of his billboard scaffolds. The latter enables him to tell Walt he is leaving and, borrowing cash and credit cards, he rejoins the adult, male world and prepares to find a woman (Jane), completing the conventional symbolic trajectory. He has also learned from Walt that their mother had died while he was in "exile" out of America. The separation would seem complete.

At Walt's house, when Travis dresses up (in a bizarre melange of his own and his brother's clothes, rounded off with a stetson) as *the* father he looks at himself in a full-length mirror, acknowledging a successful traversing of the mirror-stage. Interestingly enough, he assembles his image of *the* father (the definite article is stressed deliberately in the script to emphasize the Symbolic) from

images of the masculine in magazines in the terms of the patriarchally constructed Hispanic maid (third world woman identified with *cleaning*, and also perhaps with his mother's Hispanic roots). Carmelita, the maid, asks him if he wants to be a rich father or a poor father, telling him that "there is no in-between". She also tells him he must look up at the sky and never at the ground (linked with earth and the dirty feminine) and "you must walk very stiff", completing the phallic imagery. Many such figures in the film prepare Travis for the "real world", helping him in his quest to "forget" abjection, but each one, in some way or other, is marked by some trace of this unnameable – Walt shares the same mother, Anne is from Paris and also "mothers" him as well as suggesting desire, while Carmelita joins him in the Mexican songs he hums, as well as having a function linked to the "dirty". However much the *exile* ceaselessly seeks to separate himself from the abject it is a *land of oblivion* that is constantly remembered. In many ways, Paris, Texas signifies this land of oblivion.

At the Burbank home Travis eats very little and sleeps not at all, anxious to forestall the workings of the primary repression that opened up the spaces of the unconscious, of dream – a realm of the semiotic and of disruptive "pulsions". He is seen washing up and cleaning endless numbers of shoes (at one point measuring his son's cowboy boots against his own – a reminder of his wish to become the son), as a way of maintaining his distance from the unclean feminine. His sister-in-law Anne, contained within her stylized role as surrogate mother to Hunter and, as one gesture shows, to Travis, also acts out a glimpsed intertextual reference to *desire* as encoded in the cinematic trope of the French "seductress" – the dangerous woman. In one scene, Travis and Anne mirror each other precisely in reverse shot as they sit each with

traversing identity

an elbow on the table opposite each other; this shot further emphasizes Travis's incomplete identification with the masculine, Anne's role as reflection of the masculine in the Symbolic Order, and Travis's sublimated wish to enter the spaces of the feminine other. The shot also shows, by its reverse angle, that she is not sufficiently *othered* perhaps.

As the "child" in Travis becomes chronologically a fully separated being, the mother is still not adequately *forgotten*, which is why Anne has to "disappear" from the narrative shortly after the reverse shot just discussed, and why Jane never comes close to him again, her "danger" screened by distance. Travis sees Jane behind the glass of her car window, screened in the home movie, through the mirror in the Keyhole club, and framed in the hotel window. Interestingly, the windows of the Meridian hotel are shot in such a way as to suggest endless television screens – one of many indications throughout of overcoded, culturally mediated value.

Hunter has lived with Walt and Anne for three years ("given away" by Jane at the point when Travis's mother dies), treating them as his family and forgetting his "real" mother – watching the Super-8 footage, he says "[t]hat's not her, that's only her in a movie ... a long time, ago ... in a galaxy far, far away". In a sense, this shields him from the pulsions of abjection, the Star Wars discourse effectively jettisoning her to a great distance. He is surrounded by images of "the Name of the Father", symbolic masculinity in the form of boys' toys, Star Wars, NASA icons, the discourses of science and space travel. Unlike Travis, he is firmly settled in the Symbolic Order of the father, a fixed and model child surrounded by models: cars, planes, high technology. At one point, referring to a car he says "it's a girl's car" (it's his mother's). Walt and Anne encoding and embodying for Hunter the *middle class* home and family (but always offered as universal), and living in and off the Symbolic Order literally and figuratively, provide a clean, suburban (remote from the desert) family home where the child as speaking subject is "at home" in the patriarchal, living within familiar, safe, protected boundaries, unaware of the repression of differences.

Travis's presence opens up ambiguities (Hunter tries to explain to a friend that he has two fathers, but gives up; he also tells Travis that he could always feel him walking around and talking someplace when he had disappeared) and threatens Anne and Walt (who is unable to father a child biologically) for the first time with the spectre of "not being at home". Their space, their lifestyle, their speech and their body language are all precise, boundaried, and framed by the logic of *exclusion*. With them, Hunter would grow untroubled by the memory of abjection, always "at home" in the world. At the same time, however, the growth, insight and, possibly, creative awareness that Travis achieves (in the sense that he is able to construct a narrative of abjection) would also be denied him. As Kristeva shows, abjection has a double effect, "[t]he time of abjection is double: a time of oblivion and thunder, of veiled infinity and the moment when revelation bursts forth" (*PH* 9). Travis's motives in restoring Hunter to Jane are, therefore, complex and ambiguous. Partly it is to renew the madonna/child story, partly to put together the dyadic unity he has torn apart, but also it is to overcome his own separation from the mother, as well as, perhaps, to open up a more *provisional* sense of identity for Hunter to challenge and defy the stable essences of the Symbolic.

The Super-8 home movie shows Travis in cowboy hat, Hunter "driving", and Jane dancing (Monroe-like) *on her own*, away

roger bromley

from the family group, circling round and round. These are all, potentially, "undomesticated" images, markers of flight and mobility, yet contained within the frame of the *home* movie. It is also a *silent* movie. Anne and Walt are shown in more static and self-conscious poses.

The footage seems to help Hunter work out something of his ambiguous location. To both men he says "Goodnight, Dad" and, later, in what looks like a silent movie routine, he mimics Travis's actions when they walk home from school, separate but parallel; later, on the road, they wear similar clothes. However, the Super-8 film also prefigures the Keyhole scenes where Travis and Jane discursively trace the course of their own separation, loss of home, and break up of family. At the same time, Anne is afraid of what will happen to her marriage if they lose Hunter, and accuses Walt of promoting "all this father-son business". It is as if Anne senses that she is to become the site of abjection, the remaindered maternal body, which has been kept at bay by her clean home and suburban family. Identity, system, order are all disturbed as borders, positions, and rules are brought into question by the in-between, the ambiguous and the composite. She is reminded that Hunter is not kin and that the familiar (the space of *the* family) and the safe are imperilled.

When Anne says she loves Hunter like her own flesh and blood, while Walt insists that Travis *is* his father, Hunter *is* his son, questions are raised about biological essentialism as the only model of family available for a complex number of socio-cultural reasons, but for Walt (*image* man) it is the only model because it is a *model,* constructed within the hegemonic discourse and endorsed by the advertising and movie industries.

After a long series of interior scenes (women are rarely placed in exterior shots)

Travis decides to search for Jane based upon information supplied by Anne. The "home movie" becomes a "road movie" again as Travis buys a used Ranchero (perhaps an echo of the pick-up he crashed earlier) and, equipped with binoculars and walkie-talkies, he takes Hunter on a rite of passage to track Jane down. Travis resumes (in both senses of the word) some of his "forgotten" masculinity as he and his son, in an extended "buddy movie" sequence, stake out the (m)other in a mock thriller scenario. Each month at the same time Jane banks money for Hunter in Houston, so they are able to locate and close in on her – as *hunters* – trailing her to her place of work. In a phone call to Walt, Hunter describes the Ranchero as "a real family car" with emphasis on the "family", but equally it could have been on the "real". Significantly, they drive across the desert as though, in returning Hunter to his mother, Travis is trying not only to bridge the four-year gap but, in reprising the earlier sequences of the film with him and Walt in the car, is also putting the child through the birth/separation symbolization stages. As I have said previously, a lot of Hunter's discourse and behaviour is "adult", paternal in these scenes. He has a grasp of the dominant discourse of technological complexity and theories of creation unknown to his "borderline" male father; he is also the first to spot Jane, while Travis dozes, and it is he who tells his father which way to turn in the pursuit.

prisoners of gender

In the chapter in *Looka Yonder* called "Sam Shephard's Cowboy Mouth", Duncan Webster refers to Travis and Jane as "prisoners of gender" (Webster 1988). It is this phrase which I want to explore and, hopefully, trace culturally. *Paris, Texas* is, at many levels, concerned with gender funda-

traversing identity

mentalism – with divisions, icons, discourses which have come to inhabit individuals as though they were natural. They constitute an artificial territoriality but exist ideologically as part of an unreflexive design/model for the male, repressing continuous relations with the mother. At the simplest level Travis's clothes, the Ranchero pick-up, the drinking set-piece in the saloon, the technology, the buddy imagery, the son's name, the highway, the Red River and other intertextual references, the imaging of women in two-dimensional frames (in the gas station store at the beginning, on the dismantled billboard, as well as in the Keyhole sequences) and the road movie/Western signs, and the Mojave desert (the site for Atom bomb testing and development), all contribute towards a masculinist discourse. In other words, the highly charged visual/iconic landscape is not simply an empirical/geographical fact but culturally loaded and gendered space. At this point in the film Travis and Hunter enter what Kristeva calls men's time, or linear time – time as project, teleology, departure, progression and arrival. Early in the film Walt tells Travis he is too busy to drive and needs to take a plane. Men's time is also that of Language, enhanced here by the use of the walkie-talkies which give them power over the silent, pursued woman – pre-verbal.

Silence, the desert – prior to language – are the site of what Kristeva defines as the semiotic *chora*, an essentially mobile and extremely provisional articulation (uncertain and indeterminate), as opposed to a *disposition* that already depends on social, experiential constraints and on representation. Nevertheless the Symbolic, the disposing of the subject through language in gender, time, and space, functions in a dialogical relationship with the semiotic; each is a condition of the other. For Kristeva "the territory of the maternal is not a space confined to ... biological characteristics; it is the position a subject, any subject, can assume towards the symbolic order" (Furman 1985, 73). This positioning becomes culturally axiomatic, it fixes and reduces but it is also subject to rupture: for example, Hunter's disgust at Travis's drunkenness in the saloon and his androgynous looks; in the laundromat, however, he watches a John Wayne movie.

The *chora* precedes and underlies figuration and specularization. Jane and the other women in the Keyhole club are forced into positions of specularity – they can only see themselves, not the men – they appear solely in symbolic configuration, subject to the language of command and masculine fantasy. This is because the semiotic connects and orients the body to the mother through "drives" (energy discharges); the semiotized body is a place of permanent scission, a space, not an essence, of discontinuities and anarchies. The maternal body mediates the Symbolic law organizing social relations – home and family, for instance – and becomes the ordering principle of the semiotic chora which is on the path of destruction, aggression and death (compare Travis's relations with Jane after she becomes a mother, and her struggle against symbolization). The semiotic continuum must be split if signification is to be produced, and this is at the heart of the film's deeply conflicted narrative around home and family – Walt and Anne represent that "split" and disappear when the semiotic intercedes.

Kristeva argues that:

> Abjection preserves what existed in the archaism of pre-objectal relationship, in the immemorial violence with which a body becomes separated from another body in order to be ... thus braided, woven, ambivalent, a heterogeneous flux marks out a territory that I can call my own because the

roger bromley

Other, having dwelt in me as *alter ego*, points it out to me through loathing. (*PH* 10)

This "other" is not identifiable or "liveable with", but an *Other* which precedes and possesses the subject, and causes it to *be* through this possession.

The last quarter of the film focuses upon Travis, Jane, and Hunter. This part of the film is concerned with tracing the sources of the loathing and violence which has sundered images of home and family. The heterogeneous flux cannot inhabit the fixity of the hom(e)ogeneous, and abjection threatens famil(iarit)y. These scenes highlight the instability of the Symbolic function, in what Kristeva calls its most significant aspect, "the prohibition placed on the maternal body" (*PH* 14). The extended revelation scenes in the Keyhole club (site of the voyeur and fantasist) between Jane and Travis take

> the ego back to its source on the abominable limits from which, in order to be, the ego has broken away – it assigns it a source in the non-ego, drive and death. Abjection is a resurrection that has gone through death (of the ego). (*PH* 15)

It is also described by Kristeva as a kind of *narcissistic crisis*. Women are constantly treated in the film as the *limit* or borderline, which is why in the Keyhole club men are heavily screened from them by mirror, telephone, and "invisibility", anything but *immediacy*.

The past relationship between Travis and Jane is discursively and obliquely related by Travis, speaking of himself and her in the third person, "I knew these people ... these two people" (Kristeva refers at one point in *Powers of Horror* to the *stray* considering himself as equivalent to a third party). The location is a club predicated upon female passivation and commodification, with women domesticated in various stereotypical interiors and arranged in set poses for the male gaze, but not the touch. The woman does not return the gaze, because the mirrors in the booths only permit the men to see. To speak his violence and his love Travis turns his back on the mirror, as Jane, discursively, becomes "the untouchable, impossible, absent body of the mother" in this moment of "narcissistic perturbation" which is also the revelation referred to above. For the speaking being – almost monosyllabic until this point – it is the moment

> that secondary repression, with its reserve of symbolic means, attempts to transfer to its own account, which has thus been overdrawn, the resources of primal repression. The archaic economy is brought into full light of day, signified, verbalized. Its strategies (rejecting, separating, repeating/abjecting) hence find a symbolic existence, and the very logic of the symbolic – arguments, demonstrations, proofs etc. – must conform to it. It is then that the abject ceases to be circumscribed, reasoned with, thrust aside: it appears as abject. (*PH* 15)

The trailer life of the couple corresponds precisely with this and the revelation narrative gives it symbolic existence.

Initially, as described by Travis, Jane, in her late teens, and he, late thirties/early forties (the paternal metaphor suggests itself) enjoy an idyllic, romantic love. For reasons he cannot understand, he loved her more than he felt possible and even gave up work to be home with her. However, he describes himself as starting to get "kind of torn inside" – re-entering the space of inaugural loss, primary separation, the splitting of the subject inscribed in the Symbolic Order. The literal impossibility of origin, of return, to the "ever-absent body of the mother" renders desire insatiable. This accounts for his

traversing identity

jealousy, possessiveness, violence, drunkenness, and enslavement of Jane – he needs her to be unclean, defiled, unfaithful. Enchained to the Symbolic Order, when she becomes pregnant Jane, as mother, dreams of escape from their mobile home. There is no space for the feminine in the film's symbolization except in the domestic or the reclining, passive pose of the billboard or the pin-up calendar (there is space in Kristeva's theory for the feminine in the Symbolic, by detaching the mother function from the specificities of gender). Travis tied a cowbell to Jane's ankle (downgrading her from the human and recalling the masculine ranch of the Western genre) so he could hear her at night if she tried to get out of bed. In his turn, Travis wished he was far away, lost in a deep, vast country where nobody knew him; somewhere without language or streets. He dreamed about this place without knowing its name. Within the Symbolic it is *unnameable*; Kristeva names it as the *chora*, the maternal body.

Speaking of a non-Western hunter society, Peggy Reeves Sanday describes fear, conflict, and strife:

> In these societies, males believe that there is an uncontrollable force that may strike at any time and against which men must be prepared to defend their integrity. The nature of the force and its source are not well defined, but often they are associated with female sexuality and reproductive functions. Men believe it is their duty to harness this force, to prevent chaos and to maintain equilibrium. They go to extraordinary lengths to acquire some of the power for themselves so that they will not be impotent when it is time to fight. Men attempt to neutralize the power they think is inherent in women by stealing it, nullifying it, or banishing it to invisibility. (Sanday 164)

This, from an anthropological perspective, complements Kristeva's psychoanalytical approach by tracing the instability of the unitary male subject and the need to harness female sexuality to an extent that desire becomes mutated into the desire for violence against the very source of desire itself. Both writers are not simply talking about men and women, but about concepts and principles which constitute the "feminine" by exclusion from the realm of value. Numerous cultural spaces are rendered off limits to women as they are confined to obedient dependency. The Symbolic Order establishes cultural patterns which make the male functionally complete, but this is always a provisional "completeness" and Travis needs Jane to "fill up his emptiness". Jane refuses to use Hunter to do this for her which is why she gives him to Anne and Walt.

In an attempt to achieve some space and power, Jane burns down the trailer and escapes with the child. In the Freudian scenario, as well as having connotations of purification, fire is associated with male sexuality In "The Acquisition and Control of Fire", Freud describes how Prometheus brought fire to men, having stolen it from the gods, and is punished by being chained to a rock, with a vulture feeding daily on his liver. (Freud 187-93) Linking the liver with passion, Freud further argues that fire is a symbol of the libido. We learn from the Keyhole "confession" that Travis tied Jane to a stove – a container of fire – and perhaps she is trying to recover some "mastery" of her action, as in non-Western cultures fire is often identified with shamanic power and magic. In Dobu society, the mythical origin of fire is from the vagina of an old woman, and it is women who are thought to have the power of flight (Eliade). Whatever the significance, the fire precipitates the flight which leads to Travis's four year disappear-

110

ance. Mother, lover, other, Jane is idealized as representing the space of the semiotic for Travis, denying the psychic pain and violence (the staging of separation) which characterizes the interaction between her and Hunter. Unable to "forget" his own inaugural loss which rends and tears him, he sentimentalized the mother-child symbiosis through his paternal agency as a way of forestalling the mirror stage and restoring the undifferentiated being of the *chora*. Perhaps Hunter is unconsciously doing the same when, in the Meridian hotel, in his mother's embrace he mimes the cutting of her hair to make the two of them identical.

The only inclusive spaces for a woman in the socio-symbolic stratum are as wife and mother in the home and the family: for male, read mobile, for female, home. For Jane these discourses of gendered power demobilize and exclude her affective life as *a woman* and her condition as a social being. In response, she counter-invests the violence she has endured as the only form of *agency* available to her – the burning of the trailer renders it neither mobile nor home. Her "independence" as a worker in the Keyhole club – she switches the light on and off, the clients cannot touch her, nor does she see them – is, of course, a deeply conflicted freedom (there is a large mural of the Statue of Liberty on an exterior wall of the club as well as some racist graffiti) as she performs in yet another permitted discursive space as the object of male sexual fantasies; every man, she tells Travis, has his voice.

Throughout the film, we see Travis giving birth to himself as an I by "abjecting the mother's body". However, there is considerable instability of both fathering and mothering as I have argued, and it is this instability – that which does not respect borders, positions, rules – which renders the home unhomely (*unheimlich*) and the family unintelligible. Undisturbed, unambiguous, identity, system and order – the realm of the Symbolic – can deliver both home and family. Ironically, it is the confrontation with the feminine – the maternal body, conventionally the em-bodi-ment of home and family – that brings the abject back in "fleeting encounters". McAfee describes these encounters as "fleeting" because "we flee, horrified of falling back into the maternal body, where no difference – and thus no subjectivity – is possible" (McAfee 118). Horrified, yes, but also fascinated. With his compulsion to repeat, Travis is drawn to the uncanny – the buried and repressed – the *unheimlich*.

In a sense, the Keyhole sequences are an example of what Alice Jardine calls *gynesis* – the putting of women into discourse. Almost silent throughout, Jane (or an idea of Jane) is constructed both as a model for the unknowable, and as a figure who dominates Travis's desire which he resents (hence the violence) yet is contained by. She is both "screen goddess" (the cinematic aspects of the sequence are obvious, as are the confessional, prison visiting and analyst/analysand analogies) and "whore" in a pornography club. Jane is site of nostalgia (for the maternal body), utopia, and misogyny.

As Papastergiadis points out in *Modernity as Exile*, both the past and self-identity (for the exile, which Travis has been in a sense) begin with separation from the mother-tongue/country and discontent with the law of the father, "[h]e lies with his head between her legs ... Everything here is re-enactment, everything here is return. Home is the return to where distance did not yet count" (Papastergiadis 144). As I have argued, *Paris, Texas* is centrally concerned with re-enactment and return, as was Travis's "exile" to the spaces of his mother's roots (her father was Spanish) south of the Mexican border. The frequent use of

traversing identity

Hispanic reference in word and image, and the Mexican songs and music, rupture and puncture the growth away from the maternal and "remember" abjection.

The "homes" Travis returns to in the film are places where distance does not count. However, the composition of numerous shots indicate indirectness, screening and distance – the Super-8 movie; the mirror and telephone in the Keyhole club; the gaps between Hunter and Travis walking home from school, in the Ranchero where the child mostly travels in the back (at one point, sitting next to his father in the cab he falls asleep on his shoulder and Travis gently detaches him), in the Broadway saloon bar, and in the use of walkie-talkies and the discussions on NASA and space exploration; the gaps between brother, sister-in-law, and Travis; and the contrast between the close-up on Hunter and Jane in the Meridian hotel and the long shot of Travis watching from afar.

Giving up work so he could be close to Jane, confusing love with possession, and yet also alienating her, attaching a cowbell to her and tying her up to a stove, are all symptoms of his attempts to construct a "home" where distance did not count. Endlessly seeking a territory, he is "reterritorialized on almost anything – memory, fetish or dream ... [looking for] [w]hat will restore an equivalent of territory, valid as a home" (Deleuze and Guattari 68, 69). Yet the paradox of the mobile home, unfixed and capable of distances, their age gap even, underscores his ambivalent position. This is to say nothing of the distances travelled in the "road movie" sections of the film, the railroad tracks and the interstate which takes the time of the city to the space of the desert, and domesticate it. The ultimate, originary, distance from the mother, of course, determines Travis's final decision to leave Jane and Hunter again.

Metaphorically, he restores the distance between himself and his mother by bringing Jane and Hunter together again in the hotel. The composition of this sequence uses shots which close the distance between mother and child literally (they embrace and circle round and round in a movement both maternal and erotic – pre-abjection) and figuratively by focusing on Hunter from angles which suggest the three year old, the five year old, and, finally, the almost eight year old. It is Madonna and child, and yet also the *prohibited* love scene. At the end of the Keyhole sequence Travis turns the light on his face, and Jane switches off her light. This reverses the mirror and she sees his face. He sees the reflection of his face framed by her hair and body. The image has a gender-crossing, transgressive effect – he enters her as the maternal body, thus reversing the mirror-stage. The image also looks like Hunter, with soft, androgynous looks and longer, blonde hair. It is the only "family" portrait of the present (Travis has an old polaroid from the past), but it is also only an *image*. The three never close the distance between them.

Travis cannot live, as paternal agency, in that proximity ("with his head between her legs") but only in the distance that separates him. The final shot of the film has him driving away onto the freeway, complete with cowboy hat, into the "sunset" of neon-lit, night-time Houston; the borderlander, forever marginalized by the cultural closures of the Symbolic. He passes a billboard (made by Walt?) with the final, ironic appropriation of love discourse, "TOGETHER WE MAKE IT HAPPEN – Republic Bank". Travis has reunited Jane and Hunter by locating her at a bank, where she deposits money received in exchange for fulfilling male fantasies. It would take another essay to consider the extent to which the economy of desire is related to the Symbolic Order and the cultural dimensions of American finance capital. "Together", that home and family word, is stripped of all but its use as image.

I have mentioned the spatial gaps between Hunter and Travis. One scene which emphasizes this is the one where Hunter, framed as an extension of a television set in the hotel room (fully integrated with signs and the mediated?), listens to a tape-recorded message from Travis:

> You belong together with your mother. It was me that tore you apart. And I owe it to you to bring you back together. But I can't stay with you. I could never heal up what happened. It's like a gap. But it left me alone in a way that I'll never get over. And right now I'm afraid. I'm afraid of walking away again. I'm afraid of what I might find. But I'm even more afraid of not facing this fear. I love you Hunter. I love you more than my life. (Script 185)

Apart from echoing the "together" of the billboard, Travis is speaking "in the name of *the* Father", of symbolization; but he is also speaking of his own abjection ("gap") and separation – "walking away". Because of what Nietzsche called "creative forgetting", he can hardly remember the pre-symbolic *chora*. In order to complete his re-enactment and return to the Symbolic Order, he has to walk away from the scene of primal repression which he has staged in the Meridian (*entre-deux*) hotel. This scene is "a void which is not nothing but designates ... a defiance or challenge to symbolization" (*PH* 51). The "fear" he speaks of is of the abject:

> The phobic object has no other object than the abject. But that word "fear" – a fluid haze, an ungraspable or incomprehensible moistness – no sooner has it cropped up than it shades off like a mirage and impregnates all language with non-existence, with an hallucinatory, ghostly glimmer [the final cut

roger bromley

> omitted a number of hallucinatory scenes related to Travis]. Thus, fear, having been placed between parentheses, discourse will seem tenable only if it ceaselessly confronts that otherness, a burden both repelling and repelled, a deep well of memory that is inaccessible and intimate: the abject. (*PH* 6)

Travis's fear of the untouchable, impossible/absent body of the mother means that he can only survive in the Symbolic Order ("discourse will seem tenable only") by confronting that otherness which, for him, is configured in Jane. Nevertheless, this confronting is only oblique and, in a sense, on his terms – he tells "their" story. His attraction to Jane, initially, is that she is very young (seventeen) and, therefore, closer to the age of his mother at his own conception. Anne, his peer and not a mother (Walt says she could only have children with another man; he "fathers" images) represents a different *otherness* – a possible space for feminine desire in the Symbolic Order – but Travis is unable to respond to her, literally as his brother's wife, and, figuratively, because he is still burdened by that "deep well of memory that is unapproachable and intimate: the abject". In a sense, Anne does "give" him a family by providing clues as to the whereabouts of his child/wife and "releasing" his son.

at the borders of the unnameable

Throughout the film Travis has to work out his bearings while in the process of his return journeying but, as Jane Gallop argues, "the mother as mother is lost forever ... the mother as womb, homeland, source and grounding for the subject is irretrievably past" (Gallop 53), hence no home is ever possible as "the subject is ... in a foreign land, alienated". The "home movie" has to

traversing identity

become a "road movie" as Travis will never "arrive":

> The journey is a search for a centre, which has overcome any contestation with the peripheries, it is an "ideal" centre which knows of no outside and so can be composed only of an inside which is total and complete in itself. It is by virtue of such a centre/home [the Keyhole club for the male, perhaps?] – both abstract and concrete – that identities can ever be rendered in a static and absolute form. But it is also by virtue of its abstraction that such a centre/home is never attainable. (Papastergiadis 170)

The identities of Walt and Anne are rendered in a static and absolute form – their "ideal" centre/home is shot almost entirely in interior scenes – but as Walt "hands over" Hunter to Travis, and Anne yields information about Jane to him, they both cease to have substantive existence and are only represented, at a distance, by a collect call. They have served their purpose as agents of symbolization – surrogate parents to Hunter and Travis – and the unitary status of home and family is uprooted. Incidentally, all the positive scenes between father and son are exterior ones, except after the showing of the Super-8 footage, and when Hunter "mothers" his drunken father in the laundromat.

Travis's leaving of Burbank re-enacts his earlier leaving of America and Jane's leaving of the caravan. Jane's flight, ultimately, leads her to the site/sight of the male voyeur, structured in the booths of patriarchy. Travis's journey, however, traces what Kristeva calls the death of the name of the father:

> The exile cuts all links, including those that bind him to the belief that the thing called life has a meaning guaranteed by the dead father. For if meaning exists in the state of exile, it nevertheless finds no incarnation, and is ceaselessly produced and destroyed in geographical and discursive transformations. Exile is a way of surviving in the face of the dead father ... (Kristeva 1987, 298)

Travis's father has died in a car crash and in a scene cut from the film, there is a "vision" of Travis's own car crash shot from a subjective p.o.v. seen through the windscreen of a pick-up truck. The car is driving at an insane speed as if the driver were drunk. The car veers off the road and continues "its *suicidal path* towards rocks and a ravine" (Script 70, my emphasis). It would be possible to see the whole film as both an attempt to erase the father and a suicidal path – the drive towards death. In *Desire in Language* Kristeva, referring to Beckett's *First Love,* talks about a man experiencing love and simultaneously putting it to the test on the death of his father. Travis's father dies before his exile (the mother dies during it, unknown to him), his own car crash occurs while he is "missing" in the *land of oblivion*. Kristeva says that racked between the *father* and *Death* a man has a hard time finding something else to love. He could hardly venture in that direction, she suggests, unless he were confronted with an undifferentiated woman, tenacious and silent, preferably a prostitute. In the Keyhole club booth, Jane becomes that undifferentiated woman, passive and silent, performing for men in exchange for money.

It is in this context that Travis is able to articulate the violence and domination which has destroyed their primary love relationship, yet is facing Jane – who cannot see him – in what Kristeva calls *banishment love.* Banishment is above/beyond a life of love because "*to love* is to survive paternal meaning" (Kristeva 1980, 150). However, by re-enacting his entry into the Symbolic throughout the film Travis is actually estab-

114

lishing a relationship with the world in the image, figuratively speaking, of the dead father:

> Through this opening, he might look for woman. But the Other, the third-person father, is not that particular dead body. It is Death: it always was. It is the meaning of the narrative of the son, who never enunciated himself, save for and by virtue of this stretched out void of paternal Death, as ideal and inaccessible to any living being as it might seem. As long as a son pursues meaning in a story or through narratives, even if it eludes him, as long as he persists in his search he narrates in the name of Death for the father's corpses ... (Kristeva 1980, 150-1)

Travis's extended Keyhole narrative, his first significant "enunciation" in the film, is such a pursuit of meaning.

Although the main thrust of my argument has concentrated upon the impossibility of home and the unintelligibility of the family in respect of the prohibited maternal body, it should be remembered that not only does Travis not have his "own" name but his father's; that Hunter's nomination is similarly collapsed phonemically in the father (Hunter/Hender son, even more pronounced in American English); and also that Travis "dies" twice for son, once after the fire and then after the mother-son bonding in the Meridian. This suggests that Hunter will be caught in the spiral of abjection (metaphorically separating again from the mother) and the search that narrates in the name of Death. The re-location of mother and son in a scene of mutuality is over-determined by the absence of the paternal. At one point in the Meridian scene, the camera shows Jane swinging Hunter round and tilting him towards the window (they are several floors up) as if to jettison him. Even at the material level, how will Jane support Hunter economically, and how appropriate is her *unclean,* male-designated work, which would doubtless have to continue in the absence of any other maintenance, for this role?

In his search for the lost territory of the mother (significantly he throws away the polaroid of the vacant lot, while drinking in the Broadway saloon near the end) Travis seeks to overcome

> the unthinkable of death by postulating maternal love in its place – in the place and stead of death and thought. This love ... is perhaps a recall, on the near side of early identifications, of the primal shelter that ensured the survival of the newborn. (Kristeva 1987, 177)

He draws upon a discourse on ideal motherhood by re-constituting in the Meridian (and watching over it from a distance) the primal shelter of the bond between mother and child (it is, we notice, a hotel, like a motel a quasi-home – the space of "flight"). The whole film, as has been shown, is a "recall".

Both mother and child are figuratively reborn, Jane's wet hair confirming this. For Travis it is both a return to meaning and, simultaneously, a loss as he departs on his final drive (coded in the terms of the Western) to Death(?), surrounded by the highway. Unlike Kolker and Beicken, I do not see Travis finding "redemption in a new beginning" – the pain of loss is too sharp in the final shot – although I agree that he has achieved a significant level of understanding. The film ends on an ambiguous note (the separated male on the open road), but I would interpret this as an indicator of the obsessed man, perhaps no longer so driven by the disruptive pulsions of abjection but fortified with the assumption of Death (his first exile had been a "mock" death) driving away from the woman and child (substituting for the father) to devote himself to his

traversing identity

own "slow descents again, the long submersion" (Kristeva 1980, 152), of pursuing the meaning of the narrative of the son. It is in this sense a sacrificial ending, as Travis stands in, metaphorically, for his own son ("I love you more than my life") to enable him to survive paternal meaning.

Travis remains in the fundamental condition of abjection, heading for the boundary (again) between subject and object, the borderlands of the *entre-deux*, the cultural origins of the patriarchal west (Paris and Texas, and the Western):

> A voyager in a night whose end flees. He has a sense of the danger, of the loss that the pseudo-object attracting him represents for him, but he cannot help taking the risk at the very moment he sets himself apart from it. (*PH* 8)

He is still the subject-in-process, confronting a relation of *alterity* within. The nearer he gets to the border the closer he is to the site of inaugural loss, the boundary between the chora and the Symbolic – the not-being-at-home of the *unheimlich*. Even if this state may prefigure an opening into the new,

> the *Unheimliche* [sic] requires just the same the impetus of a new encounter with an unexpected outside element: arousing images of death, automatons, doubles, or the female sex, ... uncanniness occurs when the boundaries between *imagination* and *reality* are erased. (Kristeva 1991, 188)

In other words, the threats to identity are expelled *momentarily*, not deleted (this other form of erasure – between *imagination* and *reality* – is always present). The threats persist within the unitary status of the Symbolic as unsettling reminders, thresholds of instability threatening fixed boundaries, indicating that identity formation is a never-ending traversing, a dialogical rhythm. Not only is the feminine exiled from the Symbolic (however she may be domesticated, "homed") and banned from the transgressive (unless passively serving it), but the masculine – the name of the father – is also/always journeying. As we have seen, Travis's journey throughout is towards a place of origin. In her reading of Freud's "The Uncanny", Hélène Cixous argues that "the country from which we come is always the one to which we are returning", driven by the dialogue between separation and belonging:

> The country from which we come is always the one to which we are returning. You are on the return road which passes through the country of children in the maternal body. You have already passed through here: you recognise the landscape. You have always been on the return road. Why is it that the maternal landscape, the *heimisch*, and the familiar become so disquieting? The answer is less buried than we might suspect. The obliteration of any separation, the realization of the desire which in itself obliterates a limit; all that which in effecting the movement of life in reality, allows us to come closer to a goal, the short cuts, the crossing accomplished especially at the end of our lives; all that which overcomes, shortens, economizes and assures satisfaction appears to affirm the life forces. All of that has another face turned toward death which is the detour of life. The abbreviating effect which affirms life asserts death. (Cixous 544)

The "road movie" in *Paris, Texas* is a return road movie but the family/familiar is no longer *heimlich* but unsettling because the attempts to overcome separation, to e-*limin*-ate borders, and the abbreviating effect of the speeded-up re-enactment of the child/man stages of development are all "economies" which signal death. For Travis, arrival has always to be deferred if he is to survive.

All of Wenders' work engages with the ways in which Modernity confronts the affirmations of identity, relationships, home and family. If, as John Berger has claimed, migration is the quintessential condition of the twentieth century then both home and family are less to do with houses and the small, biologically-linked groupings of our establishment and media ideologies, and more to do with mental/cultural constructs of ever-renewable *belongings* and deep, communal, but shifting mutualities. Wenders works with allegory and fantasy but, above all, with metaphor, as defined by Kristeva, "in so far as it gives form to the infantile psychic inscriptions situated at the borders of the unnameable" (Kristeva 1992, 75).

notes

Earlier versions of this article were given as papers at Lillehammer College, Lillehammer, Norway and Cheltenham and Gloucester College of Higher Education. I am grateful to students and staff in both institutions for their helpful comments, in particular my former colleague, Shelley Ratcliffe Rogers.

1 Sam Shephard and Wim Wenders, *Paris, Texas*, Screenplay, 21 September 1983 (unpublished). This is an unpublished shooting script which includes a number of scenes omitted from the final screen version. For the purposes of my argument I have extended the conventional notion of text to include this script. Further references will be incorporated in the text as Script.

2 Julia Kristeva, *Powers of Horror*, tr. Leon S. Roudiez (New York: Columbia University Press, 1982) p8. Further references to this book will be incorporated in the text as *PH*.

roger bromley

bibliography

Cixous, H., "Fiction and its Phantoms: A Reading of Freud's 'The Uncanny'", New Literary History 7:3 (spring 1976).

Deleuze G. and F. Guattari, *What is Philosophy?* (London: Verso, 1994).

Eliade, M., *Shamanism: Archaic Techniques of Ecstasy* (London: Arkana, 1989).

Furman, N., "The Politics of Language: Beyond the Gender Principle" in *Making a Difference: Feminist Literary Criticism*, eds G. Green and C. Kahn (London: Methuen, 1985).

Gallop, J., "The Mother Tongue" in *Politics of Theory*, ed. F. Barker et al. (Colchester: University of Essex Press, 1983).

Kolker, R.P. and P. Beicken, *The Films of Wim Wenders: Cinema as Vision and Desire* (Cambridge: Cambridge University Press, 1993).

Kristeva, J., *Desire in Language*, ed. L.S. Roudiez (Oxford: Basil Blackwell, 1980).

Kristeva, J., *Powers of Horror: an Essay in Abjection*, tr. L.S. Roudiez (New York: Columbia University Press, 1982).

Kristeva, J., "Stabat Mater" in *The Kristeva Reader*, ed. T. Moi (Oxford: Basil Blackwell, 1987).

Kristeva, J., *Strangers to Ourselves*, tr. L.S. Roudiez (Hemel Hempstead: Harvester Wheatsheaf, 1991).

Kristeva, J., "Roman noir et temps présent", *L'infini* 37 (spring 1992).

McAfee, N., "Abject Strangers: Toward an Ethics of Respect" in *Ethics, Politics and Difference in Julia Kristeva's Writing*, ed. K. Oliver (London: Routledge, 1993).

Martin, B. and C. Mohanty, "Feminist Politics: What's Home Got to Do With It?" in *Feminist Studies/Critical Studies*, ed. T. de Lauretis (London: Macmillan, 1988).

Papastergiadis, N., *Modernity as Exile: The Stranger in John Berger's Writing* (Manchester: Manchester University Press, 1993).

Sanday, P.R., *Female Power and Male Dominance* (Cambridge: Cambridge University Press, 1981).

Shephard, S. and W. Wenders, *Paris, Texas*, Screenplay, 21 September 1983 (unpublished).

Taylor, M.C., *Altarity* (Chicago: Chicago University Press, 1987).

Webster, D., *Looka Yonder* (London: Routledge, 1988).

Wenders, W., *Emotion Pictures* (London: Faber, 1989).

marcus wood

NOAH'S ARK

They went into the ark with Noah, two and two of all flesh in which there was the breath of life. And they that entered, male and female of all flesh, went in as God had commanded him; and the LORD shut him in.
Genesis, chapter 6, verses 15-16

noah's ark

marcus wood

noah's ark

marcus wood

What are we looking for from Fourier, as we wake him from his sleep?

The official proclamation of a "Year of the Family", following those of the Child, Women, the Tree, the Animal, and what have you — like the Mother's and Father's Days, of Petainist origin — raises the eternal questions of *Nature* and the *Institution*. Is the family natural or conventional, good or evil, enduring or extinct? An endless source of copy, a much-repeated shibboleth. It may be wiser and more modest to recognize that, relative to the individual whose childhood unfolds within it, the family is the locus of these double constraints — the Batesonian "double bind" which traps the individual in contradictory injunctions. Despite changes born of contemporary social upheavals, and the dislocations so often reported, the family remains the closed space prescribed by experts in the psychic sciences for the harmonious development of character, the dreamed-of Eden of equilibrium.

It is from here — in another illustration of a "double bind", that psychological buzz word — that the supporters of the family are now setting off against the ever-present threat of paternal and maternal "incest". The media are making a meal of it, showing the child as victim of its own progenitors' general concupiscence! Moral order or supreme disorder? "That is the question". All of which does not prevent the unruffled defence of the couple and the household, the welcoming home for an innocent and sacred child.

Yes, why wake Fourier, if not to go beyond this short-sightedness, these contradictions, this indigent charlatanism, and, in an absolute divergence [*écart absolu*] from the spirit of the century, to begin finally to throw the family into historical perspective and into question.

rené schérer

FOURIER'S "FAMILISM" AGAINST THE HOUSEHOLD

In the *Théorie des quatre mouvements* [*Theory of Four Movements*] (1808), the reader is struck, above all, by the break Fourier proposes with the whole group of political and social ideas that, in the 18th century, constructed the nuclear family as the basic unit and ideal of life. The century of the Enlightenment, to which we are still despite everything indebted, grounded the conjugal couple in Nature and never carried its Utopias beyond a philosophy of the household.

With Fourier, the opposite occurs. The household, naturalness, the inevitability of the couple as the fate of civilization — all are over. Other destinies are outlined where the social space is decentred. The household ceases to be a privileged place of life, and appears for what it is: the arresting of a movement, the aberrant fragmenting of a circulation of individuals and their affects, which must be placed in a much larger

fourier's familism

frame, one that allows them their full play. The restricted family is not the workshop where individuals and social ties are forged. Training the passions, the attractions are the proper mechanism for establishing the order desired by Nature and the Destinies. For the derisory model of the couple in their interior, for that of its exclusive, privative, and ruinous domestic economy, one must substitute the model of "circles", "casinos", "clubs", that is, "sects" or "series" of passion, which associate through elective affinities and hold tastes and productions in common. Fourier thinks the associative principle and the extension of social ties through to its conclusion. The smallest unity (the couple or, with the child, the *ménage-à-trois*) is never fruitful for its members or for the individual it forms. It will only ever produce a poor, egoistic, "blocked" (we might say, after Freud, repressed or neurotic) subject. The space of society, not that of the monogamous family, allows the individual his or her full play. This idea — of series, of groups bonded and trained by attraction, *esprit de corps*, and enthusiasm — will permit the building of a *Nouveau monde amoureux* [*New World of Love*] founded on a multiplicity of loves in place of a single love, on the legitimacy of all tastes, all fantasies or manias [*manies*] returned — precisely because they are acknowledged, recognized and unblocked — to their proper places as supplementary social bonds, rather than remaining in a repressed state, dangerous and destructive. Fourier, then, is able to deploy in this new order the whole range of "perversions" (the "manias"), as his contemporary Sade did; but, entirely inverting Sade, the satisfied liberation of the drives' energy will lead to an augmentation of force through association with the other, rather than to force's turning back in a cruelty destructive of others.

What matters, above all, from the *Théorie des quatre mouvements* onward, is a redistribution of sexual roles that gives priority to the choice made by the woman — in opposition to the matrimonial custom which, even in the most advanced of the Enlightenment Utopian thinkers, including Restif de la Bretonne, makes the man the initiator of all decisions. "A woman can have at the same time... ", "a woman can refuse", we read in the exposition of that curious transitional institution which Fourier calls the "progressive household". The essential characteristic of such households is the separation of functions once concentrated in a single partner — those of favourite, inseminator, husband:

> A woman can have at the same time: 1. a husband by whom she has two children; 2. an inseminator by whom she has only one child; 3. a favourite who has lived with her and kept the title; and simple possessors who have no legal status.

Fourier would only be anticipating the dislocating development of the contemporary family here, if he were not ultimately opening the affirmative space of a new positivity, one not nostalgic for a disorder eternally haunted by the ideal of a normative conjugality.

What confirms this inclusive, affirmative disjunction is the paradoxical valorization from which certain types of couples profit once the nuclear family has been definitively pushed aside. The following bear witness to the rerouting of matrimony: the "angelic couple", who give themselves over to a "holy prostitution" for the happiness of the whole group, like the two young lovers described in *Le nouveau monde amoureux*; and the "pivotal" couple, safe from all jealousy, infinitely hospitable, like the one Klossowski speaks of in *Les lois de l'hospitalité* [*The*

126

rené schérer

Laws of Hospitality] – centre and home, of welcome for others, radiance, and giving.

In a word, what disappears in Fourier is less the couple itself as the instantaneous or enduring root of all love than the couple as institution. A new mechanism comes to take its place. The couple becomes a wheel within the integrated movement of the passions, no longer serving as the basis of society. Above all, it is no longer responsible for the child's education, either in infancy – because women, except for those few whose passion it may be, are liberated from the servitude of coddling – or in later childhood, whose natural milieu is *the group [la bande]* rather than the threesome [*l'être à trois*] of the parental home.

Here, undoubtedly, lies what is most important, what we (as inheritors of the stifling legacy of Freud and especially of the charlatanism of its vulgarization) most lack in rethinking childhood – a child that is not the child of parents, a family child. Our incapacity to tear ourselves from the supposedly necessary structures of the family unit keeps us from seeing that the child at liberty – omnipresent wherever society tends to anarchic dissolution, in Eastern Europe, in Latin America, in Asia, almost anywhere – becomes a child of the group [*de bande*], and that it is there that he or she develops, grows, and achieves the full play of passion. It is onto this child that Fourier, well away from the familialist lamentations that obsess us, grafts his admirable system of education, making the child the linchpin of social harmony.

Notwithstanding his abandonment of the institutional family, and of the educating and "structuring" role of the family, the family is far from absent in Fourier. It continues to exist and is even valued in what he will call "*esprit de corps*" or "*esprit corporatif*", above all in the cardinal passion of "familism [*le familisme*]", also called "paternism" or "parentism" – a passion of equal importance to the other three cardinal "affective" or "group" passions: *ambition* or *corporatism, friendship* and *love*. Like the others, familism leads to the formation of a specific group. How can it continue to exist as a passion, though, when the institution that supports and legitimates it disappears into the broader harmony of society?

The answer is that this passion, the specific and reciprocal attraction between adult and child, far from depending on the civilized institution of the family, is rather hindered by it. Its full play will carry it toward an elective paternity, founded on attraction and adoptive choice. Fourier would have subscribed to – if indeed he did not draw his inspiration from – the verses of the Latin poet Statius, consoling Melior on the death of his young favourite Glaucias: "Having children depends on fate, choosing them on our inclination [*Natos genuisse necesse est/ Elegisse juvat*]" (*Silves* II, 1).[1]

Already the natural father, the inseminator, is freer to "spoil" his children in the "Harmonian"[2] education which relieves him of repressive tasks. If he renounces the ridiculous pretension to being the "natural educator" when the children's group itself looks after this function, he gains the pure pleasure of fathering. This renunciation is already sufficient to rehabilitate familism. Yet, as always in Fourier, this passion is not to be treated by itself (as is our own, civilized propensity). Rather, it must be relocated within the movement of the whole – we might say (in the language of Deleuze and Guattari), within "the collective assemblage [*l'agencement collectif*]" – which alone can arrange its full and composite play.

Passion acquires this fullness of play

fourier's familism

through *joinings* or *rallyings* [*ralliements*]. Rallying or joining – which consists in supporting a passion with one or more of the other passions, reinforcing it, and even on occasion inducing it – changes the course of a passion without modifying it, making it serve the common good where it would otherwise be isolating or antisocial.

One of the remarkable effects of these rallyings in education is the possibility of counterbalancing harmful and destructive inclinations by emulation, group friendship, and honour. The "evil" is thus overcome by absorption.

The same goes for familism: what is injurious in it, the folding back of the family on itself, is counterbalanced by corporative emulation, the bond of industrial groups. Paternism frees itself from the exclusive tie of consanguinity, it departs from direct filiation, as it avoids conjugal cohabitation, cause of all conflicts. The full development of affect thus appears in the elective paternity of adoption. In civilization, the misfortune of fathers arises from the permanent opposition of their offspring through divergences in taste. By contrast, attraction, the community of inclinations and occupations, makes adoption one of the strongest ties of the social order. Adoption comes to give a new gloss, a highly laudable justification, to *inheritance*, which in civilization falls unjustly to the inactive descendant.

Speaking of the mechanism of the "dissemination of legacies", thanks to which the multiplicity of adoptions tends to make the Phalanx as a whole the beneficiary of inheritance, Fourier attacks the hypocrisy of current customs, that

> odious mechanism of concentrated legacies which provokes the inheritor to desire the death of his benefactor, even that of a father or, with more reason, of a brother, an uncle or a distant relative. Thus, the civilized man is pushed toward the grave by precisely those whose happiness he will provide for – nature's just reprisal for the paternal selfishness which makes heads of family iron-hearted toward the rest of humanity and persuades them that they need be concerned only for their own children.
> (*Unité universelle* [*Universal Unity*] V, 459)

Familism, which pushes for adoption outside the ties of consanguinity, transforms the family spirit into a sentiment that contributes to the common good, without connection to any moral altruism. It must be remembered, as Walter Benjamin so perceptively notes, that Fourier's world is amoral (*eine Welt der Unmoral*) and refers to combinations or complications of the training of the passions. Familism ceases to be selfish when it enters into combination with other passions which draw it outside its limits and complete it, conferring on it an affective tonality that can only be procured by shared labour, group training, the friendship from which love cannot finally be excluded: "A father is made happy only by the counterweight or competition between direct, consanguineous children and 'industrial', adoptive children, passion's continuers", Fourier writes in the same passage, rich in classical influences and allusions. An adoption which is able to reinforce itself with love conjures up the polyvalence of an attachment, the "confusion of sentiments" of which Statius sang in honour of the little freed slave of Atedius Melior, his adoptive son, servant, and lover. Only, where Roman custom remains disagreeably imprinted with relations of domination or servitude, Fourier displays the nomadic singularity (in Deleuzian language) of the affect in its free state, freely able to combine itself with love for the benefit of its chosen objects. An adoption at the same time familial and amorous might be like the one described in

rené schérer

Le nouveau monde industriel [*The New World of Industry*] in the case of Croesus, protector of the young Selima (VI, 257).

The relation in this case is not illicit, since no consanguinity prevents it and since "the tie can transform itself into a mixed one and include love after the adopted child reaches puberty" (V, 513). The logic of the mechanism of passion, however, cannot avoid absorbing or integrating *incest* as such into the reconsideration of affective and social ties as a whole – incest and its language, the sacred taboo, the archaic terror restored to a place of honour by Freud, and most recently to a penal code from which revolutionary rationality and Napoleon had expelled it. Diverging from contemporary phantasms, the healthy reading of Fourier reminds us that incest, in its mechanics, is only "the amalgam of two minor cardinal passions, of the two affectives of love and familism" (*Le nouveau monde amoureux* VII, 253). As such, it finds its place as a figure, a play, in the scale of loves. If it belongs among "existing prejudices", it is in no way contrary to nature, and its proscription is without reason once the household has disappeared. A progressive scale, classifying incests by degree, integrates them into possible relations of love. It is the rule in Harmony "to authorize anything that multiplies ties and works to the good of several people without doing harm to any one person", and incest, which "instead of causing murder produces a real tie", cannot be kept among the misdemeanours and crimes (257, 256). Besides, collateral incest, between cousins, uncles, aunts, nephews and nieces, is, according to Fourier, not only tolerated in civilization but currently prescribed: "Doesn't everyone know that aunts take the first fruits of their nephews?" This "darling incest [*inceste mignon*]", an infinitesimal incest, differs only in degree (it belongs to the seventh or infinitely small degree) and not in nature from the direct incest which forms the first degree or pivot. Simply by placing it in a graduated series, a change of meaning occurs which avoids both the repressive generalization of incest to which psychoanalysis will abandon itself and a banalization of incest which would deny its force. Relative to the common love which holds in monogamy, incest remains one of the complex, noble affections, one of the exceptions. Similarly, sapphism and pederasty are in no way perversions to be excluded, but rather subtle gearings, refining the mechanism of passion, operating the transitions between its great, visible components. In the end, in Harmony, there are only exceptions, singularities, which is why the air of the family, no less than the uniform distributing of the space of society into households, does not suit it.

To the bankrupt models of the family and education, to their imbecilic rehashing by the uncertain sciences relayed in the media, Fourier opposes his serene, inventive reason: the madness of a reasonable man which may one day substitute itself for the incoherence of our constraints.

Paris, 27 February 1994

Translated by Chris Miller and Forbes Morlock. Additional work by Anne Rançay.

notes

1 Literally, "It is necessary to have procreated; it pleases to have chosen". [Translators' note]

2 Harmony [*Harmonie*] names a new social and natural order, achieved through the free play and mutual acceptance of the passions. Fourier uses

fourier's familism

Harmony synonymously with Unity, and speaks of the inhabitants of the future Harmony or Unity as Harmonians [*Harmoniens*]. [Translators' Note]

bibliography

Fourier, C., *Le nouveau monde industriel* in *Oeuvres* vol. 4 (Paris: Éditions Anthropos).

Fourier, C., *Le nouveau monde amoureux* in *Oeuvres* vol. 8 (Paris: Éditions Anthropos).

Fourier, C., *Unité universelle* in *Oeuvres* vol. 5 (Paris: Éditions Anthropos).

Klossowski, P., *Les lois de l'hospitalité* (Paris: Gallimard, 1989).

notes on "fourier's familism against the household"

rené schérer

In response to a letter from the editors of Angelaki *requesting some elaboration on areas of the above article, and particularly on the matters of incest and child sexuality, we are pleased to comply with the author's suggestion that the following appear alongside his article.*

1. As regards Fourier and the question of the "child", Fourier does not attribute any sexuality to the pre-pubescent child. For him, sexuality and the passion of love begin only after puberty, that is, between 14 and 16.

2. It is almost certain, however, that this attitude derives from the medical conceptions of his time about infantile sexuality. Today, after Freud, Fourier would certainly have granted the child full possession of the passion of "love" that he denies him or her. To do so would have been wholly consistent with his analysis of the passions.

3. Personally I am not in favour of "Freudianizing" Fourier. The fact that he refused "love" to the child allowed him to develop an extremely rich conception of emulative friendship as the dominant passion of childhood. (See my *Pari sur l'impossible* for the development of this theme.)

4. Nevertheless, if taken seriously, the model of non-familial, non-scholastic education would not lead today to refusing children the right to love with the partner (horrible technical term!) of their choice.

5. It should be noted that the contemporary inflation of the "sexual", the emphasis on it,

rené schérer

is not present in Fourier, who speaks only of love.

6. As to incest, it goes without saying that only an idiot could imagine that I have offered an apology for it. As regards Fourier, he – in keeping with the rationalism of the Enlightenment – brings it back "into line". That is, he treats it no differently from any other amorous relation; he grants it degrees, but not a difference in nature. He abolishes the taboo; but, on the other hand, he is far from recommending incest, or from seeing it as a superior form of love. He is in favour of the pluralism of loves.

7. Why does he speak of "paternism" and not "maternism"? Because women are only too enslaved by "maternism" and mothering, and because he is writing to free them from this household servitude. He sees the woman in love as free, not shackled by children. On the contrary, paternism has a more positive sense for the man, whom society bans from taking affective care of his children.

It should be noted that Fourier everywhere takes as his guiding principle an absolute divergence [*l'écart absolu*] from civilization (equivalent today to the crass stupidity of the various leagues for moral order).

8. Reciprocity. This is the buzz word of contemporary hypocrisy, along with "abuse of power". For Fourier, there can be no love where there is no consent. He describes only consenting relationships. But it should be noted that in his conception of society children are free and consenting in all their activities. (The notion of minority – of an age at which, as a matter of principle, the consent of the child does not exist in the eyes of the law – is an aberrant one.) But consent does not mean reciprocity understood in the sense of identity or symmetry. When, for example, Fourier speaks of the relations between Selima (14 years old) and Croesus, the feeling that ties Croesus to Selima is not the same as the one that ties Selima to Croesus. The same thing goes for Urgèle (80 years old) and Valère (20). Where the attraction, in particular physical attraction, is not direct, it can be induced by gratitude, for example. This is the central theory of the rallying of the passions [*ralliements passionnels*] which is fundamental to Fourier, and without which his analysis of love (of loves in their infinite variety) cannot be understood.

In conclusion, everything rests on an idea which came into being suddenly in the late 70s, when sexual freedom seemed to be growing. This is the idea that the child cannot consent to sexual relations, that he or she is necessarily *abused*. A key idea, and one of indisputable influence, since I have the impression that you yourselves find it hard to escape. This is the absolute weapon, the unanswerable argument, the most difficult sophism to dislodge or demystify – the idea that the child, whatever he or she thinks, says, or consents to, is a victim of adult power.

We are dealing here with an abusive and scandalous hijacking of Foucault's ideas about power. Whereas Foucault thought exactly the opposite, in particular, that children had the right to sexual pleasure with whomever they desired. (He expressed this idea very clearly in a recording published in *Fous d'enfance* (*Recherches* 36).)

With this multipurpose hijacking of the idea of "power", one can say anything and everything.

The fact remains that Fourier was not talking about infants but about pubescent children aware of their own sexual desires. The fact remains, we must be absolutely

fourier's familism

clear, that it is not a question of prescribing behaviour, but of describing the variations on the theme of the passions, on the theme of love [*les amours*]. It is in this context that familism combines with love in incest (maternal, paternal, fraternal, sororal, avuncular, etc.), the governing idea – a central one in Fourier – being that nothing can be understood or analyzed except as part of a series.

Finally, for me, the issue is not to prescribe or recommend anything, but to make known, to remind people of, a different mode of thought, a way of conceiving of social relations with children and between children and adults other than that which has been imposed by current circumstances, by circumstances which are wrongly held to be *natural* [nature en soi].

> Never say it's natural –
> So that nothing ever passes for immutable...
> *Bertolt Brecht*

30 June 1994

bibliography

Foucault, M., "Fous d'enfance", *Recherches* 36.

Schérer, R., *Pari sur l'impossible, études fouriéristes* (St Denis: Presses Universitaires de l'Université de Paris VIII, 1989).

A catch is released, a clasp is undone, a hook is thumbed from the eye; a latch clicks, a lock is shot back, a handle is turned and something is opened... To reveal what: something tense and exciting; something new, other, surprising...

sotirios athanasiou

HOME EXERCISES

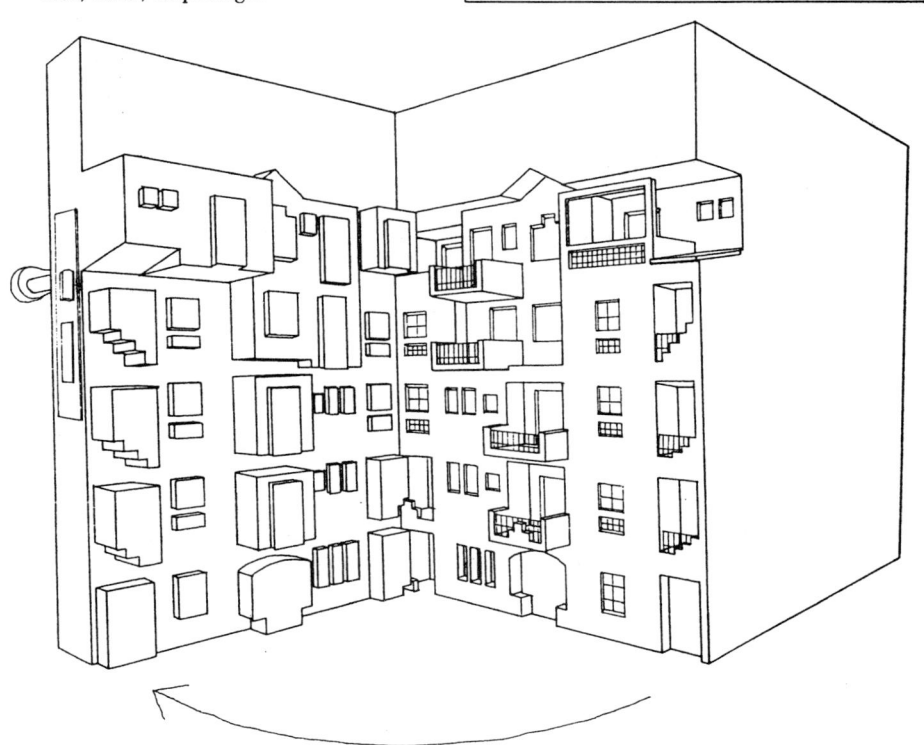

home exercises

Odd-shaped houses are of course the most charming, and perhaps most charming of all are extraordinarily thin houses – that is in relation to their occupants. Here's mine, just two metres across. What can I say: a solution in the case of extreme land scarcity, a home slimming machine...

sotirios athanasiou

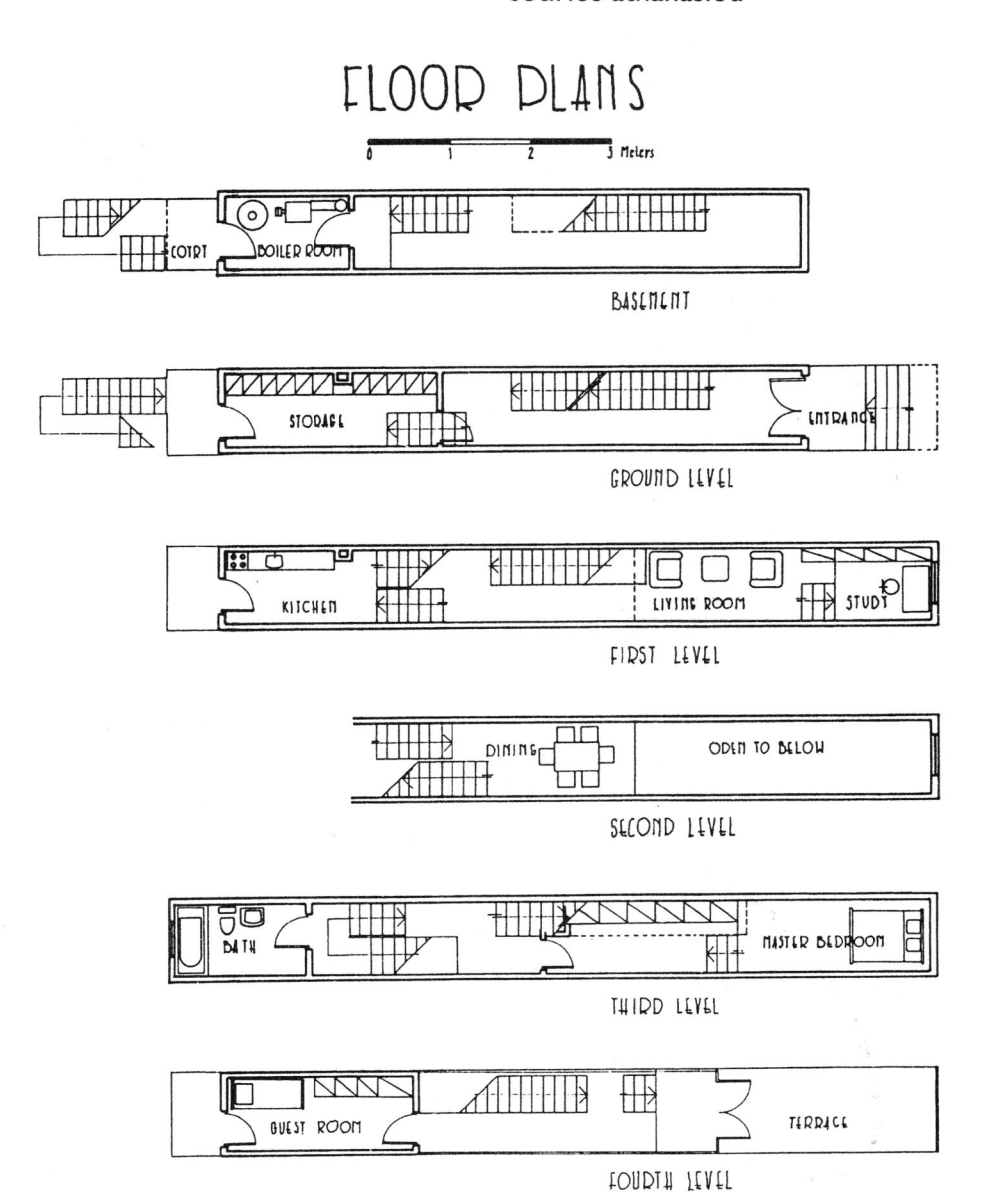

FLOOR PLANS

0 1 2 3 Meters

BASEMENT

COURT · BOILER ROOM

GROUND LEVEL

STORAGE · ENTRANCE

FIRST LEVEL

KITCHEN · LIVING ROOM · STUDY

SECOND LEVEL

DINING · OPEN TO BELOW

THIRD LEVEL

BATH · MASTER BEDROOM

FOURTH LEVEL

GUEST ROOM · TERRACE

135

home exercises

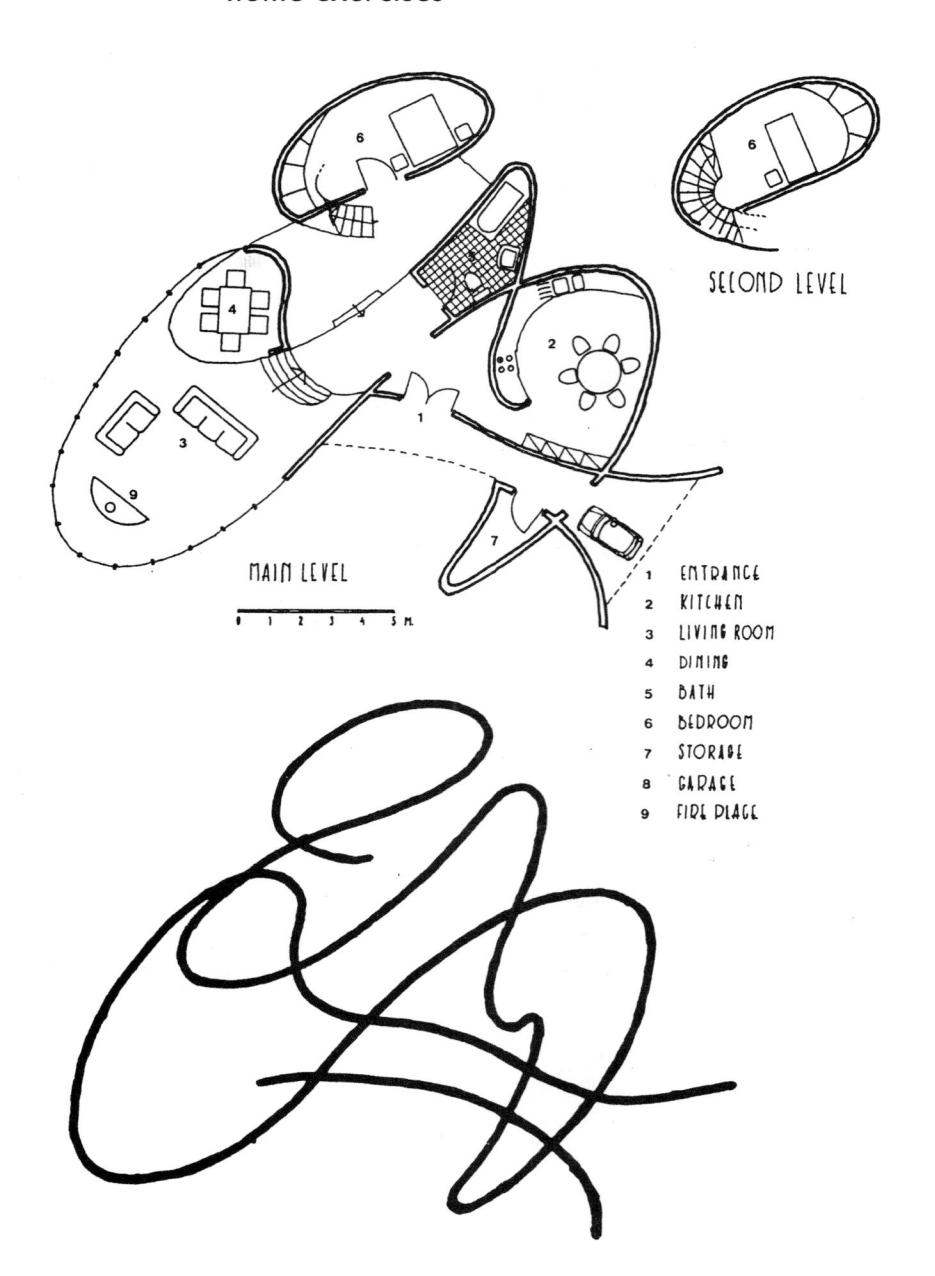

MAIN LEVEL

SECOND LEVEL

0 1 2 3 4 5 M.

1 ENTRANCE
2 KITCHEN
3 LIVING ROOM
4 DINING
5 BATH
6 BEDROOM
7 STORAGE
8 GARAGE
9 FIRE PLACE

sotirios athanasiou

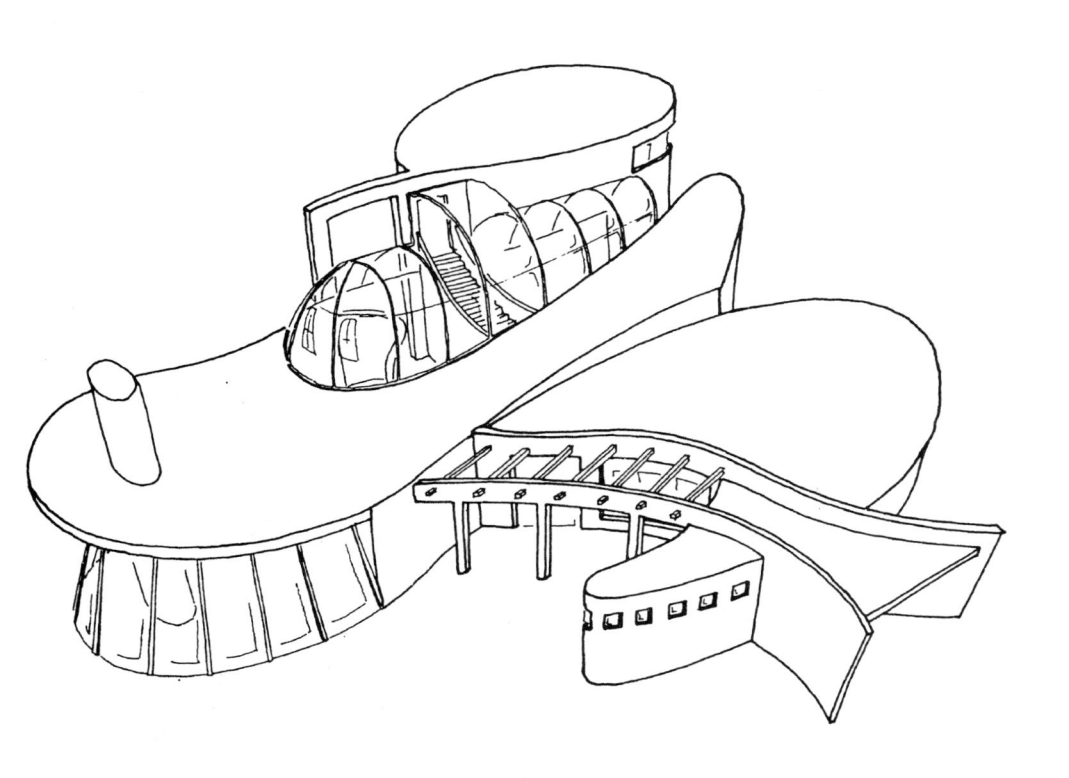

From an aleatory squiggle, a machine for living in.

From a doodle on your blotter whilst on the phone – intent and abstracted/chanceful and distracted – from the scribble of your signature – a home.

home exercises

A sketch for my cut-out *Home Encyclopedia*.

> Annoying! The same old story! When one has finished one's house one realises that while doing so one has learnt unawares something one absolutely had to know before one – began to build. The everlasting pitiful 'too late!' – The melancholy of everything *finished*!
> Nietzsche[1]

alison ainley

LUCE IRIGARAY
at home with martin heidegger?

For Luce Irigaray, as for many other contemporary thinkers, the modern age is characterised by a symptomatic and compulsive repetition of "the same"[2]: the wars, nihilistic crises and peculiar cycles of destruction which mark the era we inhabit. Deracinated by a certain failure to acknowledge the ground upon which such repetitions are built, we are in crisis, made homeless by the rootlessness of contemporary living. We also seem to lack adequate means or analysis to address the problem, except in so far as we are able to recognise it as a problem. The unique and specific problematic of modernity might be characterised in the following way: the identification of a particular set of problems and the struggle to resolve them within their own terms and, *simultaneously*, the disavowal or delegitimisation of such terms. The only possible courses of action seem to be either to seek, perhaps romantically, for a nostalgic version of what appears to have been lost or should have been known, or to adopt an ironic or strategic stance towards the perceived crisis and even towards its uniqueness. Both strands are, I think, discernible in the Nietzsche quotation above. We are doomed to build houses and to lament our lack of insight into what we needed to know, whilst we comment ironically on our problems and their limitations. Such doubling of thought, the end of philosophy perpetually deferred, may provide space for a feminist intervention into the story of "the same".

In Irigaray's work, the ground upon which dangerous and destructive repetitions are built is identified with the materiality of the female body, the symbolic instantiation of *le féminin* and the maternal. *Matière première* or prime matter ("mother-matter")[3] is explicitly figured as Mother Earth or Mother Nature, the realm of the sensible, the flesh: the conspicuous "mark" of sexual difference, maternity, is taken to express the essence of women and femininity by analogy or by extension. This ground has been objectified, devalued, suppressed or excluded, Irigaray suggests. To revalue what has been excluded is "the burning issue of our age":

> A revolution in thought and ethics is needed if the work of sexual difference is to take place. We need to reinterpret everything concerning the relation between subject and discourse, the subject and the world, the subject and the cosmic, the microcosmic and the macrocosmic. (*Ethics* 6)

Her specific slant is to look at the crisis of

139

irigaray and heidegger

the modern age as primarily a crisis of sexual relations, an inability to negotiate and comprehend sexuality in a way other than by the terms of "masculine logic". By "jamming the theoretical machinery" it might be possible to allow "a disruptive excess on the feminine side" (*This Sex* 78), the emergence of an articulation of the female sex or *le féminin* in its/her own right, and thus "true" sexual difference. If this successful negotiation could be realised, it might lead to more "fertile" relations between the sexes, mutual enrichment and an opportunity for the sexes to be more "at home" with themselves and with each other.

In other words, she offers sexual difference as both the diagnosis of the problem and the cure. But it is unclear in her writing (and perhaps deliberately unclear) whether her identification of a repressed feminine or maternal ground to Western metaphysics is a diagnosis of *fact* (a lament) or a critical, ironic and so *strategic* intervention upon patterns of thought. Such ambiguity would be in keeping with her feminist perspective on and within philosophical traditions. The acknowledgement of the contingent nature of philosophical truths would suggest that the "truth" of a feminist perspective cannot simply be substituted where other "truths" have been found lacking. The exhortation for the need (duty?) to reinterpret everything according to this basic insight (that the feminine and/or women have been excluded from and repressed within philosophy) would seem circular, except in so far as it partakes of a strand of irony, and hence has the status of a strategic, "political truth". The displacement effected by irony forces a readjustment while not claiming to substitute a wholly new order.

In a rereading which is also a refiguring, Irigaray draws upon Heidegger's analysis of philosophical content and method. Both suggest that philosophy is characterised by compulsive and repetitive patterns of thought which have failed to provide an adequate statement of the problem, let alone an adequate solution. Identifying philosophy as:

> the master discourse, ... the one which lays down the law to the others, including even the discourse held on the subject of these others; the discourse on discourses ... (149)

is the first stage in Irigaray's analysis, which suggests at once the centrality and yet distorting effects of philosophical thought. As Heidegger puts it in the Introduction to *Being and Time*:

> This question has today been forgotten ... But the question touched upon is hardly an arbitrary one ... What these two thinkers [Plato and Aristotle] gained has been preserved in various distorted forms down to Hegel's *Logic*. And what was wrested from phenomena by the highest exertion of thinking, albeit in fragments and first beginnings, has long since been trivialised.[4]

In order to think what has been obscured or forgotten, Irigaray deploys an oblique and sinuous linguistic style. The difficulties created for the reader form a strategic, poetic-philosophical brake on the idea of communication taking place through a medium of transparent clarity. Irigaray writes:

> [P]hilosophical mastery ... cannot simply be approached head on, nor simply within the realm of the philosophical itself. Thus it was necessary to deploy other languages – without forgetting their own debt to philosophical language ... so that something of the feminine at the limit of the philosophical could be heard. (150)

Thus her diagnosis of crisis and the methods

alison ainley

she adopts to respond to it are comparable in many ways to Heidegger's retracing of "the history of Being", in order to identify and address the impoverished nature of the present age and attend to the loss or misconceiving of the question of Being. For Heidegger, the forgetting of a primordial understanding, an existential-hermeneutic "as", is matched by a privileging of the theoretical subject-object assertion, the philosophical approach which occludes the very question which it sets out to explicate. As long as philosophy remains within its own territorial limitations, it will duplicate and multiply its shortcomings and mistakes.

Heidegger's search for a fundamental ontology which could readdress metaphysics in its contemporary manifestations involves rethinking what it means to dwell in the world. The possibility of "dwelling poetically", of building locations in language, in the material world and in philosophical ontology, is, for Heidegger, a re-thinking of an elemental, material basis of existence. It implies a reconsideration of the philosophical history which has housed our metaphysical questioning since the beginnings of Greek philosophy, and an attempt to readdress the destructive technological potential now threatening to annihilate our world utterly.

To dwell for Heidegger, then, is much more than the domesticity of home living. In the course of the essay "Building, Dwelling, Thinking"[5], he points out that the old meaning of building (*bauen*) was to dwell – literally to stay in the same place – but also to be at peace, to free or to spare as an activity of "letting be". Building therefore signifies dwelling, which also signifies to preserve, cherish, care for and cultivate. But building can also be read as the creating of edifices, construction and making. The latter meaning suggests a merely instrumental relation to a location if it is taken to have priority without attention to the older meaning. Cultivation, care in order to allow growth, is replaced by domination and control. According to Heidegger, the older meaning has been obscured such that we think of dwelling as contingent upon, or coming after, the buildings we have built, and fail to recognise that we build because we are first *dwellers*. The essay then calls for the recognition of the older version of dwelling which would, in "sparing the earth, set it free into its own essence" ("Building, Dwelling, Thinking" 328), and allow us to see "the real plight of dwelling":

> that mortals ever search anew for the essence of dwelling, that they must ever learn to dwell. What if man's homelessness consisted in this, that man does not even think of the real plight of dwelling as the plight? But how else can mortals answer this summons than by trying on their part, on their own, to bring dwelling into the fullness of its essence? (329)

Despite the return to the elemental (the ground of elements) which seems to characterise Heideggerian thinking, a return to an anonymous and neutral earth, Heidegger points out that it is really by virtue of human horizons of understanding that space is to be grasped at all. "[S]paces receive their essential being from locations and not from 'space'" (332). Locations are potential sites for building, and so space as such is room freed for settlement:

> [S]pace is something that has been made room for, something that is cleared and free, namely, within a boundary ... Man's relation to locations and through locations to spaces, inheres in his dwelling. The relationship between man and space is none other than dwelling, thought essentially. (335)

irigaray and heidegger

The phenomenological and hermeneutic dimensions to Heidegger's suggestions in the above quotation would suggest that the understanding of space is open for revision and interpretation, given the understanding of man (sic) as a "being who dwells". But the extent to which Heidegger's "dwelling" is actually another form of colonisation, closure, and repression is taken up in the work of thinkers who are closest to Heidegger and thus seek to distinguish their own thought from his.

Writing from a position which brings together ethics, Judaic thought and phenomenology, Emmanuel Levinas[6] attempts to separate his own phenomenological reading of dwelling from Heidegger's. He sees Heidegger's attempt to return to the elemental through a rethinking of "dwelling" as a will to return to "a peasant rootedness", "a pagan existence" entailing "a rule of power more inhuman than technology".[7] The question of being, understood from this perspective, is not merely about the "letting be" of Being, but the brutal imposition of an impersonal ontology, which Levinas links with Heidegger's Nazi connections. Levinas also suggests that in making death or mortality the horizon of Being, Heidegger foregrounds negation at the expense of the dimension of lived existence, and prioritises the individual's relation with his own death at the expense of relations with others (Levinas replaces death with "enjoyment", and his starting point is being with others). Finally, because Levinas employs a sensualised, erotic phenomenology, he is able to accuse Heidegger of making Being neutral, asexual or desexualised.[8] As Irigaray suggests, not all of these criticisms are exactly fair, although she makes use of the last for her own feminist reading of Heidegger.

> Being (être) is used to refer to a disposition which leads me to approach any being (étant) in a certain way. In this sense, the philosophy of Heidegger cannot be seen simply as an 'ethics of the "fruits of the earth"' (nourritures terrestres), nor of the enjoyment (jouissance) of objects, such as the other in sexual love. [cf. Totalité et infini 45-6, Totality and Infinity 62-4.9] The philosophy of Heidegger is more ethical than the expression conveys, than his philosophy itself says explicitly. To consider the other within the horizon of being should mean to respect the other. It is true that the definition of Being in terms of mortal destiny rather than in terms of living existence raises questions about the nature of respect. And in addition, this philosophy is more or less silent on man's sexual dimension (la dimension de l'homme comme sexué), an irreducible human dimension.[10]

In *Totality and Infinity* Levinas explicitly links the notion of dwelling with *le féminin*, as one means of elucidating the "immanent transcendence" of his thought, and as an attempt to redress the neutrality of Heideggerian dwelling.[11] For Levinas, otherness and ethical care are already present in the structures of "interiority", and already imply a feminine dimension. He suggests that "I is already an other", already self-divided within itself, and that the equation of otherness and the feminine can be taken up as an existing equation – in order to subvert it. One of his reasons for suggesting or asserting this otherness is to reproach Heidegger for what seems to have been forgotten; the question of sexuality in relation to ontology. We can rephrase the question as it was put to Derrida: Is sexuality a regional question within ontology or would sexuality challenge the very possibility of a general ontology?[12] Because Levinas identifies ontology with totality, sexuality is one way to disrupt the totalising closure of metaphysics and open it up for ethics. However,

alison ainley

Levinas's evocation of *le féminin* may be seen as instrumental, in so far as it is used as a reminder of the materiality of lived existence, but is ultimately in service to a larger conception of ethical goodness: the path of metaphysical transcendence (albeit opened through experience and through ethical relations with others). Irigaray takes issue with Levinas on this point in her essay "Questions to Emmanuel Levinas", a clarification and counterpoint to her earlier essay "The Fecundity of the Caress".[13] In "Questions" she suggests a) that Levinas "opens the feminine in philosophy" and yet still seems to "write out" the feminine, so that there is no place for women in what Levinas proposes – as she puts it: "the caress, that 'fundamental disorder', does not touch the other" ("Questions" 110); and b) that we have not yet reached an age in which onto-theological issues can simply be reintroduced with impunity – therefore she suggests that although Heidegger may have "shelved" the question of the relation between philosophy and theology, Levinas mixes them together (or rather, "intentionally fails to distinguish the foundations" (114)).

Ultimately then, Irigaray suggests Levinas is as guilty as any other metaphysician of covering over, obscuring or denying *le féminin*:

> For him, the feminine does not stand for an other to be respected in her human freedom and human identity. The feminine other is left without her own specific face. On this point, his philosophy falls radically short of ethics. (113)

From Irigaray's point of view, the same might be said of Heidegger. Irigaray's critique of Heidegger, the third of her "elemental" texts, is entitled *L'oubli de l'air chez Martin Heidegger*.[14] The element of air is used symbolically to draw attention to the neglect of the feminine, the flowing, impermanent mobility which contrasts the solidity of the earth. But the ground of earth also has feminine connotations, as "the spatiality that precedes any localisation ..." (*L'oubli* 15). Forgetting or failing to look at the ground, in so far as it is symbolically feminine, means that for Irigaray Heidegger's thought is based in "an illusion", of "solid ground ... a path which holds firm beneath his feet ... as long as Heidegger does not leave 'the earth', he cannot leave metaphysics behind" (10). The ethical implications in his work of "respect for the other" are not borne out, she suggests, because the elemental is once again symbolically feminine/maternal, a "forgotten, unthought and hated" ground.[15] Once again, the furnishing role of growth and life, equated with the feminine, is omitted and suppressed by the theoretical house of language built upon it for the masculine:

> Some creators (*masc*) of worlds, constructors of temples, builders of houses; others guardians (*fem*) of a *phuein* making its resources available, prior to any culture. (120)

The connotations of *phuein* (to grow, to engender, to come into the light) suggest not only the roots of the word *phusis* (nature), but also "unthought, left in forgetfulness", "hatred and death" (35). Hence, despite drawing attention to the destructive tendencies of building as opposed to the nurturing care for the earth implied in dwelling, she suggests that Heidegger builds his philosophical "house" at the expense of the feminine. Even though nature and the earth are the basis of dwelling, the "debt owed to the feminine" is never acknowledged, and so for Irigaray Heidegger perpetuates the immobilising, exploitative tendencies of metaphysics.

irigaray and heidegger

And yet, the "forgetting of air" itself is forgotten, as Irigaray becomes more at home with Heidegger (*chez* Martin Heidegger), and the sacred grounding of Being through poetry and song is recalled – the revealing/concealing "truth" of primordial, sensual experience incarnate. Through poetic thought, the spaces of airy song and the spaces of body and earth might be opened up in new ways. In this way Irigaray seems closer to Heidegger than she might openly admit.16

But Irigaray has to consider these questions from the point of view of one who is not "at home" in philosophy. If the feminine is providing a dwelling for man, she lacks a home for herself and is in effect "homeless". She lacks not only the interiority of self-possession, but also the means to "come and go", and the language of a being of her own.

> The house of language which for men goes so far as to supply his dwelling in a body ... woman is used to construct it, but, then, it is not available to her. (*Ethics* 15)

But homelessness is only one aspect of the problem: another is imprisonment. Irigaray suggests the feminine can become locked into the forms of representation used by the philosopher and restrictively defined as such. In exchange for what the philosopher has "borrowed" from the feminine in order to construct his spatiality

> ... he buys her a house, even shuts her up in it, places limits on her that are the opposite of the unlimited site in which he unwittingly contains her. He contains or envelops her with walls ... visibly limiting and sheltering, but at the risk of being prison-like or murderous. (11)

Either way, the result is a denial of a "proper place" for women/the feminine, whether by immobilisation or exclusion.

Irigaray characterises philosophical method as follows:

> [A] project, conscious or not, of turning away, of deviation and of reduction in the artifice of sameness, of otherness. In other words, speaking at the greatest level of generality so far as philosophical methods are concerned; of the feminine. (*This Sex* 150)

Thus, in order to address this philosophical problem philosophically, it is necessary to find an oblique approach. Irigaray's response is to turn the tables, to use seduction as a weapon: "the option left to me was to have a fling with the philosophers" – to treat philosophy less seriously, to get round the scholars, in order to know philosophical systems intimately from within. But to behave in a flirtatious manner is also to mimic the behaviour "expected" of women, a stereotypical refusal of the scholar's seriousness. This "path of mimicry" is, she suggests, one way to "get back into the philosopher's house"; to play the role of the philosopher's wife, and so take on accepted symbolic "roles" within philosophy, whether this is "like Plato's *chora*" (the black hole of chaos that is also the fertile replenishing womb) or "the mirror of the subject" (the reflection of the narcissistic self). But as she suggests, if women are to find their own way of dwelling in language they cannot simply continue to occupy the role of complementary term, secondary other. There is little solace is being the philosopher's wife as such, merely a handmaiden to the more serious business of the day, unless such a role can be subverted and transformed. Without the recognition of the mimicry inherent in this role, the "elsewhere kept in reserve" (76) the subversive masquerade is once again recuperated.

144

alison ainley

notes

1 Nietzsche, Friedrich, *Beyond Good and Evil*, tr. R. Hollingdale (Harmondsworth: Penguin, 1977) p192.

2 Irigaray, Luce, *An Ethics of Sexual Difference*, trs C. Burke and G. Gill (London: Athlone, 1993) p5.

3 Irigaray, Luce, *This Sex Which is Not One*, tr. C. Porter (London: Athlone, 1985) p77.

4 Heidegger, Martin, *Basic Writings*, tr. D. Krell (San Francisco: Harper Collins, 1977) p41-2.

5 Heidegger, Martin, *Basic Writings* p319-40.

6 See *The Levinas Reader*, ed. Seán Hand (Oxford: Blackwell, 1989).

7 Levinas, Emmanuel, *Collected Philosophical Papers*, tr. A. Lingis (Dordrecht: Martinus Nijhoff, 1987) p52

8 Although Levinas also pre-empts Irigaray's criticism when he writes: "Being directs its building and cultivating, in the midst of a familiar landscape, on a maternal earth. Anonymous, neuter, it directs it, ethically indifferent, as heroic freedom, foreign to all guilt with regard to the other." ibid. p53.

9 Levinas, Emmanuel, *Totality and Infinity*, tr. A. Lingis (Dordrecht: Martinus Nijhoff, 1977).

10 Irigaray, Luce, "Questions to Emmanuel Levinas" in *Re-Reading Levinas*, eds Robert Bernasconi and Simon Critchley (Indianapolis and Bloomington: Indiana University Press, 1991) p114.

11 Levinas, Emmanuel, *Totality and Infinity* p152-68.

12 Derrida, Jacques and Christie V. McDonald, "Choreographies", *Diacritics* 12 (summer 1982) p66-76.

13 Irigaray, Luce, *An Ethics of Sexual Difference*, p185-217.

14 Irigaray, Luce, *L'oubli de l'air chez Martin Heidegger* (Paris: Minuit, 1985).

15 See Margaret Whitford, *Luce Irigaray: Philosophy in the Feminine* (London: Routledge, 1991) p158.

16 See Caroline Burke, "Romancing the Philosophers: Luce Irigaray" in *Seduction and Theory: Readings of Gender, Representation and Rhetoric*, ed. Diane Hunter (Urbana and Chicago: University of Illinois Press, 1989) p226-40.

bibliography

Burke, C., "Romancing the Philosophers: Luce Irigaray" in *Seduction and Theory: Readings of Gender, Representation and Rhetoric*, ed. D. Hunter (Urbana and Chicago: University of Illinois Press, 1989) p226-40.

Derrida, J. and C.V. McDonald, "Choreographies", *Diacritics* 12 (summer 1982) p66-76.

Heidegger, M., *Basic Writings*, tr. D. Krell (San Francisco: Harper Collins, 1977).

Irigaray, L., *L'oubli de l'air chez Martin Heidegger* (Paris: Minuit, 1985).

Irigaray, L., *This Sex Which Is Not One*, tr. C. Porter (London: Athlone, 1985).

Irigaray, L., "Questions to Emmanuel Levinas" in *Re-Reading Levinas*, eds R. Bernasconi and S. Critchley (Indianapolis and Bloomington: Indiana University Press, 1991) p109-18.

Irigaray, L., *An Ethics of Sexual Difference*, trs C. Burke and G. Gill (London: Athlone, 1993).

Levinas, E., *Totality and Infinity*, tr. A. Lingis (Dordrecht: Martinus Nijhoff, 1977).

Levinas, E., *The Levinas Reader*, ed. S. Hand (Oxford: Blackwell, 1989).

Nietzsche, F., *Beyond Good and Evil*, tr. R. Hollingdale (Harmondsworth: Penguin, 1977).

Whitford, M., *Luce Irigaray: Philosophy in the Feminine* (London: Routledge, 1991).

forbes morlock

HOME ECONOMICS/ HOUSEHOLD WORDS
disciplining rhetoric and political economy

Of rhetoric and political economy. Of a conjunction, an exchange, an economy – rhetoric *and* political economy. *Tekhnai, artes,* disciplines – what is the relation between rhetoric and political economy? Is it essential? is it accidental? or is it, in the terms of Aristotle's *Topics*[1], proper? The question turns less on what is proper to each discipline than on what the proper (*le propre, proprium, to idion, to kurion, to prepon, to oikeion*) is to both.

Dead disciplines – rhetoric and political economy. Like certain metaphors, as institutions and pedagogies they are buried. Witnesses to the interring of another pair ("Marxism is dead!" "Deco[nstruction] is dead!"), we ask how their forebears lie beside each other. How is the answer to be figured? And what is the value – economic or linguistic – of the question?

Home, the household, in one dead language *ho oikos*. Where are the dead – disciplines, languages, and metaphors among them – at home? Rhetoric and political economy once found their homes in the law court and the agora, outside the *oikos*. Aristotle laid the foundations of their disciplined households by walling out the familial, the domestic, the proper, *to oikeion*. Still, the question of the disciplinary returns as a matter of home and of economy: economy's own first home is in household management, the household discipline, *oikonomia*. What is the discipline of the household, the home? And what is discipline itself at home to?

Such questions animate this essay, a note on a note in "White Mythology"[2], an introduction to the rhetorical reading of *Capital: A Critique of Political Economy*[3], and an examination of how a relation between disciplines is itself to be disciplined. In the name of home economics and household words, this essay is shaped by the reading of a single text, the interrogation of a critique of a discipline, and the question of a conjunction between disciplines. For their differences, these projects are too close (*proche, prope*) to allow each to speak of what is proper (*propre, proprius*) to it alone. The projects intimate one another, they interfere with one another – it can only be suggested that the specificity of this intimacy or interference is shaped (or disciplined) by the specificity of the conjunction, the "and", they would articulate.

To schematize – and schemata are already figures of speech, rhetorical figures, by an old name – the "and" between rhetoric and political economy, by the time it names itself, can articulate itself in at least three registers. To give them the names of other disciplines, these registers speak as history, philology, and philosophy. Rhetoric and political economy, a conjunction of disciplines – disciplines other than history, philology, and philosophy – articulates itself historically, philo-

home economics

logically, philosophically. Historically, the transmissions of rhetoric and political economy as regulating practices appear oddly congruent across millennia. Philologically, the technical distinctions of the disciplines as languages trace themselves to Aristotle and to a characteristic use of the proper (*to oikeion*) at the origin of each. Philosophically, the two sciences as conceptual constructions define themselves in terms of analogy and inscribe their limits in the organizing figure of an analogy missing a term. History, philology, philosophy – speaking under the signs of economy, the proper, and analogy respectively, these three disciplines organize or discipline the middle three sections of this essay.

Yet, if they are all to be assimilated to disciplines, the three registers – the registers in which the conjunction between rhetoric and political economy articulates itself – are also to be expressed in different categories of relation. Returning to a historical beginning, to the texts of Aristotle, and to the philosophy of the *Topics*, the nature of the "and" between rhetoric and political economy can be thrice figured, loosely as a relation of accident (*sumbebēkos*), of property (*idion*), and of definition (*horos* – I.4, 101b25ff.). Accidentally, the link between the regions may stand as nothing more than chance to each, sometimes belonging to it and sometimes not. Properly, the relation of the disciplines may belong to them alone, inseparable from and characteristic of each in turn, without indicating either's essence. Definitively, the conjunction of rhetoric and political economy may constitute or signify the essence of both, defining the terms it conjoins. Accident, property, and definition – alongside the disciplinary redescriptions above, these three categories of relation figure the essay's central three parts.

Still, something is missing, out of place, not at home. Such Aristotelian distinctions address the status of the "and" between rhetoric and political economy, but they do not animate it, or bring a relation between dead disciplines back to life. They enable us to figure a conjunction (figure it even as a rhetorical trope and as a political-economic calculation), but not to determine its value – the value perhaps of a conjunction between disciplines of value. Turning back, we ask to what category the different categories of belonging (perhaps *oikeios*) themselves belong? How are categories of relation themselves related? Here we are not far from home, for, even in Greek, questions of relation and relatedness (perhaps *oikeiotēs*) cannot keep relations or relatives (perhaps *oikos*) out of the house (*oikia*) altogether. In the name of *oikonomia*, how is the household to be regulated or disciplined? In the name of one discipline (*oikonomia*, for example), how is the economy between regulations or disciplines itself to be disciplined?

Framing the concerns of the centre of this essay, then, is a concern with the frame, that is, with discipline itself. The definition of discipline, as the definitions of rhetoric and political economy as disciplines, escapes this essay. The articulation of the relation between rhetoric and political economy brings talk of a particular relation between disciplines and of the general nature of the disciplinary. The two questions run alongside each other, they run into each other, but they do not quite run together. In the end, a conjunction of disciplines, this conjunction of disciplines, resists generalization in the name of the interdisciplinary and resolution in a concept of disciplinarity. As ever (for example, in the opening and closing sections of this essay), it is a matter of home. An initial inquiry into the interdisciplinary risks imagining itself without home or beyond discipline. A final inquiry into disciplinarity risks predetermining one discipline – philos-

forbes morlock

ophy (the discipline of general and particular?), for example – as the general home in which particular disciplines are to be conceived. Neither a non-home nor a philosophical home construct themselves here. Rather, the "and" of rhetoric and political economy builds its own home, a proper home, and a home in its own proper. In the end, it may find a home in the text of "White Mythology: Metaphor in the Text of Philosophy", it may find a home in that text's proper (*le propre...*), but only if proper to that proper are both the *idion* of the academy and philosophy and the unread *oikeion* of the home and family. Home and family. Rhetoric and political economy. Ultimately, their exchange may be a matter of *oikonomia*.

"regional" trade

> In signifying the metaphorical process, the paradigms of coin, of metal, silver and gold, have imposed themselves with remarkable insistence. Before metaphor – an effect of language – could find its metaphor in an economic effect, a more general analogy had to organize the exchanges between the two 'regions'. ("White Mythology" 216)

> To coin a phrase, money talks.

Money for language, language for money – two economies trade in a commonplace about the marketplace. The first exchange is intralinguistic, an exchange of grounds (or figures) between two phrases. The phrases themselves are hackneyed, over-used: their lack of verbal novelty indicates the banality of the trade between language and money. The second exchange is economic, offering for sale a truth about the money economy valid from its origin in the agorae of ancient Greece to its end in the capitalist "language of commodities" (*Capital*'s *Warensprache*).[4]

The truth is worn, almost worn out, a truism: its very lack of value marks the prevalence of the commerce between linguistic and monetary values.

So universal and everyday is the commerce between language and money that it almost defines the commonplace. Analogies between the respective circulations of words and goods have developed a currency of their own, one as debased as it is old. Marx remarks more than once that money as coin speaks different languages in different lands[5], while Nietzsche notes wearily that metaphors are worn down or effaced like the surfaces of coins.[6] As figures such figures are not proper to the texts of philosophy alone. Adam Smith finds the verbal commonplace at home in the marketplace – "there is nowhere more use made of figures than in the lowest and most vulgar conversation. The Billingsgate language is full of it"[7] – and Pierre Fontanier echoes:

> Boileau and Du Marsais have said, and it has been a thousand times repeated on their authority, that as concerns Tropes more are created in Les Halles on a market day than there are in the entire *Aeneid*, or than are created in the Académie at several consecutive sittings.[8]

Transfers between language and money, exchanges between the two "regions", are countless; yet their variety is matched by the simplicity and repetitiveness of their economy. In each case, figure and ground, what is proper to the word and what is proper to the coin, stand clear and distinct. Even as the gap between arithmetic figures and figures of speech, the difference between figures can always be told.

A great deal has rested on telling the difference between language and money and on telling it as the tale of an original and fundamental resemblance. Jean-Joseph Goux

home economics

and Marc Shell are only the latest to lay out the story of Western thought as more than an analogy — in one case as a "structural homology" — between the economies of money and writing, scrip[9] and script.[10] "Economies of literature", geneses — even autobiographies — of the coin and the concept, Goux's and Shell's would be narratives of genre themselves without genre, histories of discipline themselves without discipline.

The question of discipline presents itself otherwise as a matter of home, and of economic thought's own home. At the origin of Goux and Shell's narratives of economy (*oikonomia*), the origin of *oikonomia* lies in the home (*oikos*).[11] The homes of their respective narratives remain to be identified, indeed they remain to be constructed. In which regional science is a "sustained critique of th[e] interaction between thought and economics in the postclassical era" to locate itself (Shell, *Money* 4)? And which discipline is to regulate the tracing of "logico-historical correspondence", the elaboration of the "fundamental configuration that may perhaps have first emerged in ancient Greece (with the advent of money, of purely phonetic writing, of the philosophical concept, etc.,) and seems to have reached its height in modern Western society" (Goux, *Symbolic Economies* 108 and 4)? To continue the epigraph above:

> The analogy within language finds itself represented by an analogy between language and something other than itself. But here, that which seems to 'represent', to figure, is also that which opens the wider space of a discourse on figuration, and can no longer be contained within a regional or determined science, linguistics or philology. ("White Mythology" 216)

At issue for Goux and Shell is a non-regional science, a system of exchange that would regulate circulation between systems of exchange, an economy of economies. This general economy, an economy of generalized exchange, would govern the commerce between linguistic, monetary, and even conceptual economies. The concept of this general economy can articulate itself only in the conditional: the non-regional science, the science that would discipline all regional sciences, all disciplines, would itself be without discipline. Not undisciplined but without discipline. *Plus de discipline* — no more discipline(s), (one) more discipline.

Philosophy, the science Goux and Shell would regionalize, in Shell's case in the name of literature, is precisely the science Jacques Derrida re-inscribes otherwise in "White Mythology: Metaphor in the Text of Philosophy".[12] "Regional or determined science" may be that essay's own term, but the text is careful not to name its opposite, its other, its negation. "White Mythology" does not speak of "universal science", it does not offer philosophy as a universal science, and yet from its opening sentence, it fails to inscribe philosophy as one "regional or determined science" among others:

> *De la philosophie, la rhétorique.*
> Of philosophy [and] rhetoric.
> From philosophy, rhetoric. (209)

The translation — that interlinguistic economy, figure for the exchange of currencies as for the exchange of word and concept — is uncertain. The syntax, specifically whether the comma indicates a relation of equivalence or subordination, is undecidable. Derrida's essay explores just this undecidability. Its discussion of discipline — and it addresses a conjunction of disciplines from its first comma — is organized by its responsibility to a single discipline, a living discipline, a proper discipline, philosophy. The proper of "White Mythology" is the proper of philosophy, but, as the text acknowledges, this proper – *"idion, proprium, eigen"* (216) – is not the only proper (246). As we will see, at least one other proper has its disciplines.

Representing neither a general economy nor a re-inscribed philosophy[13], then, this essay wanders from the path of philosophical inquiry early in the text of "White Mythology". While still reading the exergue, this piece turns at the exchange between metaphor and coin. It turns to explore another disciplinary conjunction, one other than that between philosophy and rhetoric. The "and" it pursues is that between the disciplines of language and money, between their "own", "proper" disciplines. Today the question of discipline, of disciplining the exchanges between the disciplines of language and money, is most likely to be asked in terms of linguistics and economics.[14] Once, though, it was (or, more properly, was not) asked in the name of rhetoric and political economy. Under the sign of these dead disciplines, a deviation begins.

I economic discipline

How is the relation between two disciplines to be figured, represented or calculated? How is the conjunction between rhetoric and political economy to be valued? This presentation offers three different answers: in their turn, 1) historical, 2) philological, and 3) philosophical. Of course, history, philology, and philosophy are themselves disciplines, but then this inquiry remains a disciplinary matter. Its problems lie less in any lack of discipline than in the specification of its own discipline, the name of its home. Rhetoric and political economy are dead; their houses in the academy are otherwise occupied by faculties of national languages and literatures and institutes of economics and statistics. The disciplines are dead, and yet, even in their respective lives, the "and" which this essay seeks to articulate, the "and" of their conjunction, did not speak.

To articulate the conjunction, to give voice to it as a problem, this inquiry begins in death, in the death of its subjects. Rhetoric and political economy are dead. The opening line of Paul Ricoeur's *The Rule of Metaphor* [in French *La métaphore vive*] insists on nothing less.[15] Rhetoric is dead, and Ricoeur, rather than seeing rhetoric back to life like the phoenix from the ashes, is keen to pull a living metaphor from its corpse. *La rhétorique est morte. Vive la métaphore.* Metaphor lives, and yet the life or death of metaphor (not to mention living and dead metaphors) is itself only a metaphor. To announce the "death" of rhetoric would only repeat the metaphor of death and reconfirm the life of metaphor.

In what other terms can one describe the historical vicissitudes of a discipline? For Roland Barthes the period of rhetoric's life becomes "a veritable empire" (14). Barthes' narrative, for the difference in its figures, does not otherwise depart from Ricoeur's: the empire which existed for two-and-a-half millennia has declined or fallen. Histories of disciplines are perhaps limited by their very form as stories: the death (and birth) of a discipline, its fall (and rise) – the figures are relentlessly circular.[16] The trajectory of disciplines, disciplines of circulation – the circulation of goods and the circulation of figures – is itself narrated through figures of circulation.

And yet it is narrated. Political economy as a discipline, if not as a term, meets its end at the end of the nineteenth century, with the sidelining of the question of value. Rhetoric equally meets its end in the nineteenth century: its objects still circulate as texts, but they are now the objects of new subjects, that is, of classical and modern literature. A common place of birth matches

home economics

the common time of death: rhetoric and political economy are both born in ancient Greece. Political economy finds its name (*oikonomia politikē*) in the "Aristotelian" *Economics*[17]; it finds its first exposition in Aristotle's analysis of chrematistics (the art of wealth-getting) and just exchange in the *Politics* and the *Nicomachean Ethics* respectively. As a name the discipline of rhetoric (*hē rhētorikē tekhnē*) appears first in Plato's *Gorgias*; as a discipline it finds its first systematic exposition in Aristotle's *Rhetoric*.[18]

Common births and common deaths – these commonalities seem more coincidence than "logico-historical" congruence. They seem coincidental because in the long history of the disciplines' conjunction, as we narrate it now, what is remarkable is the lack of exchange between them. In the Renaissance, Antoine de Montchrétien's *Traicté de l'oeconomie politique* appears as the first rhetorics are published in English and French. Political economy achieves its fullest development during the century after the Scottish Enlightenment, at the same time as the most complete systematizations of rhetoric in its different forms appear in Britain and France. The absence of any commerce between the disciplines is not simply a question of climate: in some cases, the same men (among them Condillac, Smith, and later Whately, and de Quincey) are teaching and publishing both rhetorics and political economies[19], while others (including Turgot and Rousseau) are writing conjectural histories of both language and money.[20]

Our conjunctional history – the history of this conjunction between disciplines – must acknowledge its own limit, namely, that such congruent histories mean little to their contributors. From classical Greece to the classic texts of modern political economy and rhetoric, no attempt is made to articulate the disciplines, even by the writers and teachers working in both. The history of a conjunction, full of promising congruences, is almost completely a silent one. The exchange between the exchanges of words and goods, metaphors and money, seems not to extend beyond the commonplaces of the marketplace. An everyday "and" escapes articulation. To elaborate this absence of an articulation, we must return to the scene of its initial "non-appearance" in the texts of Aristotle.

II proper discipline

> The necessity of examining the history and system of the value of 'properness' ['*propriété*'] has become apparent to us. An immense task, which presupposes the elaboration of an entire strategy of deconstruction and an entire protocol of reading. One can foresee that such a labour, however far off it may be, in one fashion or another will have to deal with what is translated by "proper" in the Aristotelian text. That is to say, with *at least three meanings* [significations]. ("White Mythology" 246 – emphasis added)

> Aristotle's rhetoric is already a *domesticated* discipline (Ricoeur, *The Rule of Metaphor* 10 – emphasis added)

In an attempt to understand a silence, we move back from conjectural histories to conceptual histories, from dead disciplines to dead languages, from narratives of birth and death to tales of origin. As we return to the origins of rhetoric and political economy, we risk moving among philologists, even etymologists.[21] With Derrida, we acknowledge the critiques of etymologism, and note with him that the most famous of such critiques is nothing other than a story of the proper.[22] Indeed it is this proper (*eigen, proprium, to idion*) we must negotiate, even as we make ourselves at home in another proper (*to oikeion*), a proper (for Derrida, a "meaning" of the proper) entirely marginal to "White Mythology". The story that follows is thus double, properly two stories of a single word.

To define the essence of a discipline is beyond this inquiry – certainly its aim is not to provide a definition (in the terms of Aristotle's *Topics*[23]) of either rhetoric or political economy. Still, it seems possible, as well as necessary, to identify points that are proper (*idios*) to both. In the case of political economy, the concern that animates it even at its end is the determination of value. Here, with the distinction between use-value and exchange-value, Marx's critiques of political economy still begin:

> At first sight, the wealth of bourgeois society appears as a monstrous collection of commodities, its elementary unit being the single commodity. Every commodity, however, presents a double aspect – *use-value* and *exchange-value* [von *Gebrauchswerth* und *Tauschwerth*].*
> *Aristotle, *Politics*, I.9...[24]

Even in its opening sentence, Marx's critique takes up political economy's classical points of reference – value in use and value in exchange – in place since Adam Smith's *Inquiry into the Nature and the Causes of the Wealth of Nations*:

> The word VALUE, it is to be observed, has two different meanings, and sometimes expresses the utility of some particular object, and sometimes the power of purchasing other goods which the possession of that object conveys. The one may be called 'value in use'; the other, 'value in exchange'.[25]

The determination of value, its determination by labour (that is, the "labour theory of value"), will be taken up later under the sign of analogy. For the moment it suffices to mark the continuity of an opening division – indeed an originary deviation – in the texts of political economy: a division between the values, numerous and qualitative, of an object in use and the value, singular and quantitative, of an object in exchange. Political economies begin with exchange – the basis of all non-domestic economies – and with exchange's deviation from (proper) use. Political economies begin here, but so does political economy itself, for the distinction – as Marx notes – is Aristotle's own:

> Let us begin our discussion of the question [of the art of wealth-getting (*khrēmatistikē*)] with the following considerations. Of everything which we possess there are two uses: both belong to the thing as such, but not in the same manner, for one is the proper and the other the improper use [*dittē hē khrēsis estin ... hē men* oikeia *hē d'* ouk oikeia *tou pragmatos*] of it. For example, a shoe is used for wear, and is used for exchange; both are uses of the shoe. He who gives a shoe in exchange for money or food to him who wants one, does indeed use the shoe as a shoe, but this is not its proper use [*all'* ou *tēn* oikeian *khrēsin*], for a shoe is not made to be an object of barter. The same may be said of all possessions...[26]

Proper to political economy – or the discipline that will become political economy (for Aristotle refers to it here as *khrēmatistikē*)[27] – proper to its beginning is the proper itself (*to oikeion*). Proper (*idios*) to political economy is a concern with all the uses not proper (*oikeios*) to an object.[28]

Political economy is not the only discipline organized by such a proper, however. Rhetoric, concerned less with commercial property then verbal propriety, is nonetheless founded on the proper. Indeed in English and French, this proper is still known by name, for proper to – if not definitive of – the discipline is the distinction

home economics

between the ornamental and the natural, the figurative and the literal, the metaphorical and the proper (*le propre*).²⁹ Here, with the deviation from proper use, Pierre Fontanier's analysis of tropes still begins:

> The *literal meaning* [*le* sens littéral] is the one which holds in words taken to the letter, in words understood according to their sense [*acception*] in ordinary usage; it is, consequently, the one which presents itself immediately to the minds of those who understand the language.
>
> The literal meaning, which applies only in a single word, is either *primitive*, *natural*, and *proper*, or *derived*, if it need be said, and *tropological* [*ou* primitif, naturel, *et* propre, *ou* dérivé, *s'il faut le dire et* tropologique]. (part I, chap. 3, 57)

Fontanier takes up terms of reference – proper and improper – in place in French and English at least since Bernard Lamy. A contemporary translation of Lamy's *L'art de parler* explains:

> When to express a thing, we make use of an improper word, which Custom has applied to another Subject, that way of explaining our selves is figurative; and the words so transported from their proper signification, and applied to other things than what they naturally mean, are called *Tropes*, or *Changes* of Custom, as the *Greek* Verb *TREPŌ* imports. These Tropes do not signifie the things to which they are applied, otherwise than by reason of the connexion and reference that those things have with the things whose Names they do properly bear.³⁰

The determination of value in language (that is, the creation of new names) will be taken up below in the name of catachresis. Now it is enough to note the continuity in rhetorical handbooks of an opening division between the proper and the improper or metaphorical senses of a word. Rhetorics begin with metaphor – the emblem or trope for all tropological economies – and with metaphor's deviation from proper use. Rhetorics begin here, but so does rhetoric itself, for the distinction is Aristotle's own:

> In the language of prose, besides the regular and proper terms for things, metaphorical terms only can be used with advantage [*to de kurion kai* to oikeion *kai metaphora mona khrēsima pros tēn tōn psilōn logōn lexin*]. This we gather from the fact that these two classes of terms, the proper or regular and the metaphorical – these and no others – are used by everybody in conversation [*pantes gar metaphorais dialegontai kai* tois oikeiois *kai tois kuriois*].³¹

Proper to both rhetoric and political economy, appearing near the beginning of their texts as near the beginning of their disciplines, is a single proper (*to oikeion*). This proper belongs to – even makes its home in – the conjunction of disciplines as it does not belong to either individually: rhetoric (the science of figures) is as little concerned with words and their proper meaning as political economy (the science of exchange-values) is with shoes and their proper use. Proper to the structures of both sciences is an originary difference – the difference between proper and improper, proper and metaphorical. Equally proper to the histories of both disciplines is another originary difference – that in the translation between *to oikeion* and use-value, between *to oikeion kai to kurion* and the proper term or name.³² These originary differences are often narrated, the proper passages in Aristotle are widely quoted, but the doubling of an origin and an *oikeion* has gone apparently unnoted.

Indeed the property of *to oikeion* to the proper, to a general discussion of the proper, that is, to the very examination which

154

"White Mythology" seeks to initiate, seems unremarked. Derrida's essay examines the proper (its history and its values) as much as it does metaphor in the text of philosophy, and yet, for it, the proper's "meanings [*significations*]" "in the Aristotelian text" are only three: by name, *to idion*, *to kurion*, and *to prepon*. In the context of the *Rhetoric*, Derrida explores their senses at some length:

> The Aristotelian problematic of metaphor does not recur to a very simple, very clear, i.e. central, opposition of what will be called proper, literal meaning/figurative meaning [*sens propre/sens figuré*]. Nothing prevents a metaphorical lexis from being proper, that is, appropriate (*prepon*), suitable, decent, proportionate, becoming, in relation to the subject, situation, things. It is true that this value of properness remains rather exterior to the form — metaphorical or not — of discourse. This no longer holds for the significations *kurion* and *idion*, which are both generally translated by the same word: proper. Although the difference between *kurion* and *idion* is never given thematic exposition, it seems that *kurion*, ... designates the propriety of a name utilized in its dominant, master, capital sense... By extension, *kurion* is interpreted as the primitive (as opposed to derivative) sense, and sometimes is used as the equivalent of the usual, literal, familiar sense (*to de kurion kai to oikeion* — *Rhetoric*, III.2, 1404b31-32): 'By the ordinary word (*kurion*) I mean that in general use in a country' (*Poetics* 1457b3-4)... As for *idion*, which is much rarer in this context [though elsewhere, 'in the *Topics*, for example, it is at the centre of a theory of the proper, of essence, and of accident'], it seems to participate in the two other meanings... The contamination of these three values seems already accomplished in the Ciceronian notion of *verba propria* as opposed to *verba translata* (*De oratore* 2.4 [sic]). ("White Mythology" 246-247)

forbes morlock

The contamination which "White Mythology" finds in evidence in Cicero is, of course, also its own, for the three "meanings [*significations*]" of the proper noted initially are marked as three different Greek words — *to prepon*, *to kurion*, and *to idion*. It is only a process of translation or wearing away (*usure*, itself a central metaphor in Derrida's essay) that makes them three meanings of the same word, now in Latin (*proprium*), but equally now in Marx's and Heidegger's German (*eigen*) and in Derrida's French (*propre*). The passage of "the proper" between languages is also the passage of the same proper into conceptualization, and thus a passage into philosophy. "White Mythology" continues to effect these passages, even as it treats of them: as noted earlier, it trades in the syntax of subsumption from its opening sentence.

Of course, the status of the proper in the essay, as in philosophy, is not undone by such observations. Indeed, the critique of etymologism (an etymologism acted out in tracing "the proper" back to its original Greek "meanings") is the essay's own as it is Marx's. What attracts this reading is, rather, an apparent oversight in the proper's "at least three meanings". In the very passage quoted, the essay cites (as it does elsewhere — 238n) a fourth proper, *to oikeion*. It sees the word, and yet it does not read it. The proper of the private, the domestic, the *oikos*, *to oikeion* is, in effect, the proper not yet proper to a discussion of "properness [*propriété*]".[33] Certainly, it is not proper to the proper (*le propre*) of "White Mythology"; symptomatically, it is not proper to the conjunction "White Mythology" would articulate between rhetoric and philosophy. The proper *to oikeion*, then, may be proper (*idios*) only to another "and", that between rhetoric and political economy.[34] It may be proper to that "and" between disci-

155

plines precisely because, as we have seen, it is not proper to either discipline.³⁵ The proper that Derrida excludes from his analysis of the proper, in the end, is precisely the proper Aristotle excludes from rhetoric and political economy in their beginnings.

III analogical discipline and abuse

From a pursuit of the proper (*to oikeion*), the proper (*to idion*) of the disciplines of rhetoric and political economy, through the texts of Aristotle, we are left with an analogy – political economy is to the relation between improper and proper uses as rhetoric is to the relation between metaphorical and regular and proper terms:

> [P]olitical economy : *khrēsis ouk oikeia – khrēsis oikeia* :: rhetoric : *metaphora – to kurion kai to oikeion.*

To economize, we might articulate the analogy otherwise:

> [P]olitical economy : *to oikeion* :: rhetoric : *to oikeion.*

Political economy is to the proper as rhetoric is to the (selfsame) proper. At their origins, in the *Rhetoric* and the *Politics*, for example, rhetoric and political economy share a point of origin. From the outset, any attempt to conjoin them, to articulate their relation as an analogy (not to mention a structural homology, in Goux's formulation), is constrained by the absence of a discrete fourth term.

The analogy between rhetoric and political economy is limited by their common originary difference, their deviation from the same proper, even as analogy (*analogia*) itself is the principle both disciplines could be said to embody. Translated typically as analogy in one instance and as proportion in the other, Aristotle's *analogia* defines the basis of both metaphor (the metaphor of metaphors, the figure of figures) and just exchange.

Within the *Rhetoric*, as within numerous rhetorics since, metaphor (the economical comparison) serves a double function. It is both the proper name of a single trope, and a trope (a synecdoche, in fact) for all tropes insofar as they deviate from proper use. The play in metaphor at work in Aristotle's *Rhetoric*³⁶ still operates in Brooks and Warren's *Modern Rhetoric*:

> In this chapter ['Metaphor'] we have used *metaphor* in the largest and most inclusive sense. We have not distinguished metaphor proper from *simile* (an *explicit* comparison...), or *metonymy* (the use of a part to designate the whole...), or other such specializations of the metaphoric principle.³⁷

Metaphor serves as the figure for figures, and yet there are also distinct metaphors within metaphor. The *Poetics'* account of metaphor notes four types of metaphoric exchange:

> Metaphor [*metaphora*] consists in giving the thing a name that belongs to something else; the transference [*epiphora*] being either from genus to species, or from species to genus, or from species to species, or on grounds of analogy [*ē kata to analogon*].³⁸

The *Rhetoric* comments, "[o]f the four types of metaphor the most taking is the proportional kind [*eudokimousi malista hai kat'analogian*]", and goes on to note "that liveliness is got by using the proportional type of metaphor [*ek metaphoras tēs analogon*] and by making our hearers see things" (III.10, 1411a1-2, and III.11, 1411b22-23 – quoted in "White Mythology" 242). As commentators through Ricoeur note, one type of metaphor, the analogical or proportional kind, comes to enact the principle of all metaphorization. Metaphor on the grounds of analogy (*kat'analogian*) is, by analogy, to all types of metaphor as metaphor itself is to all tropes. By its own argument, that is, by analogy, the principle of *analogia* might define the essence of rhetoric.[39]

And yet, as the debate over Marx's inheritance from Aristotle's theory of value attests, *analogia* as a principle defines the essence of more than rhetoric.[40] Analogy or proportion, the basis of the understanding of metaphor in the *Rhetoric*, is also the basis of the understanding of just exchange in the *Nicomachean Ethics*. The figure, even sketched, is the same:

> [Metaphor] from analogy [*To de analogon*] is possible whenever there are four terms so related that the second is to the first, as the fourth is to the third; for one may then put the fourth in place of the second, and the second in the place of the fourth... Thus a cup is in relation to Dionysus what a shield is to Ares. The cup accordingly will be described as the 'shield of Dionysus' and the shield as 'the cup of Ares'. (*Poetics*, 21, 1457b16-22 – cited in "White Mythology" 242; cf. *Rhetoric*, III.4, 1407a15-18)

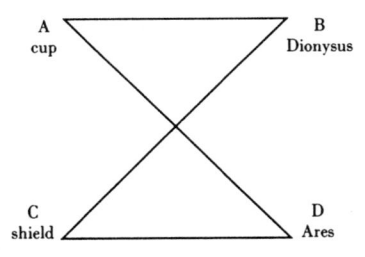

```
A                    B
cup                  Dionysus

C                    D
shield               Ares
```

Now proportionate return [*tēn antidosin tēn kat'analogian*] is secured by cross-conjunction. Let A be a builder [*oikodomos*], B a shoemaker, C a house [*oikia*], D a shoe. The builder, then, must get from the shoemaker the latter's work, and must himself give him in return his own. If, then, first there is pro-portionate equality [*to kata tēn analogian ison*] of goods, and then reciprocal action takes place, the result we mention will be effected.[41]

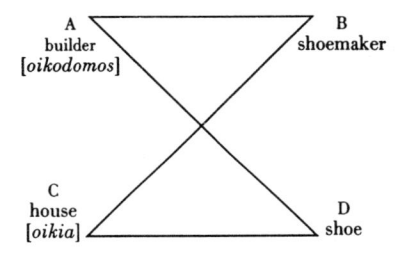

```
A                    B
builder              shoemaker
[oikodomos]

C                    D
house                shoe
[oikia]
```

Aristotle outlines economic and political relations within the city on lines that are only too visible:

> [I]n associations for exchange this sort of justice does hold men together – reciprocity in accordance with a proportion and not on the basis of equality [*to antipeponthos kat'analogian kai mē kat'isotēta*]. For it is by proportionate requital that the city holds together [*Tō antipoiein gar analogon summenei hē polis*]. (*Nicomachean Ethics*, V.5, 1132b31-35)

Analogia, the principle of analogy or proportion, both governs individual exchanges of equivalents and ensures the justice of all such equivalences, through Marx and beyond.[42] An individual economic exchange is bound to a general political bond by one principle, in one economy. By its own argument, that is, by analogy, the principle of *analogia* might define the essence of political economy.[43]

The links between rhetoric and political economy, then, are analogical in theme as well as figure. *Analogia* provides each discipline with its content, its own disciplinary principle. More than that, the very commonness of the proper name *analogia* suggests an analogy between the analogies orga-

home economics

nizing rhetoric and political economy – rhetoric is to analogy or proportion as political economy is to analogy or proportion:

[R]hetoric : *analogia* :: political economy : *analogia*.

This analogy, lacking a discrete fourth term, turns out to be no more a proper analogy than the one made possible earlier by the disciplines' respective propers, their common *to oikeion*.

Again a structure repeats itself, or perhaps still a structure endures. It remains for us to ask whether the very figure of an analogy lacking a discrete fourth term is not somehow already proper to rhetoric and to political economy. Disciplines of figure and value, linguistic and economic, the two may at their limit inscribe their limits within themselves, in their own figuration.

Rhetoric, in its concern to understand not just figures but the generation of figures, that is, the creation of linguistic value, settles firmly in the arms of a chair. The "arm" of a chair is a metaphor by analogy, figuring the proper name, the X, that is to the chair as the arm is to the body. The "arm" here is a metaphor, and yet it is also a proper name, for there is no other name, no other proper name, for that part of a chair.[44] The proper names in a language multiply by such metaphors; rhetorical handbooks, in turn, know these metaphors by the proper name "catachresis" or "*abusio*". To draw out the analogy of one such *abusio* (the body is to the arm as the chair is to its arm), proper name is to "arm" as metaphor is also to "arm":

[P]roper name : "arm" :: metaphor : "arm".

The analogy of *abusio* or abuse is, then, also an abuse of analogy – an analogy as ever missing a term.

However, what is here figured as abusive and named as *abusio* is also precisely what is productive and generative within rhetoric. Discussed as the limit of troping since Aristotle, itself named as a trope before Cicero[45], catachresis marks at its limit the origin of language, as "one of the fecund sources from which the treasures of language come" (Fontanier, part III, chap. 4, 267 – translation mine). "In multiplying the uses of words", *abusio* (the abuse of metaphor by analogy) "enriches language and renders it fit [*et la rend propre*] to express all ideas" (part III, chap. 4, 266 – translation mine). Useful is the abuse that "enriches" and brings "treasure". In the terms of the discipline's economy, catachresis names (and figures) nothing less than rhetoric's account of the creation of linguistic value.

As rhetoric finds a source of linguistic value in catachresis, political economy finds a source of economic value in labour. Catachresis, figure and proper name, names the limit of figuration in rhetoric; labour, commodity and not, in turn marks the limit of exchange or commodification in classical political economy. By the latter discipline's reckoning, labour is both a commodity among others (an exchange-value) and the standard of all commodities' value (the universal measure of exchange-value)[46]:

[E]xchange-value : "labour" :: universal measure of exchange-value : "labour".

Itself weighed in the pounds or dollars of a wage, labour in turn weighs the value of all commodities, including pounds and dollars, in the amount of it (labour) they embody.

Commodity and not, labour marks the limit not just of commodification but of political economy as well, for Marx's critique of the discipline begins precisely with the separation of concrete labour as a commodity (labour-power) from abstract labour as the measure of the value of commodities (labour proper) – suddenly, the belaboured analogy

158

finds a fourth term.[47] Yet, even within Marx's critique of political economy, "labour" remains the source of economic value. All use-values (Aristotle's "proper uses") can be excluded from the science except one: even Marx needs the use-value of labour-power to the capitalist (namely, its ability to produce more value than its own exchange-value – Aristotle's "improper use") in order to explain the source of (surplus-)value. In the labour theories of value proper to both political economy and its critique, the source of economic and disciplinary value is figured in abuse – abuse as the simultaneously proper and improper use of a commodity, the commodity at the limit of commodification, labour itself.

Between labour and catachresis, one more analogy constructs itself, because the analogies that organize both are in their turns missing a term. The analogies named catachresis and labour are hardly proper analogies. Indeed they are analogies at all only insofar as analogy itself is a proper name for a relation that otherwise has none, for a productivity that generates value in and for each discipline, as well as between disciplines. In the case of each discipline, the figure that marks its limit and names its source of value also figures its relation to the other discipline. In the case of both disciplines, the relation between rhetoric and political economy – whether articulated in the name of analogy, the proper (*to oikeion*), or economy – seems just to repeat itself, to re-iterate itself, to stutter. In two words, their own words, at every level the conjunction between rhetoric and political economy seems catachretic, even laboured.

rhetoric *and* political economy

> If Being is in effect a process of reappropriation, the 'question of Being' of a new type can never be percussed without being measured against the absolutely coextensive question of the proper. Now this latter question does not permit itself to be separated from the idealizing value of the *very-near* [*du* très-proche], which itself receives its disconcerting powers only from the structure of hearing-oneself-speak. The *proprius* presupposed in all discourses on economy, sexuality, language, semantics, rhetoric, etc., repercusses its absolute limit only in sonorous representation. Such, at least, is the most insistent hypothesis of this book. (Derrida, *Margins* xix)

> Without the displaced reinscription of this chain (Being, presence, -propriation, etc.), one will never rigorously and irreversibly transform the relation between general or fundamental onto-logy and what it masters or subordinates under the name of regional or particular science: for example, *political economy*, psychoanalysis, semiolinguistics, *rhetoric* – in all of which the value of the *proper* [*la valeur de* propriété] plays, more than elsewhere, an irreducible role – but equally spiritualist or materialist metaphysics. The analyses articulated in this volume aim at such a preliminary elaboration. (*Margins* 26 – translation modified, emphasis added)

The analyses elaborated in this essay aim preliminarily at another articulation. To re-iterate, rhetoric and political economy – the two are dead disciplines there would seem little point in disciplining. The conjunction between them should also be dead; indeed, as the focus of exchanges beyond "[t]o coin a phrase, money talks", it was never properly born. An improper birth, a bearing of the dead, an unhomely articulation of disciplines themselves without homes (now buried and on property outside the *oikos*), an *unheimlich*[48] conjunction – language runs necessarily if uneconomically toward the uncanny. Two questions, still, remain to be articulat-

home economics

ed: those of discipline (neither rhetoric nor political economy) and of value (neither linguistic nor economic).

First, it could be asked, what is the status of the conjunction "rhetoric *and* political economy" – a question of the now underlined "and"? What is the nature of the relation between two economic disciplines? What is the economy governing their exchange? To summarize, and to discipline the links between them, it could be said those links are: 1) historical but at no point institutional, 2) linguistic (or philological) but completely unspoken, and 3) structural (or philosophical) but not at all general(izable). Rhetoric and political economy, then, share: 1) coincidentally, a lifespan from Aristotle to Archbishop Whately, 2) in their conception, a home (*oikos*) and a deviation from the same proper (*to oikeion*), and 3) conceptually, a construction of, and according to, the principle of analogy. But what of the link between these links?

Framed in these terms, the three registers of our conjunction correspond as answers to the first question of "White Mythology". Of metaphor in the text of philosophy, Derrida's text inquires, "is it essential? accidental?" or, as the text forgets to ask, proper? (209). Is the conjunction between rhetoric and political economy 1) accidental, 2) proper, or 3) essential to each discipline in its turn? Accidental and coincidental? Proper and particular? Essential and definitive? The question itself may be unanswerable, at least within the regional or determined disciplines of the conjunction, within what is accidental, proper, and essential to rhetoric and to political economy. Of his text's and philosophy's own proper (*to idion*), Derrida writes:

> We know that in the *Topics*, for example, it is at the centre of a theory of the proper, of essence, and of accident. Now if metaphor (or *mimēsis* in general) aims at an effect of cognition, it cannot be treated without being placed in relation to a knowledge that bears on *definitions*: on what the thing of which one speaks is, properly, essentially, or accidentally... The space of language, the field of its divisions, is opened precisely by the difference between essence, the proper, and accident. (247)

The space of a conjunction, the discipline of its determinations, is also opened by the difference between the accidental, the proper, and the essential. It can be opened, and yet it cannot be contained, defined, or essentialized by the conjunction's own terms. Despite a flirtation with the mode of expression proper or peculiar to philosophy[49], our subjects are a non-philosophical proper, and disciplines, *artes*, *tekhnai*, other than philosophy.

The last question to be asked, then, is one of value, specifically what the worth of a conjunction like that between rhetoric and political economy might be. Once more, we return to the matter of dead disciplines, much written in dead languages, more often than not inscribing dead metaphors. And at the side of the grave (perhaps *oikēsis*), disciplinarity – the definition or concept of discipline, perhaps the generality of particular disciplines – appears. Or rather, precisely not disciplinarity but a relation between disciplines, for to speak of disciplinarity as such may be to have decided among the graveside attendants – history, philology, philosophy – already. If the interdisciplinary (as the enterprise of Goux and Shell) attends too little to the question of its own home and its own proper, disciplinarity, or "technicity" by another name, may bear too strongly the mark of one particular home and one particular proper (the proper, say, that would assimilate *to idion*, *to kurion*, and *to prepon* into three meanings of the same word). Philosophy, as it inscribes itself even in "White Mythology", is never on offer as one *tekhnē* or discipline among oth-

forbes morlock

ers ("*De philosophie*,..."); the latest invitation to "Think technics" is the sales pitch only of a philosopher.

Instead, an exemplary apparition, a ghostly conjunction, hovers above a double grave. Rhetoric and political economy may not be able to decide, as they have not even needed to articulate, the status of their own "and". Yet, as regional sciences, they enable us – as readers of rhetoric and political economy, and indeed of metaphor in the text of philosophy – to inquire, under the sign of their "and", into relations between regional sciences, and to articulate an answer not fully assimilable to a central policy of regionalism, let alone a "general or fundamental onto-logy". The relation between rhetoric and political economy may be accidental to each, proper to each, and definitive of each, but what it exemplifies remains beyond each, indeed beyond both. Like the X of a chair, what the conjunction of rhetoric and political economy would figure remains beyond their economies and exchanges, outside proper names, the bounds of propriety and the boundaries of property, past any particular adventure of analogy. Beyond economies but not yet economy proper, after the names translated by "proper" but still before the proper [*le propre*], between analogies and the principle of *analogia*, X marks a spectre. One more discipline (*une discipline de plus*) would name the mark.

From rhetoric and political economy,...

By a certain economy, even the economy of economy, we come home to *oikonomia* – in Greek, the name for household management, home economics[50]; in Latin, a technical division of rhetoric[51]; in French, as domesticated by Derrida, a household word for the law-of-the-proper in philosophy.[52] *Oikonomia* – in the name of its economy, on the economy of its name, we could turn once more a note on "White Mythology", an introduction to the "tekhnical" challenges of reading *Capital: A Critique of Political Economy* rhetorically, and a singular instance of improper discipline.

notes

1 Aristotle, *Topics*, I.4-I.5, tr. W.A. Pickard-Cambridge, in *The Complete Works of Aristotle* – all references to Aristotle will be to this edition.

2 Jacques Derrida, "White Mythology: Metaphor in the Text of Philosophy" [1971] in *Margins of Philosophy* p207-271, esp. n. 13, p216-217; "La mythologie blanche: la métaphore dans le texte philosophique" in *Marges de la philosophie* p247-324.

3 Karl Marx, *Capital: A Critique of Political Economy*, vol. I [1867].

4 *Capital*, chap. I, sec.3, p144.

5 *A Contribution to the Critique of Political Economy* [1859], chap. 2, tr. Salo Ryazanskaya, in Karl Marx and Frederick Engels, *Collected Works* [hereafter *CW*], vol. 29 (1987) p342, and "Outlines of the Critique of Political Economy (Rough Draft of 1857-58) [*Grundrisse*]", tr. Ernst Wangermann, in *CW*, vol. 28 (1986) p159 – the former cited in "White Mythology" p216.

6 Friedrich Nietzsche, "On Truth and Lies in a Nonmoral Sense" [written 1873] p84 – cited in "White Mythology" p217.

7 Adam Smith, *Lectures on Rhetoric and Belles Lettres* [recorded 1762-63] p34.

8 Pierre Fontanier, *Les figures du discours* [1821-27], part III sec. 3, chap. I, p157 – quoted in "White Mythology" p244n. Cf. Dumarsais, *Des tropes ou des différents sens* [1730], chap. I, art. I, p62-63.

9 Originally a small bag or wallet, now a collective term for share certificates, in American usage "scrip" also denotes a paper currency.

10 Goux, *Symbolic Economies: After Marx and Freud* [1973/1978] p4, for example; Shell, *The Economy of*

Literature, and Money, Language and Thought: Literary and Philosophic Economies from the Medieval to the Modern Era.

11 The etymological narrative of "economy" has been related again and again, for example by Jean-Jacques Rousseau at the beginning of his "Discours sur l'économie politique" in the Encyclopédie [1755]:

> ECONOMY or OECONOMY, (Moral and Political.) This word comes from *oikos*, house, and *nomos*, law, and originally signified only the wise and legitimate government of the household for the common good of the whole family. The meaning of the term was subsequently extended to the government of the large family which is the state – "Discourse on Political Economy" p140.

And by J.R. M^{ac}Culloch in the first note to *The Principles of Political Economy* [1825]:

> Economy, from *oikos*, a house, or family, and *nomos*, a law – *the government of a family.* Hence, Political Economy may be said to be to the State what domestic economy is to a family – Introduction, p1n.

12 There are readings, like Paul Ricoeur's, which see Derrida's essay regionalizing philosophy in the name of metaphor (if not literature), but these readings seem blind to the text's own program – for example, its statement that "Neither a *rhetoric* of philosophy nor a *metaphilosophy* appear to be pertinent here – such is the hypothesis" – p230: Ricoeur, "Metaphor and Philosophical Discourse" in *The Rule of Metaphor: Multi-disciplinary Studies of the Creation of Meaning in Language* [1975] p257-313, 354-367. Derrida's response to this particular reading continues in "The *Retrait* of Metaphor" [1978].

13 A rhetoric of political economy and a political economy of rhetoric do not appear to be pertinent here, either. The former might develop on the figure of "commodity" or the function of a seller's verbal ability as a source of exchange-value. The latter might develop on persuasion as an object of commercial exchange and (with the sophists) the first subject of paid instruction; as Roland Barthes notes of the discipline's own source, "[r]hetoric (as a metalanguage) was born in the legal actions concerning property" – "The Old Rhetoric: an aide-mémoire" [1970] p16. Even together, the two projects leave us some way short of a full articulation of the "and" between rhetoric and political economy.

14 See, for example, the discussions of value – economic, linguistic, and aesthetic – in Saussure and Mallarmé, cited in "White Mythology" p217-219. On the question of economic and aesthetic values figured as a fraternal relation, in fact, as the relation between brothers Charles and André Gide, see Goux, *The Coiners of Language* [1984].

15 The historical paradox of the problem of metaphor is that it reaches us via a discipline that died towards the middle of the nineteenth century, when it ceased to be part of the collegial *cursus studiorum*. This link between metaphor and a dead discipline is a source of great perplexity: does not the return of contemporary thinkers to the problem of metaphor commit them to the hopeless project of resurrecting rhetoric from its ashes? – Ricoeur p9.

16 Indeed the figures circulate further, between Barthes and Ricoeur, for example: Barthes notes of rhetoric, "moribund since the Renaissance, it has taken three centuries to die", while Ricoeur's account is entitled, "The Decline of Rhetoric: Tropology" – Barthes p15 and Ricoeur p44.

17 Properly, "the economy of the city" – *Economics*, II.1, tr. E.S. Forster, 1346a6. The *Economics* is not Aristotle's own.

18 *Gorgias*, 449a4-5. See also Thomas Cole, *The Origins of Rhetoric in Ancient Greece* p2 and *passim*.

19 Étienne Bonnot de Condillac, *De l'art d'écrire* in *Cours d'études pour l'instruction du prince de Parme* [1775], and *Le commerce et le gouvernement considérés relativement l'un à l'autre* [1776]; Adam Smith, *Lectures on Rhetoric and Belles Lettres*, and *An Inquiry into the Nature and Causes of the Wealth of Nations*

forbes morlock

[1776]; Richard Whately, *Elements of Rhetoric* [1828], and *Introductory Lectures on Political Economy* [1831]; and Thomas de Quincey, "Elements of Rhetoric" [1828], and *The Logic of Political Economy* [1844].

20 Anne Robert Jacques Turgot, "Tableau philosophique des progrès successifs de l'esprit humain" [1750], "Valeurs et monnaies" [1769], and *Réflexions sur la formation et la distribution des richesses* [1766]; Jean-Jacques Rousseau, *Essai sur l'origine des langues* [completed 1761], and *Discours sur l'origine et les fondemens de l'inégalité parmi les hommes* [1755]. Cf. Condillac, *Essai sur l'origine des connaissances humaines* [1746]; and Smith, "Considerations Concerning the First Formation of Languages, etc." [1761].

21 It may be worth noting that, among all the meanings or senses of a word to be examined, the word's "original sense" (in Greek *to etumon* – the very word or sense at the origin of our "etymology") escapes articulation here.

22 Marx, *The German Ideology* [written 1845-46], vol. I, part III, tr. Clemens Dutt, in *CW*, vol. 5 (1976) p228-231 – quoted in part in "White Mythology" p216-217n.

23 Aristotle distinguishes between essential definition and characteristic property:

> Now every proposition and every problem indicates either a property or a genus or an accident [ē *idion* ē *genos* ē *sumbebēkos*] ... Since, however, of what is proper [*tou idiou*] to anything part signifies its essence, while part does not, let us divide the proper [*to idion*] into both the aforesaid parts, and call that part which indicates the essence a definition [*horos*], while of the remainder let us adopt the terminology which is generally current about these things and speak of it as a property [*idion*] – *Topics*, I.4, 101b17-23 – translation modified; see also I.5, 101b37-102b26 – the latter cited in "White Mythology" p249-250.

24 The footnote is Marx's – *A Contribution to the Critique of Political Economy*, chap. 1, p269 – translation modified; *Karl Marx Friedrich Engels Gesamtausgabe* [hereafter *MEGA*], ser. II, vol. 2 (1980) p107 – original spellings retained throughout. Cf. *Capital: A Critique of Political Economy*, chap. 1, p125-126.

In the footnote, Marx goes on to quote in Greek the same passage from Aristotle's *Politics* that this essay quotes below in English. The passage also appears in a German translation in *Capital*, chap. 2, p179n.

25 *Wealth of Nations*, Book I, chap. 4, p44. To trace the passage of use-value and exchange-value from Marx to Smith, see, for example, John Stuart Mill, *Principles of Political Economy* [1848], Book III, chap. I, p436-437; de Quincey, *The Logic of Political Economy* p187; J.R. Ma̧cCulloch, *The Principles of Political Economy*, Introduction, p3-4; and David Ricardo, *On the Principles of Political Economy and Taxation* [1817], chap. 1, sec. 1, p11.

26 *Politics*, I.9, tr. Benjamin Jowett, 1257a5-14 – emphasis added.

Aware of the passage's heirs, Jowett marks it "Value in use and value in exchange" – *The Politics of Aristotle*, tr. Jowett (1885) marginal analysis.

As mentioned above, Marx quotes all but the first sentence of this passage in Greek on the opening page of *A Contribution*, chap. 1, p269n; and in German at the beginning of chap. 2 of *Capital*, p179n. In the second instance, Marx translates proper (*oikeia*) inconsistently as *eigen* and *natürlich* (as in "Der eine ist dem Ding als solchem eigen, der andere nicht", and "Aber nicht in ihrer natürlichen Gebrauchsweise"), while glossing *khrēsis* [use] in one case as *Gebrauchswerth* [use-value] – *Das Kapital*, *MEGA*, ser. II, vol. 5 (1983) p52n – emphasis added.

On the significance of the shoemaker and the exemplary shoe in political thought from Plato's *Republic* on, see Jacques Rancière, *Le philosophe et ses pauvres*.

27 Marx takes up Aristotle's distinction between *oikonomia* and *khrēmatistikē* in *A Contribution*, chap. 2, p370n (cf. p488) and in *Capital*, chap. 4, p253-254n. Derrida, in turn, takes up the distinction in *Given*

home economics

Time [1991] p158. A distinction between Marx's and Derrida's elaborations of Aristotle's distinction is itself elaborated in Egide Berns, "Monnaie et non-violence".

28 Thus, "[u]se-value in this indifference to the determined economic form, i.e. use-value as such, lies outside the sphere of investigation of political economy" – Marx, *A Contribution*, chap. 1, p270. Cf. MacCulloch's definition of the discipline:

> Political Economy might, indeed, be called the *science of values*; for, nothing destitute of exchangeable value, or which will not be received as an equivalent for something else which it has taken some labour to produce or obtain, can ever properly be brought within the scope of its inquiries – p3.

29 Rhetoricians and readers, including Ricoeur, have objected to a tropological characterization of rhetoric. Certainly the analysis of metaphor, and figures more generally, is not central to, essential to, or definitive of, all rhetorics. On the other hand, there are no rhetorics without such analyses; they are, in Aristotle's term, at least proper to the discipline.

30 *The Art of Speaking* [1675; translation 1676], part II, chap. 1, sec. 1, p214. To trace the path of the proper from Fontanier to Lamy at least in French, see, for example, Dumarsais, chap. 1, art. 6, p73-74.

31 *Rhetoric*, III.2, tr. W. Rhys Roberts, 1404b31-35 – emphasis added – quoted in part in "White Mythology" p247.

32 "Proper name" is used here rhetorically rather than grammatically, as the opposite of "metaphor" and not of "common noun" (the synonym of "proper noun"). In English rhetorics there seems to be no single term, name or common noun for the opposite of metaphor, in the way that "proper" opposes "metaphorical" and "literal" "figurative". "Proper meaning", "sense", "use", "expression", "term" and "name" all appear – often on the same page – without the difference in their own proper meanings, senses or uses ever being accounted for. In effect, "proper name" serves here as a marker – a figure for a name, term, expression, use, sense and meaning which in English has no proper name of its own.

33 Economy and the proper may be proper to Derrida's writing from *Writing and Difference*, but their articulation in "the law-of-the-proper, the *economy* of the source", for example, appears only after "White Mythology" – *Margins* p285n. In *Signéponge/Signsponge* [1976-77]:

> It is easier still to identify in its *economic* form, that is, under household law or the law of property [*sous la forme* économique, *entendez sous la loi de la maison ou du propre*], in a manufactured, manipulable, and domesticated form – p82-83.

To speak economically of economy, "The *Retrait* of Metaphor" invokes:

> b. Economy in order to articulate this possibility about the law-of-the-house and the law of the proper, *oiko-nomia* – p17.

Made possible by the work of "White Mythology", *oikonomia* often returns in Derrida's subsequent writing to articulate economically an economy and the proper; in each case, though, the proper of "the law-of-the-proper", the proper of the *oikos*, *to oikeion*, remains unread. Even *Politiques de l'amitié*, with its extended discussion of *oikeiotēs* (relationship, domesticity, marriage, intimacy, friendship), can only cite without reading the proper of *to oikeion* – p178n.

A full discussion of the proper and "properness" in the text of "White Mythology" would need also to account for the extravagant, even uneconomic, array of proper nouns within it.

34 To close this section on a philological note, we could again remark that the root of *oikeion* – *oikos*, the house or household – is also the root of *oikonomia*, household management or economy. Here, in the *oikos*, belong questions of "home", as well as of "economies", including the "economy of economies". Here, too, the metaphors of metaphor ("a borrowed dwelling [*une demeure empruntée*]", for example) come home – Dumarsais, chap. 2, sec.

164

X, p136 – quoted in "White Mythology" p253 and "The *Retrait* of Metaphor" p17.

Neither, among such homecomings, should the exemplary presence of *hē oikia*, the house, be ignored. Houses are constructed as objects of exchange in political economy from Plato to Marx, just as rhetoric at least from Quintilian builds its discourses on foundations and floorplans. See, in the first case, Plato, *Republic*, book II, 369dff., the Aristotelian *Magna Moralia*, I.33, 1194a6ff., and Aristotle, *Nicomachean Ethics*, V.5, 1133a5ff. – the last cited in *Capital*, chap. 1, sec. 3, p151; in the second case, Quintilian, *Institutio Oratoria*, XI.ii.17-21, and Frances A. Yates, *The Art of Memory* [1966], chap. 1, p18-19 and *passim*. For exemplary rhetorical houses, see Aristotle, *Rhetoric*, II.18, 1392a15, Cicero, *De Oratore*, III.xlii.168, and George Campbell, *The Philosophy of Rhetoric* [1776], Book III chap. 1, p307n.

35 Disciplines that depart from the *oikos* and *oikeion* – the proper as the familiar, the familial, the domestic, and the private – towards metaphor and improper use, rhetoric and political economy mark in their meeting in the public sphere (in the agora and the law courts) the gendering of public space, discourse, and exchange as male in Western thought from Aristotle on.

36 Noted by Cicero and Hugh Blair [1783], and elaborated by Derrida – "White Mythology" p231n.

37 Cleanth Brooks and Robert Penn Warren, *Modern Rhetoric* [1949], chap. 12, p435n.

38 *Poetics*, 21, tr. I. Bywater, 1457b6-9 – cited in *Rhetoric* III.2, 1405a3-6, and quoted in "White Mythology" p231.

39 Beyond the essence of metaphor, analogy (*analogia*) within rhetoric extends to language's correspondence (*analogon*) to its subject:

> Your language will be *appropriate* if it expresses emotion and character, and if it corresponds to its subject [*To de prepon exei hē lexis, ean ē pathētikē te kai ēthikē kai tois hupokeimenois pragmasin analogon*]. 'Correspondence to subject' [*To d'analogon*]

means that we must neither speak casually about weighty matters, nor solemnly about trivial ones; nor must we add ornamental epithets to commonplace nouns – *Rhetoric*, III.7, 1408a10-14 – cited in "White Mythology" p247n.

40 Of course, the claims staked by the principle of *analogia*, and by analogical reasoning, extend beyond the discipline of political economy as well. Cf., for example, the analogical chain of being (*analogia entis*) anchored in Aristotle's *Metaphysics*: Ricoeur, chap. 8, p259-280. On analogy in the text of "White Mythology", see Rodolphe Gasché, *The Tain of the Mirror* esp. p296-307. On analogy and knowledge beyond Aristotle, see Derrida, *The Archaeology of the Frivolous* [1973], originally published as a preface to Condillac's *Essai sur l'origine des connaissances humaines*.

41 *Nicomachean Ethics*, V.5, tr. W.D. Ross, rev. J.O. Urmson, 1133a5-12.

42 For all the criticism of the capitalist mode of production it may inscribe, the analysis of *Capital* still assumes that surplus-value is not the product of theft or persuasion.

43 For a different, but perhaps analogous, elaboration of the relation between Aristotle and Marx in terms of analogy, see Luce Irigaray, "Women on the Market" [1976]:

> Will it be objected that this interpretation is analogical by nature? I accept the question, on condition that it be addressed also, and in the first place, to Marx's analysis of commodities. Did not Aristotle, 'a great thinker' according to Marx, determine the relation of form to matter by analogy with the relation between masculine and feminine? Returning to the question of the difference between the sexes would amount instead, then, to going back through analogism – p174n.

As analogy or proportion organizes political relations, that is, relations in the *polis*, so it organizes relations between the domestic and the political –

on the basis of the analogy between master and household [*oikos*], and monarch and state [*polis*, itself "made up of households [*ex oikiōn*]" – *Politics*, I.3, 1253b2-3]:

> [M]aster : household :: monarch : state
> – *Politics*, I.7, 1255b19-20.

After the departures from *to oikeion* narrated above in the name of the proper, it may not be a coincidence that the principle of analogy or proportion has no place in the household [*oikos*] itself.

44 Andrzej Warminski, in an exemplary reading, marks such arms as "metaphors that are also not metaphors but markers, figural substitutions that are also proper names, figures that are not figures (for anything but the impossibility of figure)" – *Readings in Interpretation* pliii.

On the analogous "sowing" of the sun's rays, see "White Mythology" p230-245.

45 Cicero, *Orator*, xxvii.94.

46 The value of any commodity, therefore, to the person who possesses it, and who means not to use or consume it himself [*sic*], but to exchange it for other commodities, is equal to the quantity of labour which it enables him to purchase or command. Labour, therefore, is the real measure of the exchangeable value of all commodities – *Wealth of Nations*, chap. 5, p47.

47 Marx notes of *Capital*:

> The best points in my book are: 1. (this is fundamental to *all* understanding of the FACTS) the *two-fold character of labour* according to whether it is expressed in use-value or exchange-value, which is brought out in the very *First* Chapter – letter to Engels, 24 August 1867, tr. John Peet, in *CW*, vol. 42 (1987) p407.

and:

> Economists, without exception, have missed the simple fact that, if the commodity has the double character of use-value and exchange-value, then the labour represented in the commodity must also have a double character; thus, the bare analysis of labour *sans phrase*, as in Smith, Ricardo, etc., is bound to come up against the inexplicable everywhere. This is, in fact, the whole secret of the critical conception – letter to Engels, 8 January 1868, tr. Christopher Upward, in *CW*, vol. 42 p514.

48 "Unhomely" in one translation, "uncanny" in another: on the matter of the word and the question of its conceptualization, see Sigmund Freud, "Das Unheimliche" [1919].

49 Derrida's own philosophical writing certainly flirts with the mode of expression peculiar to Marx the political economist, as the latter's *Capital: A Critique of Political Economy* earlier flirted with the mode of expression peculiar to Hegelian philosophy: "I therefore openly avowed myself the pupil of that mighty thinker, and even, here and there in the chapter on the theory of value, coquetted with the mode of expression peculiar to him" – *Capital*, "Afterword", p102-103. On Derrida's coquetterie with the language of use-value, exchange-value, surplus-value, capital, and capitalization, see Gayatri Chakravorty Spivak, "Limits and Openings of Marx in Derrida" [1981].

50 As in Xenophon's *Oeconomicus* [*Oikonomikos*] (eg., I.1 and I.2), and Aristotle's *Politics* (eg., I.3, 1253b2).

51 As in Quintilian:

> Hermagoras places *judgment, division, order* and everything relating to *expression* under the heading of *economy*, a Greek word meaning the management of domestic affairs which is applied metaphorically to oratory and has no Latin equivalent [*oeconomiae, quae Graece appellata ex cura rerum domesticarum et hic per abusionem posita nomine Latino caret*] – *Institutio oratoria*, III.iii.9 – emphasis added in Latin; cf. I.viii.9 and 17.

Oikonomia also figures as a synonym for *taxis* or *dispositio* – Nietzsche, "Description of Ancient Rhetoric (1872-73)" p151; cf. p19.

52 See note 33 above.

bibliography

Aristotle, *The Complete Works of Aristotle: The Revised Oxford Translation*, 2 vols, ed. J. Barnes (Princeton: Princeton University Press, 1984).

Aristotle, *Ars Rhetorica*, ed. W.D. Ross (Oxford: Clarendon Press, 1959).

Aristotle, *De Arte Poetica Liber*, ed. R. Kassel (Oxford: Clarendon Press, 1965).

Aristotle, *Ethica Nicomachea*, ed. I. Bywater (Oxford: Clarendon Press, 1894).

Aristotle, *The Oeconomica* in *Metaphysics (Books X-XIV), Oeconomica, and Magna Moralia* (Cambridge MA: Harvard University Press (Loeb Classical Library), 1935).

Aristotle, *Politica*, ed. W.D. Ross (Oxford: Clarendon Press, 1957).

Aristotle, *The Politics of Aristotle*, tr. B. Jowett, 2 vols (Oxford: Clarendon Press, 1885).

Aristotle, *Topica* in *Topica et Sophistici Elenchi*, ed. W.D. Ross (Oxford: Clarendon Press, 1958).

Barthes, R., "The Old Rhetoric: an aide-mémoire" in *The Semiotic Challenge*, tr. R. Howard (New York: Hill and Wang, 1988) p11-93.

Berns, E., "Monnaie et non-violence" in *Le passage des frontières. Autour du travail de Jacques Derrida*, ed. M.-L. Mallet (Paris: Galilée, 1994) p211-213.

Blair, H., *Lectures on Rhetoric and Belles Lettres*, 2 vols, ed. H.F. Harding (Carbondale: Southern Illinois University Press, 1965).

Brooks, C. and R.P. Warren, *Modern Rhetoric*, 3rd ed. (New York: Harcourt, Brace and World, 1970).

Campbell, G., *The Philosophy of Rhetoric*, ed. L. Bitzer

forbes morlock

(Carbondale: Southern Illinois University Press, 1963).

Cicero, *De Oratore*, 2 vols, trs E.W. Sutton and H. Rackham (Cambridge MA: Harvard University Press (Loeb Classical Library), 1942).

Cicero, *Orator*, tr. H.M. Hubbell, in *Brutus and Orator* (Cambridge MA: Harvard University Press (Loeb Classical Library), 1939).

Cole, T., *The Origins of Rhetoric in Ancient Greece* (Baltimore: Johns Hopkins University Press, 1991).

de Quincey, T., *The Logic of Political Economy* in *The Collected Writings of Thomas de Quincey*, ed. D. Masson, vol. 9 (Edinburgh, 1890).

Derrida, J., *The Archaeology of the Frivolous: Reading Condillac*, tr. J.P. Leavey, Jr (Pittsburgh: Duquesne University Press, 1980).

Derrida, J., *Given Time: I. Counterfeit Money*, tr. P. Kamuf (Chicago: University of Chicago Press, 1992).

Derrida, J., *Marges de la philosophie* (Paris: Minuit, 1972).

Derrida, J., *Margins of Philosophy*, tr. A. Bass (Chicago: University of Chicago Press, 1982).

Derrida, J., *Politiques de l'amitié* (Paris: Galilée, 1994).

Derrida, J., "The *Retrait* of Metaphor", tr. F. Gardner et al., *Enclitic*, vol. 2, no. 2 (fall 1978) p4-33.

Derrida, J., *Signéponge/Signsponge*, tr. R. Rand (New York: Columbia University Press, 1984).

Dumarsais, C.C., *Des tropes ou des différents sens* (Paris: Flammarion, 1988).

Fontanier, P., *Les figures du discours* (Paris: Flammarion, 1977).

Freud, S., "The 'Uncanny' [Das Unheimliche]", trs J. and A. Strachey, in *The Standard Edition of the Complete Psychological Works of Sigmund Freud*, ed. J. Strachey, vol. 17 (London: Hogarth Press and the Institute of Psycho-Analysis, 1955) p217-256.

Gasché, R., *The Tain of the Mirror: Derrida and the*

home economics

Philosophy of Reflection (Cambridge MA: Harvard University Press, 1986).

Goux, J.-J., *The Coiners of Language*, tr. J.C. Gage (Norman: University of Oklahoma Press, 1994).

Goux, J.-J., *Symbolic Economies: After Marx and Freud*, tr. J.C. Gage (Ithaca: Cornell University Press, 1990).

Irigaray, L., "Women on the Market" in *This Sex Which Is Not One*, tr. C. Porter with C. Burke (Ithaca: Cornell University Press, 1985) p170-191.

Lamy, B., *The Art of Speaking* in *The Rhetorics of Thomas Hobbes and Bernard Lamy*, ed. J.T. Harwood (Carbondale: Southern Illinois University Press, 1986).

MacCulloch, J.R., *The Principles of Political Economy*, 4th ed. (Edinburgh and London, 1849).

Marx, K., *Capital: A Critique of Political Economy*, vol. 1, tr. B. Fowkes (New York: Vintage, 1977).

Marx, K. and F. Engels, *Collected Works* (London: Lawrence and Wishart, 1975-).

Marx, K. and F. Engels, *Karl Marx Friedrich Engels Gesamtausgabe* (Berlin: Dietz Verlag, 1975-).

Mill, J.S., *Principles of Political Economy* (Fairfield NJ: Augustus M. Kelley, 1987).

Nietzsche, F., "Description of Ancient Rhetoric (1872-73)" in *Friedrich Nietzsche on Rhetoric and Language*, eds and trs S.L. Gilman, C. Blair, and D.J. Parent (New York: Oxford University Press, 1989) p2-206.

Nietzsche, F., "On Truth and Lies in a Nonmoral Sense" in *Philosophy and Truth: Selections from Nietzsche's Notebooks of the Early 1870's*, ed. and tr. D. Breazeale (New Jersey: Humanities Press, 1979) p77-97.

Plato, *The Collected Dialogues of Plato*, eds E. Hamilton and H. Cairns (Princeton: Princeton University Press, 1961).

Plato, *Gorgias* in *Opera*, vol. 3, ed. J. Burnet (Oxford: Clarendon Press, 1903).

Quintilian, *Institutio Oratoria*, 4 vols, tr. H.E. Butler (Cambridge MA: Harvard University Press (Loeb Classical Library), 1920-22).

Rancière, J., *Le philosophe et ses pauvres* (Paris: Fayard, 1983).

Ricardo, D., *On the Principles of Political Economy and Taxation* (Cambridge: Cambridge University Press, 1951).

Ricoeur, P., *The Rule of Metaphor: Multi-disciplinary Studies of the Creation of Meaning in Language*, tr. R. Czerny et al. (Toronto: University of Toronto Press, 1977).

Rousseau, J.-J., "Discourse on Political Economy" in *The Collected Writings of Rousseau*, vol. 3, eds R.D. Masters and C. Kelly, trs J.R. Bush, R.D. Masters, C. Kelly and T. Marshall (Hanover: University Press of New England, 1992) p140-170, 200-205.

Shell, M., *The Economy of Literature* (Baltimore: Johns Hopkins University Press, 1978).

Shell, M., *Money, Language, and Thought: Literary and Philosophic Economies from the Medieval to the Modern Era* (Berkeley: University of California Press, 1982).

Smith, A., *An Inquiry into the Nature and the Causes of the Wealth of Nations* (Oxford: Clarendon Press, 1976).

Smith, A., *Lectures on Rhetoric and Belles Lettres* (Oxford: Clarendon Press, 1983).

Spivak, G.C., "Limits and Openings of Marx in Derrida" in *Outside in the Teaching Machine* (New York: Routledge, 1993) p97-119, 303-305.

Warminski, A., *Readings in Interpretation: Hölderlin, Hegel, Heidegger* (Minneapolis: University of Minnesota Press, 1987).

Xenophon, *Oeconomicus: A Social and Historical Commentary*, tr. S.B. Pomeroy (Oxford: Clarendon Press, 1994).

Yates, F.A., *The Art of Memory* (London: Pimlico, 1992).

She liked to speak French and to play the piano, but what do these things mean?
Jeanette Winterson[1]

fran sendbuehler

THE ART OF DOING NOTHING

What is it that causes us to see such accomplishments as piano playing and speaking French – the stock in trade, if you will, of the "socially acceptable" woman – as meaningless? Perhaps this sense of meaninglessness derives from our conventional perception of these "talents" as the direct result of "doing nothing", that sort of "nothing" that occurs when a woman of a particular social class occupies her position in society. But perhaps Winterson's question can take on another, rather unconventional, force as we read Jane Austen's *Mansfield Park* (1813). Perhaps it is actually a question of what it is that these things do mean.

The "nothingness" of the socially accomplished woman, the woman of the private sphere of the eighteenth and early nineteenth centuries, is central to the writings of Jane Austen. The sense of female idleness arises in her novels from the fact that the women *do* things, and yet seem to accomplish little that might be perceived as substantive from the point of view of how men *do* things. Idleness is thus what might make the women of the domestic, or the private, sphere noticeable. The female accomplishments of upper-class society have achieved a sense of meaninglessness for us: of what value is it to play the piano unless one is a pianist? of what value is it to speak French unless the language is used for effective communication? What then is it that causes us to *notice* the idleness, the nothingness, of a woman of society in Austen's *Mansfield Park*? Why is it that these things *do* mean? And what do they mean?

Perhaps it is the play of propriety and property: we see in *Mansfield Park* the cultural system that considers the private woman as property; she is also supposed to be a model of propriety. If not, she becomes something other, that is, a public woman. In order for the upper-class woman to be valued as a model of propriety she must do nothing that might jeopardize her standing. She must, that is, do nothing. Austen's female characters occupy themselves with various tasks and chores, yet it is worthwhile noticing that the Bertram daughters and Mary Crawford are noticeably idle, filling their days with tours in the country and evenings with family in the parlour. These women long to do something, yet in that longing risk becoming public women.

The structure of understanding that situates the upper-class woman's activities as "nothing" rests upon the notion that privilege allows those with an income to be bastions of society precisely by doing nothing. Austen presents the reader with "doing nothing" as one of the most essential elements of *Mansfield Park*. Idleness represents the

the art of doing nothing

privilege and propriety of the upper classes, their "good example", that underpins taste and good breeding in society. "Doing something", in reference to the upper classes, represents impropriety, moral emptiness, and insensibility; for women this impropriety extends into activities that decrease the worth of a woman in society. A public woman becomes a courtesan, a barmaid, a laundress, a whore. Activity in the upper classes is allowable only when there is some sort of financial or aesthetic improvement in progress, and then these activities may only be carried out by men, unless that improvement relates strictly to the household and the education of very young children. So, examples of this type of activity are those that are somehow occupational without having a negative effect on one's propriety as a member of the landed classes.[2]

What I want to discuss within the structure of the opposition – of doing nothing as opposed to doing something, and the play of property and propriety that goes with this – is the social background of the stratification that makes women become "other". I will not attempt an exhaustive examination of *Mansfield Park*; rather I will examine why it is that doing nothing becomes an art: something that is learned as a talent and is seen as respectable; and how this relates to an exploration of the opposition between the public and private spheres. What I would like to show is that there is more to *Mansfield Park* than the busyness, the eventfulness of this novel – but how that activity is limited to occupations that are not really more than a use of time. This opposition is crucial to the structure of the novel: Fanny is saved from the potential difficulties of growing up in Portsmouth (as a woman who risks becoming a part of the public sphere in order to survive) by being taken into the household at Mansfield Park; the reputations of the Bertram sisters are jeopardized by their collective or repeated refusals to be quiet, acceptable daughters. Indeed, both become, in their quite deliberate loss of propriety, public women and are, therefore, no longer acceptable as mistresses of a place such as Mansfield Park. In addition to having significance within the structure of the novel, the opposition between the public and private spheres is an element that draws the reader's attention to the causal relationship between propriety and property. Women become representative of propriety through their status as property; a woman is a good example as long as she is seen to do nothing. Within the structure that sees the play of property and propriety, the reader notices how this otherness of women is perceived as nothing, and how Jane Austen turns this into an art of doing nothing. Austen's women do nothing in order to maintain propriety; they are "good" examples of "breeding" provided that they adhere to certain strict rules. A woman, therefore, does not make a good piece of property if she cannot display a certain sense of propriety. In *Mansfield Park*, Austen draws out this play of property and propriety in the habits of the day, and does so in terms that parody and play with the notions of worth and marriageableness.

Jürgen Habermas[3] discusses the inception of the demarcation between the public and private spheres as parallel with the "invention" of the bourgeoisie from its very earliest beginnings to the eighteenth century and details this development in relation to the genesis of finance and trade capitalism. Terry Eagleton, in *The Function of Criticism*, discusses these developments and the social demarcation of the bourgeoisie in relation to literary culture and the development of the English public sphere, in particular, around that culture. Eagleton uses the opposition of the public to the private sphere within his arguments without saying much about the private sphere. Thus he neglects aspects of Habermas's work that discuss the importance of those activities of the rational-critical public which are nonetheless located within private spaces. Indeed, with Habermas it is the public which becomes transparent — for him, the public sphere represents society, and the private sphere represents culture: he sees the growth of the avant-garde as based on the critique which originates within the private sphere. Yet, the private sphere appears as nothing in Eagleton's analysis of British social conventions:

> The public sphere acknowledges no given rational identity *beyond its own bounds*, for what counts as rationality is precisely the capacity to articulate within its own constraints; the rational are those capable of a certain mode of discourse, but this cannot be judged other than in the act of deploying it. (Eagleton 15, emphasis mine)

It seems that, for Eagleton, the private sphere is of little importance in the formation of culture in British society. What "is at stake in the public sphere, according to its own ideological self-image, is not power, but reason. Truth, not authority, is its ground, and rationality, not domination, its daily currency" (17). I would argue that authority and domination are *precisely* the currency of the public sphere: the public sphere is, in an extrapolation of Eagleton's assessment, nothing but a thin veneer of truth and rationality in order not to appear to be the *diktum* and *ukases* of authoritarian politics. The nothing that the private sphere represents, therefore, becomes something worthy of notice, although, according to Eagleton, the private sphere holds little or no importance in the formation of culture. He reminds us that "the interests of the propertied classes are in a real sense all that politically exists; the boundaries of the public sphere are not boundaries at all, for beyond them, as beyond the curvature of cosmic space, there is nothing" (35). There is nothing, much as there is nothing for the woman of the time, locked in the private sphere. But perhaps we move too fast, and miss Austen's talent for black comedy, if we simply accept Eagleton's account of the private sphere as blank. Austen's women are totally limited by their societal position, by their political position, so that, indeed, outside the public sphere, there is nothing and they are nothing:

> To the education of her daughters, Lady Bertram paid not the smallest attention. She had not time for such cares. She was a woman who spent her days in sitting nicely dressed on the sofa, doing some long piece of needlework, of little use and no beauty, thinking more of her pug than her children, but very indulgent to the latter, when it did not put herself to inconvenience, guided in everything important by Sir Thomas, and in smaller concerns by her sister. Had she possessed greater leisure for the service of her girls, she would probably have supposed it unnecessary, for they were under the care of a governess, with proper masters, and could want nothing more. (Austen 18)

These women can do nothing *other than* do nothing: that is, nothing more beyond occupying their time in proper ways for young ladies and women of the manor, who, if they marry well, will be fortunate enough to have a man to do their thinking for them.

The public sphere in the eighteenth and nineteenth centuries included a wide range of social institutions: business circles, coffee houses, and the disreputable classes of women. It was claimed to be a "place of free and equal exchange of reasonable dis-

the art of doing nothing

course"[4], and a place wherein participants "direct themselves into a body whose deliberations assume the form of a powerful political force" (Eagleton 9). Within an historical context, the development of this formal sphere of activity began in the "thirteenth century with the emergence of early finance and trade capitalism" (Habermas 14) and thence evolved into the familiar structure of the seventeenth and eighteenth centuries. This development, being synchronous with the development of a modern economy and the development of a wide-ranging publishing culture: books, pamphlets, and newspapers, led to the development of what Eagleton calls a "sphere of cultural discourse" which was closely related to the sphere of social power. This language of what is spoken or written developed a sort of reciprocity with a class-bound consciousness of control. What is controlled and by whom is the basis of this element of power; patriarchy in general, and, specifically, the patriarchal representatives of the upper classes become the element that set the tone of what is expected in all spheres. Eagleton, in his concentration on the public sphere, misses the issue of gender. This division, then, between the public and private spheres, becomes strictly gendered. In the public sphere of the eighteenth and nineteenth centuries, the control of information and business interests was conducted strictly by men. Other functions such as gaming, drinking, and socializing at men's clubs, were conducted without the company of the women who normally occupied the private sphere, but were often conducted in the company of "public" women – women who, for one currency or another, were bought and sold. The topic of public women is particularly relevant in the discussion of *Mansfield Park* in order to situate the public woman and her place within society, and to understand the relevance of what is, precisely, a public woman. The situation of this distinction applies particularly to *Mansfield Park* in the performance of the theatricals. The Bertram daughters not only risk becoming public women in their simple performance of a play, but they approach becoming equivalent to whores in the eyes of their father as their sin is much greater than merely intending to perform a risqué play; they also threaten the name of their father's house. Their value as women of good name, of valuable political or financial ties is diminished by their becoming public women. The idea of "how things appear" is, therefore, something that must be taken into account in order to fully appreciate what it is that so damages the proprietous demeanor of the Bertram daughters.

The importance of "how things appear" is emphasized by the activities surrounding the theatricals and by the reaction of Sir Thomas on his return to *Mansfield Park*: these cause much discontent and endanger the once-tranquil family harmony. All are affected by the play in one way or another: Crawford flirts with Maria, annoying Rushworth and Julia. Edmund is insulted by the moral tone of the play in general, and would rather not participate, however, he risks the wrath of the whole group by not joining in. Mary Crawford, then, has an opportunity to flirt with Edmund, and Edmund is insulted again, this time by the moral tone of their scenes together in particular, which scenes, in turn, offend Fanny. Tom and Yates seem like instigators of the whole thing: their motivation appears to be to have their way as Yates's fun was previously spoiled elsewhere. The feeling that Edmund, Fanny and Rushworth have, that the play was generally a bad idea, is embodied in the return of Sir Thomas, the one person in a position to demonstrate the social necessity of maintaining the propriety of the women of his household. His reaction underscores the importance, for him, of maintaining a private household: his daughters must not become public women, in any sense of the word: his reputation is endangered by their so doing, as is their value as marketable wives in the assistance of obtaining valuable political or monetary connections.

The presentation of women in this novel depends entirely on the social structuration of sexual difference. (Although I would prefer to argue that it is men and the public sphere that constitute the evident differences about which we write, current discourse reminds me that it is woman that is different or other.) What we see portrayed in Austen, then, is a successful public imposition of boundaries of difference as fixed gender roles rather than as the matter of tragedy; these boundaries are at their highest juncture at the point at which Austen writes, just moments before the Industrial Revolution.

Attitudes towards upper-class marriages change markedly following the Industrial Revolution. What does not change until well into the mid-twentieth century is the delineation of the public and private spheres and the places that women occupy within those spheres; it is arguable, in fact, that there have not been many changes at all. For example, it is certain that a present-day discussion of the issues involved in pornography would touch on many of the same questions of the value of woman as chattel and woman as the subject of the male gaze. There is not much difference in the many permutations of the issues that discuss the buying and selling of women: the issue of marriageableness of women in Austen's work becomes a part of the discussion of value and worth.

If doing nothing can be seen as a cultivated practice, and is thus an "art of doing

fran sendbuehler

nothing", we see in *Mansfield Park* that women and men are asymmetrically related to their social and economic value: thus doing nothing is, in essence, a material practice. Women are chattels, yet also represent a foundation of value in their status as mistresses of estates and mothers of those who help to perpetuate the patriarchy. Upper-class women's nothingness is related to their ability to do nothing (and how well they do nothing), hence their value as a commodity that does nothing. This position and repositioning is curious in its diametric opposition: doing nothing becomes a substance of value. However, if this same structure were to be applied to men, within Austen, a man who does nothing is certain to have no value at all. For example, Fanny's father in Portsmouth does little that may be considered of use, hence, he is useless. In terms of this comparison, we can see just how skewed is the concept of the private woman and what it is that delineates her worth. It is, of course, the gendering of the idea that skews this concept: here we see the reinforcement of the idea that a woman who "does" in the public gaze cannot be of value as a good wife, and so cannot be an example of propriety. A man who "does nothing" in the public gaze is valued as worthless, and also cannot be an example of propriety.

The date of the publication of *Mansfield Park* situates the novel within the period of this controlling and forming division of life into the public and private spheres. Austen, however, maintains a certain distance from all that touches on the public sphere. By no means is she unaware either of the distance she maintains, or of the public sphere; it is obvious that the public sphere is not her domain, yet her awareness of this element is that which controls and guides the formation of this novel. That Austen should have restricted herself quite deliberately to work-

the art of doing nothing

ing on those elements that constitute the private sphere tells us that it is obvious that it is not "proper" for her to work outside this realm: her own physical sphere was limited. Austen remains trapped by her class and yet her writing seems to demonstrate clearly that she perceives the limitations of vapidity, in the sense that she clearly notices that "doing nothing" actually adds nothing to society. Others, such as Emerson, clearly believed Austen's own art to be itself vapid:

> I am at a loss to understand why people hold Miss Austen's novels at so high a rate, which seems to me vulgar in tone, sterile in artistic invention, imprisoned in the wretched conventions of English society, without genius, wit, or knowledge of the world. Never was life so pinched and narrow. (Emerson 146)

Emerson continues, commenting upon the importance of marriageableness, which is indeed a key element of Austen's novels, and a significant indication of the importance of the public and private spheres in her work. Austen poses valid questions about society in her novels; that she focuses on what Emerson calls the "wretched conventions of English society"[5] is a key indication of the importance that propriety plays as a focus for her wit. Within the body of her work, it is easily supposed that she expresses a degree of discomfort with those very same "wretched conventions" of which Emerson complains. It was Austen who took such pains to remind the reader of this and the "pinched and narrow" constraints that are their result. The first pages of *Mansfield Park* may very well be those which put off Mr Emerson so thoroughly: they detail the marriageableness and financial circumstances (arguably the same thing) of the previous generation, thereby setting the tone for the novel and preparing the reader for the "present-day" scenario: who married so-and-so, and for how much (money and social standing) – all of which reinforces the cultural view of woman as chattel, no doubt one of those "wretched conventions":

> About thirty years ago, Miss Maria Ward, of Huntingdon, with only seven thousand pounds, had the good luck to captivate Sir Thomas Bertram, of Mansfield Park, in the county of Northampton, and to be thereby raised to the rank of a baronet's lady, with all the comforts and consequences of an handsome house and large income. All Huntingdon exclaimed on the greatness of the match, and her uncle, the lawyer, himself, allowed her to be at least three thousand pounds short of any equitable claim to it. She had two sisters to be benefitted by her elevation; and such of their acquaintance as thought Miss Ward and Miss Frances quite as handsome as Miss Maria, did not scruple to predict their marrying with almost equal advantage. But there certainly are not so many men of large fortune in the world, as there are pretty women to deserve them. (Austen 5)

Austen, however, remained so tightly within the structure of the private sphere that she, within her novels, never enquires too curiously about sources of income, yet is obliged, in a curious kind of way (Emerson's "wretched social conventions"?), to comment on amounts. It seems that the lower the station of the man in question, the simpler it is to comment on his occupation and fortune. We never know more about Sir Thomas than that he has a plantation in Antigua; yet Mr Norris's position, with all his lack of family fortune, is known to us, as is Fanny's father's worth as a Lieutenant in the Marines.

And so, any act of "doing" has little interest for Austen, with the possible exception of

174

a lack of activity being attributable to male laziness, particularly lower-class male laziness. In this case, however, this lack takes on a threatening aspect, much as female activity becomes threatening. It seems that Austen simply is not interested in the accumulation of any information from outside the sphere that she knows so well, especially if it might have anything to do with unethical activity or brutality of any sort. An example of a profound unwillingness to know, (which is, no doubt, a symptom of doing nothing) is Sir Bertram's plantation in Antigua. Little is said about it, yet it is virtually certain that this is where a great portion of the family money comes from. The reasons for Sir Thomas's lengthy stay in Antigua are even more vague, if that is possible: it is highly likely that Austen refers obliquely to the slave uprisings at the turn of the nineteenth century, and that this property was probably a sugar plantation. Closer to home, rural work is only referred to in passing, when Mary Crawford cannot, for all her money, hire a cart to transport her harp. Nothing more objectionable than the making of hay is referred to in this passage. Austen's disinterest in the accumulation of information from outside the private sphere allows her to focus on issues of the household.

Jean-François Lyotard discusses the household as the basis of society in his essay "*oikos*".[6] He says that the *oikos* is not a place of safety (certainly not, if one can be bought and sold in one's own house):

> The *oikos* is above all the place of tragedy. I recall that one of the conditions of the tragic enumerated by Aristotle is precisely the domestic condition: relationships are tragic because they occur in the family; it is within the family that incest, patricide, matricide occur. Tragedy is not possible outside this ecologic or ecotragic framework. (Lyotard 97)

fran sendbuehler

The relevance of such a notion of domestic tragedy in *Mansfield Park* becomes clearer if we consider that what happens to Austen's female characters is akin to tragedy, especially as regards the play of property and propriety. The woman's only control over her situation is to observe propriety so that she will remain valuable as property. Hence the tragic conflict: woman has little or no control over the society within which she is supposed to function.

Lyotard later delineates a very clear opposition between the *oikeion* and the *politikon*: everything that can be called domesticity is the *oikeion*: women, children, "everything that is not *offentlich* [public]" (101). This opposition draws attention to the private (Lyotard's "secluded"), that is, "the shadowy space of all that escapes the light of public speech [and in which] darkness ... tragedy occurs" (102). Tragedy and narrative[7] together and separately form a pattern that establishes our place within culture and society, particularly since tragedy and narrative are common to all human cultures. Thus, with the narrative form that we know as the novel, we see a pattern of learning and of reinforcement of our place in society through the exploration of those positions and conflicts that occur within the *oikos*, within society. This analogy helps us to focus once more on Austen's private sphere of the household as the place where tragedy occurs. Tragedy, that is, is linked essentially to gender difference and to the dissymmetrical positioning of men and women. This inequality appears in the public sphere as a political difference of position but it arises in the private sphere as a tragic *aporia*, as a gap which is both everything and nothing. Why is it that the public sphere is that element which is of primary importance in determining what it is that we call "society"? Might not society be that which is found at home,

the art of doing nothing

and not that which is outside the home? If, as Lyotard says, the *oikos* is the seat of tragedy, this tragedy is common to all. "Tragedy" is, perhaps, what we see in action in *Mansfield Park*; the discovery of that which can be called "society", its discovery as something that involves differences as irreconcilable as that of gender, although it happens within the home. Austen's novel is the recounting and enumeration of all possible domestic tragedies as parts of a learning experience that relates her characters to male-dominated society. This she describes without touching – or touching only very lightly – on the public sphere. Can it also be said, then, that these experiences count for nothing? (Again, we have arrived at something of value that is perceived as counting for nothing.) Is this question of "experience as nothing" that which is raised by Austen when it is quite clear that the social function of the family revolves around doing nothing? The division of the public and private spheres can be seen to problematise this category of action in the novel. What women "do" in the domestic sphere is "doing nothing" in the eyes of the male-dominated public sphere.

Mansfield Park of course, is an idealized image (or is it?) of a particular social class that is controlled by the question of propriety and inaction, among which the keeping of women, and keeping them in their place, is a paramount objective. It becomes important that the women not only do nothing, but are capable of doing nothing. It is preferable (to Sir Thomas) that Lady Bertram decorate her sofa as a great stupid lump of satin and feathers than that she actually think about anything; in fact, it is of the very greatest importance that her husband do her thinking for her. Of the marriageable women in the household, Fanny is the most "worthy" of the three and is the one who is not capable of doing anything, her worth being determined by her value as nothing. Physically feeble, Fanny limps from scene to scene, doing nothing more than a woman of the house *should* do, and saying little. She seems to be barely noticed, and indeed, she seems to have lived in the house for about ten years before anyone (of course, it is Sir Thomas) thought to light a fire in her room. Fanny must first be perceived as having some marriageable worth before she is worthy of even this small degree of attention. The Bertram daughters, in their longing for activity: to do something other than to decorate a landscape or to sing at the piano, risk becoming public women. One of them is, in the end, cast out for her adulterous liaison. Austen seems to say, in the portrayal of Mary Crawford's "doing", and of her longing to not live sitting still, that there is something amiss with a woman who, with her standing in society, takes it upon herself to be the bad example that a public woman (a courtesan, perhaps) comes to represent. If a public woman is a woman who is not acceptable to polite society, then a woman who wants to "do", such as Mary Crawford, should also represent that unacceptable sort of woman, regardless of her wealth and breeding – things that have little value if they are accompanied by a lack of acceptable behaviour.

What role does the novel play in the establishment or encouragement of social identity – class structure – that a novel such as this perpetuates? One problem that the reader is presented with is the difficulty of *Mansfield Park* as critique. This is evident in that there has been much discussion of whether Austen's novels are simply a presentation of society as she saw it, or whether they are a critique of that which she saw surrounding her. It is evident throughout her writing that Austen has a keen wit and an acute sense of the ridiculous and that there is a clear delineation of society as she saw it within the pages of *Mansfield Park*; Austen gives us a remarkable view of the private sphere, the representation of which is all but ignored as being insignificant. The questions which the value and validity of the private sphere and the notion of nothingness-as-value provoke are significant in determining nothingness's referential value.

Perhaps this novel is meant to be a kind of portrait of a society and order that were about to vanish. Certainly, the portrayal of the art of doing nothing, in its brutal subtlety, opens up many possible avenues of exploration, yet does not determine strictly whether what we have here is a reproduction or a critique; perhaps what we have is something that is somehow both. Austen seems more and more to have been an incredibly astute critic of the lesser importance ascribed to the private sphere. She seems to speak for the advantages of propriety and the importance of setting a good example, but she also seems to question most or all of the baggage that accompanies expectations of propriety. Austen's commentary also speaks about private life; her novels do not praise it but rather explore its twists and turns. She does seem to be asking: "what does it all mean?" Society has, in setting political discourse outside the domestic sphere, relegated to woman that which is other, hence woman's value as an object of commodification: if her husband is an individual concerned with or committed to propriety, his wife or daughter has value as property. It is very important, though, that she be careful to do nothing.

fran sendbuehler

notes

1 Jeanette Winterson, *Oranges Are Not the Only Fruit* (London: Pandora, 1985) p9.

2 We should also pay attention, briefly, to the ambiguous figures of the companion and the governess and the roles both these occupations fill within upper-class society. Women in such positions are in a kind of nether world in that they fill certain requirements (good breeding, perhaps a certain level of education) in order to hold such positions, yet the positions themselves hold little honour and, very often, considerably less dignity. It was poverty, in its many forms, that often placed women in this kind of employment. It would not be out of place to speculate that the embarrassment of poverty itself contributed to the sense of loss of dignity that these women often suffered. cf. *Jane Eyre*.

3 Jürgen Habermas, *The Structural Transformation of the Public Sphere*, trs Thomas Burger and Frederick Lawrence (Cambridge: MIT Pr., 1989). Translation of *Strukturwandel der Öffentlichkeit* (Darmstadt and Neuwied: Hermann Luchterhand Verlag, 1962).

4 Again, I find it pertinent to inquire why it is that a "place of free and equal exchange of reasonable discourse" *must* take place outside the household? It seems obvious to me that the household should be the first place wherein this exchange takes place.

5 Emerson's comments refer to *Pride and Prejudice* and *Persuasion*. He says "all that interests in any character introduced is still this one, has he or she money to marry with, & conditions conforming? Tis 'the nympholepsy of a fond despair', (Byron, *Childe Harold*) say rather, of an English boarding-house. Suicide is more respectable". We can, therefore, guess that this is the reason he did not continue to read Austen's other works.

6 This essay is to be found in Lyotard's *Political Writings* (Minneapolis: University of Minnesota Press, 1993).

7 J. Hillis Miller in "Narrative" asks the question: "Why do we need the same story over and over?"

the art of doing nothing

and states that narrative has a kind of culture-making function; that narratives offer a sense of structure to our sense of the world.

bibliography

Austen, J., *Mansfield Park* (Markham, Ont.: Penguin Books Canada, 1964).

Eagleton, T., *The Function of Criticism from the Spectator to Post-Structuralism* (London: Verso, 1984).

Emerson, R.W., *Journals and Miscellaneous Notebooks of Ralph Waldo Emerson 1803-1882*, vol. 15, 1860-1866, eds S. Sutton Smith and H. Hayford (Cambridge Mass.: Belknap Press of Harvard University Press, 1960).

Habermas J., *The Structural Transformation of the Public Sphere*, tr. T. Burger (Cambridge, Mass.: MIT Press, 1989).

Lyotard, J.-F., "oikos" in *Political Writings*, trs B. Readings and K.-P. Geiman (Minneapolis: University of Minnesota Press, 1993) p96-107.

Miller, J.H., "Narrative" in *Critical Terms for Literary Study*, eds F. Lentricchia and T. McLaughlin (Chicago: University of Chicago Press, 1990) p66-79.

Winterson, J., *Oranges Are Not the Only Fruit* (London: Pandora, 1985).

> This thing of darkness I
> Acknowledge mine.
> *Prospero, in* The Tempest 5.1[1]

> To be more demonstrative, in the effusiveness of my praise, I shall now bring out the resoluteness with which he will have taken sides with the proper [*le propre*] against the dirty [*le sale*], or rather against the soiled [*le sali*], the sullied [*le souillé*], a distinction which reveals a whole story [*toute une histoire*], one that takes time and decomposes itself...
> Jacques Derrida, Signéponge/Signsponge 36-37

roy sellars

THEORY ON THE TOILET
a manifesto for dreckology

(a) redeeming the time: a fable

In Joyce's Dublin, on 16 June 1904, Mr Leopold Bloom ends the first chapter of his day ("Calypso") on the toilet. On his way to the "jakes", Bloom thinks of manuring the garden with hen droppings or cattle dung (*Ulysses* 65-66). Neither of these is the best form of manure according to Varro, the learned Roman who, in his treatise on agriculture written around 36 BC, recommends pigeon dung and "human excrement" (*stercus ... hominis*, 264-65); but then *Ulysses* is not a treatise. Bloom is generally unperturbed by authorities. "Reclaim the whole place", he thinks, noting also the use of dung to clean kid gloves. "Dirty cleans" (*Ulysses* 66). Such is the power of reclaiming and recycling in Joyce's text that there seems to be no possibility that dirt may be left over, unaccounted for. *Dreck*, on the other hand, would present more of a problem to the reader or economist. Is the distinction between dirt and *Dreck* decidable, and if so, how? One purpose of this manifesto is to interrogate the concepts of dirt and manure [*stercus*] presupposed in the heterogeneous economies of Leopold Bloom and Marcus Terentius Varro.[2] A textual economy will be called "heterogeneous" not because of the conflictual variety of its representations, but because of what disturbs its identity while resisting representation. The distinction here is between opposition and difference. The heterogeneity of the latter implies a crisis of the proper which marks both property and propriety in a most unsettling way. As distinct from dirt and the dirty, *Dreck* cannot be read (or defined) as such: the study of *Dreck* produces a phenomenon, certainly, but this phenomenon itself occludes the waste product whose disfiguration is at stake, thus blindly repeating a process in which readability is a lure. Where *Dreck* was, there dirt shall be. But dirt that is to be reclaimed will always run the risk of falling into the irrecuperable event of *Dreck*. This history takes time.

Bloom's reclaiming is ambitious, not limiting itself to thoughts of gardening and

theory on the toilet

cleaning. Most importantly of all, as we shall see in the next section, he attempts to reclaim time. We should not forget that he works in advertising, in the representation of commodities, where time itself is the greatest commodity. But the principles of time management are not new. Towards the end of "De l'expérience" (the last of his *Essais*), Michel de Montaigne tells a story which demands to be repeated:

> Esope, ce grand homme, vid son maistre qui pissoit en se promenant: "Quoy donq, fit-il, nous faudra-il chier en courant?" Mesnageons le temps; encore nous en reste-il beaucoup d'oisif et mal employé. Nostre esprit n'a volontiers pas assez d'autres heures à faire ses besongnes, sans se desassocier du corps en ce peu d'espace qu'il luy faut pour sa necessité. ("De l'expérience" 327)

> Aesope, that famous man, saw his master pisse as he was walking; what (said hee) must we not, &c. [*chier*], when we are running? Let us husband time as well as wee can, yet shall we employ much of it both idly and ill; as if our minde had not other houres enough to doe hir businesse without disassociating hir selfe from the body in that little space which shee needeth for her necessity. ("Of Experience" 574-75)

The uncanny figure of "Esope" – slave, phantasm, allegorist, and purveyor of minor literature – will return at later stages of this project, in stories to be told of Chaucer's cock and hen, Henryson's cock and jewel, Spenser's mole, and Milton's wen. Aesop remains uncanny because his signature produces fables of ascription and inscription, and because we can never be sure that we have outgrown him.

Montaigne here draws on the ancient Life of Aesop, already a remarkable Aesopic fable in itself (Patterson 15-26), so as to allegorise Aesop's scurrilous question: Montaigne gives it another meaning, so that the question can coincide with his own argument against transcendental experience and the disassociation of the body. Montaigne is also a master allegorist or manager of time. But when the allegorist refers to Aesop as authority, he also disassociates his own text from itself. As he had written near the beginning of his essay, "nous ne faisons que nous entregloser" ("De l'expérience" 279); "[w]e do but interglose ourselves" ("Of Experience" 548). In citing and interglosing, Montaigne courts the permanent risk that the text cited may run away with itself or from itself – that is, that the "tweezers" of his quotation marks may not be strong enough to keep it in its proper place (Derrida 44-45, "quoting" Francis Ponge). This is a fable about allegory, a fable which will question the propriety of describing any place as proper to a text. A new ethics of citation is urgently needed to displace the literary husbandry which has often passed for criticism (see Derrida 20-27). What is it that the writer/intergloser presumes to hold between his or her tweezers? Does a text have a postal or legal address of its own? Can a text ever be domesticated, or kept on a leash? Can there be a hygiene of reading? Like Aesop's master, one should husband one's time and property carefully in order to guard against the disturbing ramifications of such questions. To take sides with the proper demands a certain resolution. So the slave should not be let loose. Moreover, it is clear that one should not let the slave speak. Instead of redeeming the time, in Montaigne's story, the master opened himself up to ridicule by ignoring this elementary law of philosophy.

(b) a fine and private place

More intelligent than the philosopher,

roy sellars

Leopold Bloom knows better than to think of opening his bowels while running down to the butcher's shop for his morning pork kidney. If there is to be no waste of time, as he contemplates a retreat to the private place of the jakes, there appears to be only one effective strategy open to him: reading. The jakes emerges as a pre-eminent site of reading – as it had been since at least the sixteenth century (Pops 46). Danny Lamarcq's illustrated history of the toilet shows that a classic eighteenth-century design formed a *trompe l'oeil* in which the bowl of the toilet itself appeared to be set into a pile of books; in the case of a particularly luxurious privy built for a Dutch nobleman in 1770, the walls of the privy were then filled with fake books (88, 94-95). To the reader, it looks like a scene in poor taste from a novel by Tom Sharpe (to be studied in due course), but it is not: it is a *trompe l'oeil*. On such a toilet, is one inside or outside literature? Literary criticism needs to be able to answer this question in order to sit comfortably.

So-called pierced chairs [*chaises percées*] were very common among "les classes possédantes" [literally, "the possessing classes"] of the seventeenth century, as Roger-Henri Guerrand points out (38). The man of affairs, now pressed by the clock, could not afford to be tied down to the fixed medieval privy. An inventory of the 274 such mobile possessions at Versailles, under the personal rule of Louis XIV which began in 1661, includes some featuring "un guéridon permettant de lire et d'écrire" ["a pedestal table allowing one to read and write"]. The threat to the temporal continuity of reading and writing could thereby be suspended. Guerrand notes here that other pierced chairs were catalogued at Versailles "avec le siège en forme de gros livres portant l'inscription suivante: 'Voyage aux Pays-Bas'" ["with a seat in the form of large books, bearing the following inscription: *Journey to the Nether-lands*"] (38; illustrated 11). Another *trompe l'oeil*, the French design could be mistaken for a prolepsis of the fourth book of *Gulliver's Travels*, published in 1726. (Swift's writing will haunt and vex later parts of this project.)

Leopold Bloom's voyage to the netherlands does not involve the literary furnishings of high culture. "A paper. He liked to read at stool" (*Ulysses* 65). As Joyce's "biografiend" Richard Ellmann points out[3], the story which Bloom reads – "Matcham's Masterstroke", by a Mr Philip Beaufoy – is based on a piece of Joyce's own juvenilia (50). The text is recycled, as text within the text of *Ulysses*. But it is far from clear what it means to recycle a text, or what it means for a text to be "within" another text. Joyce intergloses himself, or rather, Bloom in some sense intergloses Joyce as Beaufoy. Like a well-trained literary critic, Bloom remarks on the material conditions of production of the story before beginning to analyse its structure, style and theme, its *dispositio* and *inventio*. But what exactly has the work of recycling accomplished – and disbarred? Can its products be framed so as to become readable as such? What is a frame?

Let us return to the problem of time, which indeed we have never left, since the temporal articulation of this manifesto inevitably dislocates the punctual time of the theses and positions that might be expected from it. Bloom has clearly heeded Bill Oddie's injunction that, since the average person spends eleven and a half minutes per day on the toilet – "the always open university" (1) – this time ought to be devoted to self-improvement (vi). The ineluctable modality of the temporal holds Bloom in its grasp, but at least he can attempt to reclaim this time as his own, time for private reading, at the start of his

theory on the toilet

day. "Something new and easy. No great hurry. Keep it a bit" (*Ulysses* 66). As the syntax of the following sentence indicates, the rhythm of the text before him, in its printed columns, is made to follow the rhythm of the column inside him: "Quietly he read, restraining himself, the first column and, yielding but resisting, began the second."[4] His approval of the story as "neat" here coincides with the moment at which he can best appreciate the performance of his own masterstroke: "He read on, seated calm above his own rising smell. Neat certainly."

The uses of literature are far from exhausted. Bloom imagines writing a story of his own, in which he could recycle Molly's casual remarks into a prize-winning narrative (compare the prize-winning technique of the final chapter of *Ulysses*, "Penelope"). In the "Circe" chapter, in fact, Mr Philip Beaufoy himself makes a brief appearance – a prosopopeia of the author with a vengeance. Beaufoy speaks as a witness at Bloom's trial, accusing him of plagiarism and other sins and mocking him as "too beastly awfully weird for words" (435). Beaufoy's imputation that Bloom is *Dreck* is unjust. The postscript to the latter's masterstroke in "Calypso" had merely involved using Beaufoy's text in such a way as to remind us that toilet paper has a history of its own (which this project proposes later to examine): "He tore away half the prize story sharply and wiped himself with it" (67).

At this climactic moment, as the text of "Matcham's Masterstroke" disappears from literary history, the reader may come dangerously close to falling into *Dreck*. If this "moment" is taken as a place, however, it can still safely be recuperated. This is a mistake, but it is a mistake programmed into any system of critical reading, as system. It could easily be argued in Ellmann's humanistic system that the moment in question has a use-value, like everything else represented in the scene, to which it is subordinate: namely, justifying the commonplace in proper words as not beastly, not awful, not weird. The imposition of meaning onto textual articulation which has mostly been the task of the Joyce industry would thus have been further facilitated.[5] The productivity of this industry is measured in terms of its totalising knowledge. As the sceptical Leo Bersani asks concerning Bloom, "[h]as any fictional character ever been so completely known?" (157) In other words, has any fictional character ever become such a commonplace, such a topos? Bloom's appropriation by the Joyce industry threatens to banalise the adventure of reading altogether. The industry has achieved excellence, but at the cost of pollution on a scale to which it must remain structurally blind in order to continue functioning. If the knowing impositions of criticism are to be displaced, it will not be sufficient to point to different thematic identifications or topoi in the text as if they had power to challenge those impositions. Instead, this manifesto calls readers to the experience of the impossible, to hear the inaudible remaindering which characterises the temporality of the reading process. In that process is a remainder or remnant which resists appropriation. This remnant is unspeakable, not because of its intrinsic content, but because it confounds the system of spatial enframing which would allow a content to be distinguished and addressed as intrinsic (compare Mary Douglas's systemic analysis of dirt, 35-37). *Dreck* interferes with the constitution of the text. The hermeneutic system cannot be kept clean from such interference, as Gordon Teskey shows in a powerful argument concerning the history and performance of allegory and irony (401). The system's remnant acts as an event, and cannot be reduced to a dirtied prize story or to any represented object, phenomenon, character, or thematisation whatsoever. The remnant is not a topos.

The provocation to the literary critic, who deals in topoi, is clear. Bloom seems to offer the critic the gift of his consciousness, in which anything can be named and known, and yet the nature of such a gift is called into question by this scene of reading and excreting. It is evident that "Matcham's Masterstroke" itself, the text upon which the scene depends, remains unreadable, even if a biographer could reproduce it for us as evidence. The reproduction of textual evidence in this way is a growing problem. Freud's warning of the epistemological impossibility of biography (*Letters of Freud and Zweig* 127) is routinely ignored by the biography industry; and, more generally, the drive towards totalised archives of "evidence" is accelerating. To reproduce a text is not equivalent to reading it, however, and the mechanical act of reproduction merely calls attention to the enigmatic materiality of the text being (re)produced. In that enigma of materiality lies the difference between dirt, which can be understood phenomenally, and *Dreck*, which cannot. To reiterate, *Dreck* is not reducible to imagery or the level of the thematic: it is in constructing what passes for an "image" or a "theme" that the possibility of *Dreck* is produced, or by-produced, if such a verb is possible.

Dreck is not to be found by searching a text for a content, whether scatological, biographical, or psychological. This manifesto is not Freudian in any recognisable sense. Despite Freud's predilection for archaeological metaphors, criticism cannot legitimate its enterprise of metaphorical excavation by appealing to psychoanalysis. Such an appeal would imply that the content of psychoanalysis itself had already been excavated and classified, which is certainly not the case – as much of this project will try to demonstrate. Perhaps the only aspect of excavation which is relevant to the reading process is the potentially interminable surprise to which both are subject. The suspension of knowledge with which the reader confronts the non-phenomenal work of the text means that the texts of literature, agricultural economy, psychoanalysis, and so forth, become "occasions for the unprecedented" (Wood 65). The provocation of *Dreck* does not derive from something which is recognised, such as an indecorous representation; rather, *Dreck* provokes reading epistemologically, in the sense of being a permanent danger to the stability of textual knowledge. At the moment when *Dreck* enters the economy of literature, knowledge is about to go down the drain, and the proliferation of this effect is not to be limited to what is recognisable under the institutional label of "literature". If, for the sake of exposition, *Dreck*-ology has to be given a beginning, Bloom's scene of reading suggests that it will remain deprived of ending, linear continuity, determinate position, and even object. Instead of pursuing an argument "about" an object, writing about *Dreck* will inexorably turn into writing about or around writing.

(c) *veni, vidi, vici*

To describe the episode from "Calypso" sketched above as Bloom's scene of reading could be taken to imply that, in some basic sense, it is proper to Bloom as subject. After all, the scene appears to be graphically founded on a place which, as Freud reminds us, is cathected [*besetzt*] or at least occupied [*besetzt*] by every subject. It would then be tempting to take Bloom in the jakes as an emblem, an emblem of the position of the literary theorist.

theory on the toilet

Rodin was no fool
When he cast his Thinker,
Cogitating deeply,
Crouched in the position
Of a man at stool.
(W.H. Auden, "The Geography of the House" lines 28-32)

The theorist tries to be one on whom nothing is lost and for whom anything can be recycled. Even if neither objective is in fact possible, the position which sustains the attempt could be seen as relatively secure. The potential scope of Bloom's vision seems to be suitably comprehensive. To be sure, this is a seeing which cannot be publicly certified, and hence it can never arrive at the level of theoretical authenticity in the traditional Greek sense (Godzich xiv-xv). But why should Bloom care for external certification? Literary criticism can do that for him. So it could be argued that Bloom theorises in security, and that the reader's position, equally private, repeats this security.

Yet this emblematic interpretation is thoroughly misleading. For even in the emblem, that apparently most static of literary forms, temporality cannot be excluded. The emblem emerges as a ruse of allegory, presenting the *trompe l'oeil* of static meaning which criticism is only too willing to accept as a terminus in order to be able to arrive somewhere. This manifesto declines to arrive, at the risk of becoming entangled in perpetual detours, simply because the dislocation it attempts to describe must also dislocate the teleology of arrival. Even Auden, in the mostly very conservative poem quoted above, recognises that "Mind and Body run on / Different timetables" (lines 73-74). Allegory offers the reader the alarming prospect of a system in which the "timetables" cannot be synchronised because they do not correspond to themselves in the first place.

In one of the epigrams of Sir John Harington, collected posthumously in 1618, we read of a "godly Father" at stool somewhat resembling Martin Luther. He is disturbed in his prayers by the appearance of the devil, rebuking him "that it prou'd he was deuoyd of grace, / To speake to God in so vnfit a place" (*Letters and Epigrams* 166, lines 1-8). This epigram, which was represented as an emblem with appropriate illustration in Harington's *Metamorphosis of Ajax* (*A New Discourse* 93-95), concludes with the following decisive rejoinder to the devil on the part of the "reuerend man", underlined by an alliterative concluding couplet:

> Thou damned Spirit, wicked, false, and lying,
> Despayring thine owne good, and ours enuying:
> Each take his due, and me thou canst not hurt,
> To God my prayer I meant, to thee the durt.
> Pure prayer ascends to him that high doth sit.
> Downe falls the filth, for fiends of hell more fit.
> (lines 11-16)

The mere fact that the emblem is recirculated in Harington's cloacinean treatise suggests that the repudiation of the devil is never finished. *The Metamorphosis of Ajax*, which will be a focus of attention in this project, is often read as if it were reducible to a homiletic development of such a gesture of repudiation. But this reading presumes that the text is based on an emblem in which one can separate a figurative tenor from a material vehicle, so to speak. The problem here is that the crucial separation between "pure" apotropaic "prayer" and material "durt" remains unstable. In order to secure the emblem of Leopold Bloom as theorist, the reader would have to repeat what is supposed to be Bloom's gesture of separating thought from its material supplement. But the theorist whose faith is not as "strong" as that of Harington's divine can hardly avoid the difficulty that thought is contaminated by the mire of language. Through its entanglement in that mire, reading tends to undo the categorisations necessary to keep any emblem as such in its place.

In the process of reading Joyce's text, one sees Bloom fall between dirt and prayer, between the invisibly private and the accountably public, and so on, leading to the decomposition of these fundamental oppositions. Inasmuch as it can be treated as a theory, Dreckology is an originary fall or falling which emerges from the difficulty of establishing a theory of decomposition that does not itself decompose or fester (cf. de Certeau, "The Institution of Rot" 45-46). The sense of smell in reading should not be neglected. If Leopold Bloom's scene of reading is in any sense emblematic, it is emblematic of allegory, here taken as the (impossible) writing of such decomposition. Milton's Satan, in *Paradise Lost*, will furnish commentary on this gnomic assertion in a later section of this project comparing work on Satanic allegory by Walter Benjamin (226-33) and Harold Bloom (19-45). *Paradise Lost* is also notable because it tries to give a definitive ending to the story of *Dreck* – the apocalypse.

It must be repeated that Dreckology is in no way equivalent to scatology. But even scatology has been too much for some readers of Joyce to stomach. Ezra Pound – whose own work is not untouched by the scatological – wanted some twenty lines deleted from Joyce's "Calypso", for its magazine publication in 1918, because of their "excessive" character (Ellmann 421-22). A reviewer of the *Portrait of the Artist as a Young Man*, the year before, had commented that "Mr Joyce is a clever novelist, but we feel he would be really at his best in a treatise on drains" (Beja 78). H.G. Wells, also reviewing the *Portrait*, accused Joyce of harbouring a "cloacal obsession" typical of Irish writers. What particularly disgusted Wells was that Joyce "would bring back into the general picture of life aspects which modern drainage and modern decorum have taken out of ordinary intercourse and conversation" (cited by Jeri Johnson, *Ulysses* 812-13). The story is waiting to be told of how the work of Thomas Crapper and others led, in the late nineteenth century, to the possibility of this institutionalised alliteration of "drainage" and "decorum" (for a biography of Crapper, see Reyburn). Here it should simply be noted that Wells has produced the general picture of an authorial "obsession" of which he complains. It is not self-evident that either the *Portrait* or *Ulysses* forms part of a "general picture of life"; nor is Joyce's intention self-evident in writing them. In constructing his "general picture", in imposing the normative violence of a frame, it is Wells himself who has produced *Dreck*. The reduction of writing to a function of a "cloacal obsession" is surprising because it tends to eliminate reading, which is generally assumed to be one of the main tasks of a book reviewer. Such a reduction collapses the difference between Leopold Bloom and Thomas Crapper, for example. The irony is that the transparency of meaning which Wells presupposes is called into question by the very explicitness of his own gesture in identifying what is unspeakable or beyond the pale. It is only through an attachment to the law of drainage and decorum that the ending of "Calypso" can be considered transgressive, and yet that law appears as a problem of reading at the very moment it is taken for granted. Nevertheless, it would be a mistake to ridicule Joyce's reviewers for their naive attachments. To value transgression for its own sake, as this manifesto does, is to forget that transgression precisely depends on

theory on the toilet

some form of attachment to law or limit (Foucault 33-35). An analysis of Spenserian allegory and English colonialism in Ireland, with its famous pale, will attempt to address this problem.

Joyce had revenge on his reviewers, appropriately or not, by recycling Wells's phrase in the "Aeolus" chapter of *Ulysses*. The verbose professor MacHugh, master of languages and high culture, is contrasting Hebrew civilisation with that of the Romans, "Vast ... but vile" (126). He warns that "[w]e mustn't be led away by words, by sounds of words." As if in response to Wells, the professor continues his speech by reflecting on a familiar noun inherited from Latin, the *latrina lingua* – to borrow a relevant but discourteous pun from Castiglione's *Book of the Courtier* (168; see Harington, *A New Discourse* 61-62):

> Cloacae: sewers. The Jews in the wilderness and on the mountaintop said: *It is meet to be here. Let us build an altar to Jehovah.* The Roman, like the Englishman who follows in his footsteps, brought to every new shore on which he set his foot (on our shore he never set it) only his cloacal obsession. He gazed about him in his toga and he said: *It is meet to be here. Let us construct a watercloset.* (126, Joyce's italics)

J.J. O'Molloy adds that "we have also Roman law", to which the professor responds "[a]nd Pontius Pilate is its prophet." The law of colonialism – Roman, and by extension, British – thus appears to be bound up with a particular system of cleanliness which is held in place by the *Dreck* it produces. The administration of colonial law, which has included allowing Jesus Christ to be condemned to death (Derrida 110-11), could be said to rely on the institution of the water-closet. And now wash your hands. In his *Histoire de la merde*, a book which has yet to receive the attention it deserves, Dominique Laporte analyses the "lien qui unit l'impérialisme d'un Etat à sa police du déchet" (54; see 51-53), the links which bind the imperialism of a state to its regulations concerning rubbish and waste. Jean-Marie Le Pen, leader of the French *Front national*, appeared on an election poster in 1993, beaming, with the slogan "Mains propres" ["Clean Hands"]. Is it only neo-fascists who have clean hands?

If to see is to conquer, as Julius Caesar put it, then the task of the *Dreck*ologist should be to make the visible a little hard to see. This disturbance of vision begins with the texts cited here already, opposing Richard Ellmann's presupposition that Joyce is to be conquered by the reader, for instance (6). Imperialistic literary criticism has proved itself quite capable of surviving the death of other empires. The paradigm of reading as conquest is not easy to displace.

(d) the history and epistemology of the water-closet

In recent years, cultural historians such as Guerrand and Lamarcq have begun to excavate some of the complexities of the institution of the toilet. The main documentary focus of such work, inevitably, lies on the past hundred years or so: the modern flushing valve water-closet as defined by Thomas Crapper, Sanitary Engineer by appointment to His Majesty Edward VII, is so recent as to be a novelty in the history of western domestic culture (Reyburn 11-14, 29-31). Bloom's outside jakes, in the Dublin of 1904, would probably not flush and not be connected to a public system of drainage. After the Romans, whose most fundamental contributions can be summarised under the convenient heading of abjection (see Kristeva,

Pouvoirs de l'horreur 7-39; "Approaching Abjection"), almost the only notable reformer before the eighteenth century was John Harington – poet, classicist, translator, Elizabethan courtier and colonialist. This apparent gulf between the Romans and Harington calls for further study. Harington's work will receive particular consideration: his *Metamorphosis of Ajax* ["A jakes"], written under the pseudonym *Misacmos* ["Hater of filth"] and published in the same year and by the same printer as *The Faerie Queene* (1596, Richard Field), is one of the most remarkable treatises of the English Renaissance. A mock encomium whose margins are continually invading the already questionable body of its text, and whose irony remains undecidable, it reveals the Renaissance as a renaissance of the cloaca (Laporte 33).

Harington's work had little practical effect, however. Queen Elizabeth, Spenser's Gloriana, may have been one of the very few Elizabethans privileged to test Harington's invention out, since, according to another of his epigrams, a water-closet was installed following his model in Richmond Palace (*Letters and Epigrams* 165; see Craig 19, Lamarcq 63-64). According to the anonymous author of the relevant entry in the *Oxford Junior Encyclopaedia*, the first British patent for a flushing water-closet was not granted until 1755 ("Sanitation" 400, Lamarcq 90); and, until the triumph of the U-bend and the efficient cistern in the time of Thomas Crapper, the stench of the underlying cesspool or sewer could not effectively be kept out of private domestic space. Technology has now separated base from superstructure, of course, so that there appears to be almost no relationship between them.

The author of this admirably lucid encyclopaedia entry structures his or her work as a narrative of progress from medieval filth to modern enlightenment, seeking to reassure its mainly young audience that the base dirt and horrors of pre-modern sanitation belong to history. Now, we read, local authorities in Britain are "responsible" for ensuring that "proper" standards of sanitation are maintained ("Sanitation" 401; on the French adjective *propre* in this context, see Derrida 28-33, 42-47 and Laporte 32-33). The configuration of patriotism here is strong.

> Think of what our Nation stands for,
>   Books from Boots' and country lanes,
> Free speech, free passes, class distinction,
>   Democracy and proper drains.
> (Betjeman, "In Westminster Abbey" lines 19-22)

But to the distress of John Betjeman's speaker, praying for protection against the Germans in 1940, history refuses to stay in its proper place. What is needed here is a treatise on history and drains.

A recent report by the British Member of Parliament Jon Owen Jones, "Not at Your Convenience", notes that local authorities are regularly failing to meet their statutory responsibilities in providing and maintaining public toilets. This is an indicator of what has become familiar to the subjects of post-Thatcherite Britain as the disintegration of the "public" sphere. It is largely a question of power. Councillor Ian Arnold points out that the town planners of today do not have the same powers as their illustrious Victorian precursors. He explains the difficulties which the London Borough of Lambeth has experienced in implementing its proposal for obliging major developers to provide public conveniences: at the inquiry into the proposed plan, Tesco stores successfully objected to being "expected" to provide anything. In the light of such a refusal, what does Britain "stand for"?

Whatever its historical vicissitudes, it

theory on the toilet

might be assumed that the privy has always functioned as an anchor of the private. It would appear to be one of the most secure points of reference in the domestic economy. Roger-Henri Guerrand's historical investigation is entitled *Les lieux* ["places", an abbreviation of *lieux d'aisances*, "conveniences"]. This could lead the unsuspecting English reader to presume that Guerrand will be writing about topography or indeed rhetorical topoi. As one of Joyce's washerwomen puts it, "I know by heart the places he likes to saale, duddurty devil! Scorching my hand and starving my famine to make his private linen public" (*Finnegans Wake* 196). But in fact the borderline between "private" and "public", where dirt and privies are concerned, turns out to be quite unstable (see Harris, and Lamarcq 11-12).

This project is only secondarily concerned with cultural history, because this mode of "history" is too easily reduced to a metanarrative based on documentation in which texts function as mere purveyors of knowledge. Several so-called histories of the privy in English operate on the level of the more or less facetious anecdote, and then lose the potentially subversive local power of their anecdotes by assimilating them into a narrative of progress or mere entertainment. Such historians assume that their historiography is based on an object of knowledge – ultimately, the self-identical turd – which could always be named as such. This assumption amounts to an elimination of history, in the sense of history as that which resists representation and identity. To be serious where others have been facetious will change little; this distinction itself is not to be taken too seriously, as the rhetorical categories that underlie it cannot be secured. Tone can indeed play a decisive role, but, as Derrida asks in a question it would be facetious to call rhetorical, who will decide whether tone forms part of a discourse or not (2-3)? The problem is rather that the construction of private space, like the construction of history, passes through the incontinent temporal detour of the text, in which what is proper or identical can never contain itself. The impossible task of Dreckology is to follow that detour as a detour without repeating the elimination of its incontinence and aberrance.

(e) the merchant and the letter: fragments of a tale

Once upon a time, and a very bad time it was, there was a merchant travelling to Canterbury. In his first words to the group of pilgrims, Chaucer's Merchant tries to establish a notion of community based on marital suffering (lines 1-5). He claims to speak on behalf of "[w]e wedded men" (line 16) in their misery, a misery allegedly caused by the "difference" between the ideal figure of patient Griselda, in the preceding Clerk's Tale, and his own wife (lines 11-13). But difference is in fact absent from his account of women. The Merchant's misogyny could be defined as the annihilation of difference, in the definitive character he gives to his wife – to whom he has been married for all of two months (lines 21-22) – and in the gross generalisation by which all "wedded men" are presumed to suffer from the same cause, namely woman. So one might expect that the Merchant will give a straightforward *exemplum* to show his audience that "[a] boy is a boy, but a girl is *drek*", as Kirk Douglas's mother explained this potent *sententia* to her young son before he left for college (Kirk Douglas 53).

Such an expectation is frustrated, of course. This project will study the Merchant's Tale in its disruptions of patriarchy, *sententia* and hermeneutics. The

188

roy sellars

action of the tale can be said to turn on another scene of reading. Damyan the squire writes a letter to May (lines 666-72), who is newly married to – or rather, acquired by – the *senex amans* Januarie. Great emphasis is laid on the secrecy necessary for desire to be communicated:

> She feyned hire as that she moste gon
> Ther as ye woot that every wight moot neede;
> And whan she of this bille hath taken heede,
> She rente it al to cloutes ['fragments'] atte laste,
> And in the privee softely it caste. (lines 738-42)

The Merchant's direct address to his audience here seems to ground the privy in common knowledge, just as he attempts to ground woman in common knowledge, but the tale itself, disseminating scenes of reading and interpretative conflict, calls into question such economies. Moreover, what happens to the materiality of the text or "bille", in reading?

This question will lead to a comparative analysis of two poems by Thomas Hardy, "The Torn Letter" (313-14) and "The Letter's Triumph" (898-99). The former, in which the speaker tears a love letter into fragments and thereby loses the co-ordinates of the sender, is the object of an important essay by J. Hillis Miller. Hillis Miller applies work by Jacques Derrida to the difficulties of reading Hardy's text. It is an interesting gesture, but it tends to suggest that Derrida has sent a message to Hillis Miller, whether via Hardy's or Derrida's text, which can then be expounded and exemplified: this is a problem, because it is the aberrance of the very structure of address, message and delivery which is at stake. Despite his thematisation of literature as litter, there is not much room for *Dreck* in Hillis Miller's system of reading. "The Letter's Triumph", as its title suggests, disturbingly presents a letter as agent, acting literally in the place of the sender and lover.

It will be argued that the material letter of the tales told by Joyce, Chaucer and Hardy institutes a triumph, or a fall, which is quite irrecuperable – even by an allegorical reading of a text such as "The Letter's Triumph".

(f) the phantasmic monarchism of the subject

"I'll wring the neck of any fucking bastard says a word against my bleeding fucking king" (*Ulysses* 554). The violence of Private Carr's expostulation or expectoration, in "Circe", might lead the reader to dismiss it as merely carnivalesque raving. But if Private Carr is the most fervent monarchist in this scene, he is certainly not the only one. As Montaigne reminds us, in a passage added to "De l'expérience" and published in the posthumous edition of 1595, "avons nous beau monter ... au plus eslevé throne du monde, si ne sommes assis que sus nostre cul" (327); "sit we upon the highest throne of the world, yet sit we upon our owne taile" ("Of Experience" 575). The "throne" and the "taile" function in a system of figurative exchange in which the one may silently take the place of the other.

The training of the modern subject offers him or her the lure of a throne – as if, in a democratic state, every subject were free to establish her or his own self as a monarchy in miniature, within certain predetermined limits. But the act of accession to this phantasmic monarchy of the toilet only serves to reinforce the subjection of the subject to a law which is all the more powerful since it is not open to inspection, having always already been incorporated. How did this disaster overtake us? It seems history is to blame.

"The king was in his countinghouse", we read as Bloom, in the jakes, looks up through a gap in the wall at the back window of the house next door, presumably checking

theory on the toilet

that his entry has been unobserved (*Ulysses* 66). It is impossible to determine either the source or the reference of this grammatically simple sentence. We do not know whether it is external or internal to Bloom's consciousness – if indeed we can ever properly use these terms in writing about a text – and we do not know whether the "king" is Bloom's neighbour, Bloom himself, Edward VII, a figure in a nursery rhyme ("The king was in his countinghouse, / Counting out his money"), or all or none of these. In this indeterminacy lies the power of the economic system which arbitrarily assigns value to its units of exchange: the law of this "king" defies resistance precisely because of its arbitrariness, as he counts up the tributes which his loyally excreting subjects guarantee him (Laporte 29-33). Private Carr's "king" can be located, even if, confusingly, he has two bodies; he could be addressed; a word could be said against him. The "king" who is "in his countinghouse" cannot be located, and if he could be addressed and resisted, it would only be through that most unreliable trope, prosopopeia. The sentence may reassure Bloom that all's right with the world, but it can hardly reassure the reader.

One of the most venerable manuals of baby and child care is that of Dr Benjamin Spock, first published in 1946, which by the time of its 1969 edition had sold over twenty million copies. Spock places considerable emphasis on the act of toilet training. He begins his section on bowel training with a paragraph entitled "What does it mean?" Spock's apparently open hermeneutic gesture is – like most hermeneutic gestures – a ruse, for it systematically forecloses itself, thereby sustaining a powerful institutional structure. What does it mean? Here is Spock's answer to this potentially embarrassing question from the liberal parent's catechism:

Learning to use the toilet is an important *forward* step for a child – in several ways. He [sic] gains *control* of two apertures of his body that previously functioned automatically, and this gives him a lot of pride... He is accepting the first serious *responsibility* that his mother assigns to him... You may think of this shift as primarily meaning no more soiled nappies. That's important, all right. But the preference for cleanliness that a child gains at a year and a half or two *means a lot more than that*. It's actually the foundation for his lifelong preference for unsticky hands, for clean clothes, for a neat home, for an orderly way of *doing business*. It's from his toilet training that he gets some of his feeling that one way of doing things is *right* and another way is not; this helps him to develop a sense of obligation, to become *a systematic person*. (228, my italics)

This genealogy of the "systematic person" keeps meaning safely in the hands of the parent – or more precisely, in the hands of a liberal system first administered by the parent and then by the systematic person him- or herself. The child's excretions are to be properly controlled by the parent, acting for the good of the child and of capitalist society, only until such "control" can operate independently. At that point, anal control can become the basis for responsibility, morality, order, good business practice, and much else. Liberated from "soiled nappies", the liberal subject can discover freedom in voluntary submission to a just (and invisible) law. Babies of the world unite, you have nothing to lose except your nappies (as long as you accept the hegemony of the toilet, needless to say).

In the wake of Spock and others, the genre of the toilet training manual flourishes. One of the more imaginative illustrated narratives currently available is *I Want My Potty*, by Tony Ross. It tells the story of how a "little roy sellars

princess" negotiates the move from nappies, which she describes as "'YUUECH'" (Ross 1), to the potty. After strenuous resistance, she comes to love it (8), and she is assured while she performs that she "would grow up to be a wonderful queen" (11). But the admiral of the fleet purloins the potty to add to his navy, causing general distress as the entire royal court searches for it. The potty is eventually restored to the princess "... a little too late", as the final illustration shows her shamefacedly standing in a pool of urine (23). The monarchist rhetoric of this family romance is clear and effective, encouraging the child to identify with the heroine who outgrows her dependence but still remains subject to the permanent risk of *Dreck*. Reading the text is a vital heuristic experience, offering the reader the lure of autonomy but subject to similar risk. When I first heard of this book, it was as something which had already been devoured by the children to whom it was given: they had read it to bits.

In Freud's analysis of narcissistic fantasy, the figure of "'His Majesty the Baby'" plays a crucial role (*Standard Edition* 14: 91 = *Pelican Freud* 11: 85; *Studienausgabe* 3: 57, English in the original). This figure has a double, "His Majesty the Ego [*das Ich*]", whom we meet in Freud's paper on "Creative Writers and Day-dreaming" (*Standard Edition* 9: 150 = *Pelican Freud* 14: 138; *Studienausgabe* 10: 176). The relationship between the two is hard to conceptualise, though, because conceptualisation itself tends to be dominated by the systematic misreadings of the ego. Freud was, of course, one of the first creative writers to show the complicity of bowel training and subject formation. But it remains difficult to distance his work objectively, for we can never be quite sure if we are behaving monarchically when we read.

(g) the dream of theory

According to the Flaubert of Julian Barnes, reading the newspapers of 1850, we are "dancing ... on the wooden seat of a latrine, and it seems to me more than a touch rotten. Soon society will go plummeting down and drown in nineteen centuries of shit" (Barnes 179). This manifesto will resist the temptation to offer any such prophecy, leaving the work of imaginative apocalypse to more competent texts – such as *Paradise Lost* (see 10.597-640). Instead, it will attempt to sketch a choreography for some dances on the seat of Flaubert's latrine.

Writing on the question of affect in dreams a few decades after Flaubert, Sigmund Freud found himself obliged to analyse "a short dream, which will fill every reader with disgust [*Ekel*]". He is initially puzzled that he himself felt no disgust during the dream. Here is its text – or rather, here are its textual leftovers:

> *A hill, on which there was something like an open-air closet* [*etwas wie ein Abort im Freien*]: *a very long seat* [*Bank*] *with a large hole* [*Abortloch*] *at the end of it. Its back edge was thickly covered* [*besetzt*] *with small heaps of faeces* [*Häufchen Kot*] *of all sizes and degrees of freshness. There were bushes behind the seat. I micturated* [*uriniere*] *on the seat; a long stream of urine washed everything clean* [*ein langer Harnstrahl spült alles rein*]; *the lumps of faeces* [*Kotpatzen*] *came away easily and fell into the opening* [*fallen in die Öffnung*]. *It was as though at the end there was still some left* [*Als ob am Ende noch etwas übrigbliebe*].

> (*Standard Edition* 5: 468-69 = *Pelican Freud* 4: 605; *Studienausgabe* 2: 452, Freud's italics)

Incidentally, one has to admire the determination of James Strachey to clean up

theory on the toilet

Freud's act, as it were, for the benefit of anglophone readers. Instead of finding excrement or turds [*Kot*] in the present tense, Freud the dreamer now finds the more scientific "*faeces*", in the past tense. Instead of urinating, as Freud the dreamer does in German with the gusto of Captain Gulliver in Lilliput (to whom he refers in his analysis), he now has to limit himself to micturation.

Even when he comes across the *Kot*, then, Freud experiences no disgust. In the free association to the dream text, he immediately produced the image of the Augean stables as cleaned by Hercules. Freud has overgone Hercules, in other words, by succeeding in his position and cleaning out psychological errors and prejudices. To a certain extent, he is cheering himself up, as indeed the dreamer is supposed to do.

The seat "(except, of course, for the hole)" was an exact reproduction of a present given to Freud by "a grateful woman patient". The dream is a kind of gift. Proper interpretation soon brings its rewards, in the immediate aftermath of the dream: "even the museum of human excrement could be given an interpretation to rejoice my heart" [*selbst das Museum menschlicher Exkremente ist einer herzerfreuenden Deutung fähig*]. The self-congratulation here is not as straightforward as it may seem, however, and it would be a serious mistake to see Freud as the curator of a museum, whether of excrement or anything else. The congratulation which Freud has won is like that which Derrida gives to Francis Ponge writing about the Augean stables: "he does not run away from dirt, he writes with dirt, against dirt, on dirt, about dirt. It is his matter [*C'est sa matière*]" (44-45). The Augean stables are not to be cleansed, but to be written.

It should be remembered that Freud paid careful attention to the theory of the dream as a form of psychical excretion: in the end, he agrees with the theory as regards the function (but not the structure) of dreams (*Standard Edition* 5: 579 = *Pelican Freud* 4: 735; *Studienausgabe* 2: 551). But the textual leftovers cited above call into question the act of excretion which supposedly preceded and produced them. Excretion is dramatised in the text as an event, so that the text becomes an allegory of excretion which – despite Freud's archaeological endeavours – does not have a determinate origin. Freud's work repeatedly produces leftovers which do not know their own place. As far as psychoanalysis is concerned, there will always be "*still some left*". It is striking, in fact, that Freud does not refer to this final sentence of the dream text, about the leftover, in the course of his laborious and detailed analysis. The sentence itself is left over. It is also striking that, on the day of the dream, Freud had felt frustrated and "longed to be away from all this grubbing about in human dirt [*Wühlen im menschlichen Schmutz*]" (*Standard Edition* 5: 470 = *Pelican Freud* 4: 606; *Studienausgabe* 2: 453). Freud is burrowing away in the soil like a mole, or wallowing in the mire like a pig – *wühlen* is a rich verb – whose longing to escape from its environment must remain frustrated. According to Jacques Lacan, indeed, the psychoanalyst can work in the transference only by means of being cast as *Schmutz* or "trash [*déchet*]" (15-16).

It would be easy to assume that work on *Dreck* will become mired in the banality of an excrement that is identical to itself. A weak reading of Freud might lend support to such an assumption. After all, Freud quotes the following lines by Heine with approval, to explain how his method of dream interpretation functions:

Selten habt ihr mich *verstanden*,
Selten auch verstand ich Euch,
Nur wenn wir im *Kot* uns fanden,
So verstanden wir uns gleich.

[Rarely have you *understood* me, and rarely too have I understood you. Not until we both found ourselves in the *mud* did we promptly understand each other.]

(*Standard Edition* 5: 513 = *Pelican Freud* 4: 657-58; *Studienausgabe* 2: 492, Freud's italics)

Strachey describes his translation of Heine, given in a footnote, as literal; but in one important aspect it is not literal enough, since *Kot* is "excrement" rather than "mud". Understanding promptly takes place, it appears, when Freud and his material find themselves in the shit together. But what does "understand" mean here? Freud explains that interpretation begins by thinking about "the most trivial elements" in the dream, because they turn out, surprisingly, to be the most "indispensable". The apparently indispensable is in fact trivial or misleading, we learn in this passage, and the apparently trivial is in fact indispensable. Such is the process of psychoanalytic understanding. *Dreck* haunts the position of comprehensible *Kot*; *Dreck* takes place when understanding can no longer be understood and when the distinction between indispensable and trivial becomes incoherent. *Dreck* is other.

What is proposed, then, is not another academic treatise but a return to a form of writing and reading in which otherness is perpetually invoked even as it is displaced, in which the remnant of materiality is recycled and reworked in order to produce meaning even as the impossibility of joining that meaning to the event of the text is acknowledged. Dreckology demands the study of a practice which works on such

roy sellars

impossibility — namely, allegory. The Dreckologist is an allegorist.

The term *Dreck-ologie* was originally a private joke between Freud and his confidant Wilhelm Fliess, as this project will show in some detail (see *Complete Letters to Fliess* 291; *Briefe an Fliess* 317). Dreckology is not a science of anything: it foregrounds a crisis of terminology, in fact, as it explicitly fails to name an object (see Benjamin 37).

Moreover, this will not have been a manifesto in any familiar sense. The form of "manifest" text which it ought properly to have presented is described by Freud in *The Interpretation of Dreams* as pure dissimulation, for the superficial coherence and intelligibility of the manifest is a measure of how far it has been distorted by the dream-work. The most deceptive aspect of the manifest text is that readers will naturally tend to excavate it and grasp what appears to be latent — whereas the task of reading concerns the figurative work between, with, against, on, or about such an opposition (*Standard Edition* 5: 506-07n2 = *Pelican Freud* 4: 649-50n2; *Studienausgabe* 2: 486n1).

In contrast to the domesticity of Auden in "The Geography of the House", in which anything can be recycled and dirt is merely a comforting sign of the human, Freud explains that the ego is not master in its own house or even on its own toilet. Auden implies that Freud was right about anality (lines 41-48), but this is beside the point. Freud's dream of theory is important here not for its results, whatever they may be, but because it includes a point at which meaning falls irreparably into the unknown (*Standard Edition* 5: 525 = *Pelican Freud* 4: 671-72; *Studienausgabe* 2: 503). Psychoanalytic theory is itself a falling in which *Dreck* is inextricably entangled. Through prosopopeia, there may be a voice caught up in this

193

theory on the toilet

process of entanglement [*Verstrickung*], but it is a voice which resists categorisation and even recognition. The demand of this voice must nevertheless be heard. As Freud wrote to Fliess shortly before finishing *The Interpretation of Dreams*, "filth [*der Dreck*] is unavoidable and asks to be treated humanely [*bittet um humane Behandlung*]" (*Complete Letters to Fliess* 370; *Briefe an Fliess* 405, Freud's emphasis). It is no wonder that Freud complained so eloquently about being obliged to have dirty hands.

notes

1 Anne Barton points out in her edition that this sentence – in which Prospero speaks of Caliban – does not necessarily imply that *The Tempest* is "an interior drama", as some critics have claimed (Shakespeare 176). The aim of the present manifesto is not to offer another interpretation of Prospero's act of acknowledgement. Instead, it takes issue with the notion of interiority that would support the classification of a drama or thing as "interior". Neither interior nor exterior, our "thing of darkness" is ectopic.

2 Varro was a scholar whom Julius Caesar appointed as the first librarian of the Roman public library (Radice 245). This essay is an advertisement for a work in progress provisionally entitled *Figures of Dreck*, the first volume of which investigates the privatisation of excrement and the unreadability of *Dreck* in textual economies from Varro to *Paradise Lost* (1667). Georgics fall apart; meaning cannot hold.

3 The term "biografiend" derives from *Finnegans Wake*, where it is found in a parenthesis warning that *bio-graphy* may be an oxymoron, insofar as it kills its own object in the process of writing (55). Ellmann cites the term, rather at his own expense, in the Introduction to his monumental biography of Joyce (7). According to Ellmann, Joyce's work is "humanistic" because it is dedicated to "the justification of the commonplace", which is both "dear and dirty" (5-6). Doubting Ellmann's belief in the "joining of event and composition" (3), this manifesto declines to justify the ways of literature to man and rejects the assumption that Joyce wishes his readers to "conquer" him (6).

4 This observation about Bloom's rhythm has been made by Martin Pops in his essay "The Metamorphosis of Shit" (35-36), whose own somewhat breathless rhythm is notable as it produces one textual example of defecation after another – a rich and seamless flow of exemplification. While the examples are valuable, the difference promised by his title turns into an elaboration of the same.

5 For a recent discussion of the scene in relation to Joyce criticism (and Kristeva), see Anspaugh, "Powers of Ordure".

bibliography

Anspaugh, K., "Powers of Ordure: James Joyce and the Excremental Vision(s)", *Mosaic* 27:1 (1994) p73-100.

Arnold, I., Letter to the Editor, *Independent* 22 April 1994, p17.

Auden, W.H., "The Geography of the House" in *Selected Poems*, ed. E. Mendelson (London: Faber, 1979) p261-63.

Barnes, J., *Flaubert's Parrot* (London: Jonathan Cape, 1984).

Beja, M., ed., *James Joyce, Dubliners and A Portrait of the Artist as a Young Man: A Casebook* (London: Macmillan, 1973).

Benjamin, W., *The Origin of German Tragic Drama*, tr. J. Osborne (London: New Left Books, 1977).

Betjeman, J., "In Westminster Abbey" in *The Oxford Anthology of English Literature*, eds F. Kermode and J. Hollander, 2 vols (New York: Oxford University Press, 1973) 2: p2138-9.

roy sellars

Bersani, L., *The Culture of Redemption* (Cambridge, Mass.: Harvard University Press, 1990).

Bloom, H., *The Anxiety of Influence: A Theory of Poetry* (New York: Oxford University Press, 1973).

Castiglione, B., *The Book of the Courtier*, tr. G. Bull, rev. ed. (Harmondsworth: Penguin, 1976).

Chaucer, G., *The Merchant's Prologue and Tale*, ed. M. Hussey (Cambridge: Cambridge University Press, 1966).

Craig, D.H., *Sir John Harington* (Boston: Twayne-Hall, 1985).

de Certeau, M., *Heterologies: Discourse on the Other*, tr. B. Massumi (Manchester: Manchester University Press, 1986).

Derrida, J., *Signéponge/Signsponge*, tr. R. Rand (New York: Columbia University Press, 1984).

Douglas, K., *The Ragman's Son* (London: Simon and Schuster, 1988).

Douglas, M., *Purity and Danger: An Analysis of the Concepts of Pollution and Taboo* (London: Routledge, 1966).

Ellman, R., *James Joyce*, rev. ed. (Oxford: Oxford University Press, 1983).

Foucault, M., "A Preface to Transgression" in *Language, Counter-memory, Practice: Selected Essays and Interviews*, ed. D.F. Bouchard, tr. D.F. Bouchard and S. Simon (Ithaca: Cornell University Press, 1977).

Freud, S., *Briefe an Wilhelm Fliess, 1887-1904*, ed. J.M. Masson and M. Schröter (Frankfurt: M. Fischer, 1986).

Freud, S., *The Complete Letters of Sigmund Freud to Wilhelm Fliess, 1887-1904*, ed. and tr. J.M. Masson (Cambridge, Mass.: Harvard University Press, 1985).

Freud, S. and A. Zweig, *The Letters of Sigmund Freud and Arnold Zweig*, ed. E.L. Freud, tr. E. and W. Robson-Scott (New York: Harcourt, 1970).

Freud, S., *The Pelican Freud Library*, ed. A. Richards et al., tr. J. Strachey et al., 15 vols (Harmondsworth: Penguin, 1973-86).

Freud, S., *The Standard Edition of the Complete Psychological Works of Sigmund Freud*, ed. and tr. J. Strachey et al., 24 vols (London: Hogarth Press, 1953-74).

Freud, S., *Studienausgabe*, ed. A. Mitscherlich et al., 11 vols (Frankfurt: M. Fischer, 1969-75).

Godzich, W., "Foreword: The Tiger on the Paper Mat" in *The Resistance to Theory* by P. de Man (Manchester: Manchester University Press, 1986) pix-xviii.

Guerrand, R.-H., *Les lieux: Histoire des commodités* (Paris: La Découverte, 1985).

Hardy, T., *The Complete Poems of Thomas Hardy*, ed. J. Gibson (London: Macmillan, 1976).

Harington, Sir J., *The Letters and Epigrams of Sir John Harington, Together with The Prayse of Private Life*, ed. N.E. McClure (Philadelphia: University of Pennsylvania Press, 1930).

Harington, Sir J., *A New Discourse of a Stale Subject, Called the Metamorphosis of Ajax*, ed. E. Story Donno (London: Routledge, 1962).

Harris, M., *Privies Galore* (Stroud: Alan Sutton, 1990).

Hillis Miller, J., "Thomas Hardy, Jacques Derrida, and the 'Dislocation of Souls'" in *Taking Chances: Derrida, Psychoanalysis and Literature*, ed. J.H. Smith and W. Kerrigan (Baltimore: Johns Hopkins University Press, 1984) p135-45.

Jones, J.O., MP, "Not at Your Convenience" (Cardiff: privately printed, 1994).

Joyce, J., *Finnegans Wake*, 4th ed. (London: Faber, 1975).

Joyce, J., *Ulysses*, ed. J. Johnson (Oxford: Oxford University Press, 1993).

Kristeva, J., "Approaching Abjection", tr. J. Lechte, *Oxford Literary Review* 5 (1982) p125-49.

theory on the toilet

Kristeva, J., *Pouvoirs de l'horreur: Essai sur l'abjection* (Paris: Seuil, 1980).

Lacan, J., *Television*, ed. J. Copjec, tr. D. Hollier et al., with *A Challenge to the Psychoanalytic Establishment*, tr. J. Mehlman (New York: Norton, 1990) p1-46.

Lamarq, D., *Het Latrinaire Gebeuren: De Gescheidnis van de W.C.* (Ghent: Stichting Mens en Kultuur, 1993).

Laporte, D., *Histoire de la merde (prologue)* (Paris: Christian Bourgois, 1978).

Milton, J., *Paradise Lost*, ed. A. Fowler (London: Longman, 1971).

Montaigne, M. de, "De l'expérience" in *Essais*, ed. A. Micha, 3 vols (Paris: Flammarion, 1969) 3: p275-328.

Montaigne, M. de, "Of Experience" in *The Essays of Michael Lord of Montaigne*, tr. J. Florio (London: Routledge, [1885]) p546-75.

Oddie, B. and L. Beaumont, *The Toilet Book* (London: Methuen, 1984).

Patterson, A., *Fables of Power: Aesopian Writing and Political History* (Durham: Duke University Press, 1991).

Pops, M., "The Metamorphosis of Shit", *Salmagundi* 56 (1982) p26-61.

Radice, B., *Who's Who in the Ancient World: A Handbook to the Survivors of the Greek and Roman Classics*, rev. ed. (Harmondsworth: Penguin, 1973).

Reyburn, W., *Flushed with Pride: The Story of Thomas Crapper* (London: Pavilion, 1989).

Ross, T., *I Want My Potty* (London: Andersen, 1986).

"Sanitation, History of" in *Oxford Junior Encyclopaedia*, ed. L.E. Salt et al., rev. ed., 13 vols (London: Oxford University Press, 1974-75) 11: p399-401.

Shakespeare, W., *The Tempest*, ed. A. Righter [A. Barton] (Harmondsworth: Penguin, 1968).

Spock, Dr B., *Baby and Child Care*, rev. ed. (London: New English Library, 1969).

Swift, J., *Gulliver's Travels*, eds P. Dixon and J. Chalker (Harmondsworth: Penguin, 1967).

Teskey, G., "Irony, Allegory, and Metaphysical Decay", *PMLA* 109:3 (1994) p397-408.

Varro, M.T., *On Agriculture*, with *On Agriculture* by M.P. Cato, tr. W.D. Hooper and H.B. Ash, rev. ed. (Cambridge, Mass.: Harvard University Press; London: Heinemann, 1935) p159-529.

Wood, S., "Surprise in Literature", *Angelaki* 1:1 (1993) p58-68.

notes on the contributors

alison ainley
is Lecturer in Philosophy at Anglia Polytechnic University, Cambridge and author of a forthcoming book on Luce Irigaray.

sotirios athanasiou
is an architect, designer and committed folk dancer, based in his much loved home town of Xanthi, northern Greece. A restless scientist pitted against the provincial banality of his native place, his work ranges from village squares, shops and summer houses, to articles of furniture in a vibrant neo-deco style. His designs have appeared in a number of periodicals, including the *Architect's Journal*.

roger bromley
is a Professor in International Cultural Studies at the Nottingham Trent University, having previously taught at Portsmouth University and Cheltenham and Gloucester College of Higher Education. He has been involved in the field of Cultural Studies for twenty years, and is the author of *Lost Narratives* (1988), *Policing the Carnival: Popular Cultural Forms and the National Process, 1880-1914* (forthcoming), and co-editor of the *Cultural Studies Reader: History, Theory, Practice* (forthcoming). His current research interests are in borderline writings and cross-cultural studies.

sara guyer
is a doctoral student in the Department of Rhetoric at the University of Berkeley. She has edited *Stories from the Nerve Bible: A Twenty Year Retrospective* by Laurie Anderson.

stephen keane
is a doctoral student at the University of Sussex.

chris miller
is a freelance writer and translator. He studied Lit. Hum. at Oxford and lived for four years in Paris. A contributor to *PN Review* and *European Photography*, he has written on Barthes, Hill and Curnow. Co-founder of the Oxford Amnesty Lectures, he is working on a novel.

forbes morlock
is completing a dissertation about reading and *Capital* at the University of Oxford. He teaches at the Syracuse University London Centre.

bill readings
is author of *Introducing Lyotard: Art and Politics* (New York and London: Routledge, 1991) and *The University and the Idea of Excellence: Beyond Culture* (forthcoming from Harvard University Press). He edited Jean-François Lyotard's *Political Writings* (Minneapolis: University of Minnesota Press, 1993) with Kevin-Paul Geiman, and *Postmodernism Across the Ages* (Syracuse: Syracuse University Press, 1993) with Bennet Schaber.

nicholas royle

is an editor of the *Oxford Literary Review*. He is the author of *Telepathy and Literature* (Oxford: Basil Blackwell, 1991) and *After Derrida* (Manchester: Manchester University Press, 1995). He is co-author, with Andrew Bennett, of *Elizabeth Bowen and the Dissolution of the Novel* (London: Macmillan, 1995) and *An Introduction to Literature, Criticism and Theory: Key Critical Concepts* (Hemel Hempstead: Harvester-Wheatsheaf, 1995).

roy sellars

teaches English at the University of Geneva. He holds a doctorate from Oxford, and has published in the field of literary theory. He recently co-translated *Text and Memory*, by Renate Lachmann, for Minnesota, and is completing an annotated bibliography of Harold Bloom, for Garland. His essay in the present volume is an advertisement for a book provisionally entitled *Figures of* Dreck.

fran sendbuehler

is a doctoral candidate and instructor in the département d'études anglaises at the Université de Montréal. She is currently completing her master's thesis entitled *Image Object Text*, and is author of an essay on Milton entitled "Silence as Discourse".

rené schérer

is Professor of Philosophy at the University of Paris VIII. His recent publications include *Zeus hospitalier* (Paris: Armand Colin, 1993), *Pari sur l'impossible* (Paris: Presses Universitaires de l'Université de Paris VIII, 1989) and, with Guy Hocquenghem, *L'âme atomique* (Paris: Alain Michel, 1988).

dan stone

is a doctoral student at Lincoln College, Oxford, working on the historiographical representation of the Holocaust. He was involved in organising the exhibition "Representation of Auschwitz" held in Cracow, summer 1995, part of the three year Tempus Project, "Civil Society and Social Change in Europe After Auschwitz".

robert white

is a doctoral student at St John's College, Oxford, writing a dissertation on psychoanalysis and history.

marcus wood

is a painter and printmaker who also writes academic books about propaganda. He is married to Sarah Wood and is the father of Miss Rose Wood. The family will soon be moving to Manchester to find a new home.

sarah wood (editor)

has taught at Cheltenham and Gloucester College of Higher Education, Oxford University and London University. She is a founder-member of the editorial board of *Angelaki* and is writing a book about Robert Browning.

ANGELAKI

Established in 1993, *Angelaki* is a tri-annual journal edited by researchers in philosophical, literary and social theory, publishing thematic book collections. The journal seeks to publish advancing work from contributors in different centres in the UK and internationally, and to foster a spirit of vigorous debate within and between disciplines.

Angelaki encourages a critical engagement with theory in terms of disciplinary development and intellectual and political usefulness; the inquiry into and articulation of culture, and the complex determination of change and its relation to history.

The journal especially strives to foster the theory of minor movements, recognising their significant impact on and dynamic relation to the development of cultures, political spaces and academic disciplines, and emphasising their formative power, rather than their oppositional entrenchment.

Angelaki provides a forum for the inquiry into questions of existential and political definition and agency, on the personal, collective, institutional and policy-oriented levels, and promotes the work of spirited and experimental theoretical writing in all areas of value-production.

call for papers / issue proposals

Angelaki invites the submission of original articles of 2-10,000 words, review articles, and proposals for translations and interviews. Typescripts should be in duplicate, double-spaced. The editors also encourage the submission of publishing proposals from individuals prepared to assume responsibility for producing an issue of the journal. Issue proposals should be at least 500 words, and should make clear the kind of publication envisaged, and the way in which it will contribute to *Angelaki*'s project.

debate

Readers are invited to submit responses to pieces published in the journal to be considered for publication in the debate section. Responses should be no more than 3,000 words, and should be sent in duplicate, double-spaced.

style

Angelaki follows the *MLA Handbook for Writers of Research Papers*.

Angelaki 44 Abbey Rd
Oxford OX2 0AE UK

Angelaki is a refereed serial.

Angelaki is abstracted in the *MLA Bibliography*.

back issues

vol. 1, no. 1
the uses of theory

Publication: September 1993. Pages: 144.
New Edition: October 1995.

Editors: Pelagia Goulimari
and Gerard Greenway

Contents
On the Line of Flight: How to be a Realist?, *Pelagia Goulimari*. Crisis in Politics, *Barry Stocker*. Reflections on the Politics of Time and Space, *David Howarth*. Surprise in Literature, *Sarah Wood*. Title without Colon, *Robert Smith*. Yuli's Birthday Party: A Philosophical Short Story, *Mozaffar Qizilbash*. Never Mind the Ballads, Here's Thomas Percy, *Nick Groom*. Interview with Félix Guattari. Félix Guattari: Towards a Queer Chaosmosis, *Josep-Anton Fernández*. William Burroughs Between Indifference and Revalorisation: Notes Towards a Political Reading, *Timothy S. Murphy*. In the Shadow of Cybernetic Minorities: Life, Death and Delirium in the Capitalist Imaginary, *Charlie Blake*.

vol. 1, no. 2
narratives of forgery

Publication: April 1994. Pages: 176.

Editor: Nick Groom

Contents
Rewriting Plagiarism, *Don Nichol*. The Isle of Pines and the Problem of Genre, *Daniel Carey*. Forgery or Plagiarism?, *Nick Groom*. Chatterton in Bristol, *Jonathan Barry*. What Thomas Knew, *Michael F. Suarez S.J.* The Macaroni Parson and the Marvellous Boy, *Paul Baines*. Forgery Discovered, *Randall McGowen*. Identity, Authenticity, Class, *John Goodridge*. Arthur as Artefact, *Inga Bryden*. Thomas Chatterton: Early Sources and Responses, *Review Article*.

vol. 1, no. 3
reconsidering the political

Publication: January 1995. Pages: 200.

Editors: David Howarth and Aletta J. Norval

Contents
Politics, Ethics, Identity: Reconsidering the Political, *David Howarth and Aletta J. Norval*. Tracing the Political, *Benjamin Arditi*. Enacting the Political, *Michael Cholewa-Madsen*. Negotiating the Paradoxes of Contemporary Politics, *Interview with Ernesto Laclau*. Herculean Tasks, Dionysian Labor, *Timothy S. Murphy*. Postmodern Law and the Withering of Civil Society, *Michael Hardt and Antonio Negri*. Civil Society: The Traumatic Patient, *Yael Shalem and David Bensusan*. Curiosity, *Sue Golding*. Fascination with Foucault, *Rudi Visker*. Agonal Thought: Reading Nietzsche as Political Thinker, *David Owen*. Rorty's Pragmatism, *Michael Reid*. The Reinvention of Democracy in Eastern Europe, *Jelica Sumic and Rado Riha*. The Politics of Homecoming: Contending Identities in Contemporary South Africa, *Aletta J. Norval*. Post-Democracy, Politics and Philosophy, *Interview with Jacques Rancière*. The Aims of Radicalism, *Michael Reid*.

forthcoming issues

vol. 2, no. 2
authorizing culture

Publication: winter 1995.

Editors: Gary Hall and Simon Wortham

For many, criticism is currently trapped in a struggle whereby the representation of popular culture is restricted to a choice between what appear to be two equally unacceptable positions: on the one hand, a traditional position of cultural critique and critical distance; and, on the other, a denial of distance and difference in favour of a simple celebration of cultural forms. It is this impasse that *Authorizing Culture* will explore. In what ways does this problem affect contemporary forms of cultural criticism? Can cultural criticism really take no other form than an opposition between optimism and pessimism, inside and outside, critical objectivity and populist celebration? And is a change in attitude needed toward those commonly considered to be the modern masters?

Contents
Interdisciplinarity and its Discontents: Editorial Introduction, *Gary Hall and Simon Wortham*. The Dialectics of Cultural Criticism, *Robert J.C. Young*. 'It's a Thin Line Between Love and Hate': Why Cultural Studies is so 'Naff', *Gary Hall*. The Glasse of Majesty: Reflections on New Historicism and Cultural Materialism, *Simon Wortham*. Rethinking Authority, *Interview with Homi K. Bhabha*. Value, Tradition and the Place of the Present: The Disputed Canon in the United States, *Graham Macphee*. The Paradox of Authority: Psychoanalysis, History and Cultural Criticism, *Graham Dawson*. The Epistemology of Mastery, *Jonathan Derbyshire*. 'Something Still More Exact': T.S. Eliot's 'Traditional Claims', *Elizabeth Beaumont Bissell*. Liberalism After Nietzsche and Weber, *Barry Stocker*. 'Come and Keep Your Comrade Warm': Stories of Jacques Derrida and the Beatles, *Stephen Jarvis*.

vol. 2, no. 3
intellectuals and global culture

Publication: spring 1996.

Editors: Charlie Blake and Linnie Blake

Whether the issue is institutionalisation or degeneration (Jacoby, Bloom), genealogy or delegitimation (Turner, Baumann), specificity or universality (Spivak, Said), or redundancy (Johnson, Carey), the intellectual is now a species under anxious, largely autolectic, scrutiny. This number will consider the broad issue of the intellectual as both regional and global phenomenon – as visualiser of the *world* as much as the *locality*, the *universal* as much as the *specific*. The issue will examine the mutable status of the intellectual in different periods and, importantly, in different parts of the world; in the corporation and the revolutionary cell; in the imagination of artists and dreamers.

The editors invite papers and proposals from all points of view (nation, gender, sexuality, class, cultural identity in general) on themes relating to intellectuals and global or local culture.

Provisional Contents
Falling Down, *Tim Shakesby*. And Now Here Comes a Book that Makes Everything Easy: Intellectual History and the Field of Intellectual Production, *John Beasley-Murray*. Critical Mass: Intellectual Politics and the Mode of Complexity, *Charlie Blake*. The Jew, the Red, the Whore and the Bomber, *Linnie Blake*. The African-American Intellectual Abroad, *James Wilie*. The Impertinence of Intellectuals: Democracy and Post-Modernity in Latin America, *Joanildo N. Burity*. Soyinka and Cultural Politics: The Politics of Culture, *Caroline Ukoumunne*. On Bulgarian Intellectuals, *Yanna Popova*. Bugger Bentham: Sodomy and the Panoptic Intellectual, *Elaine Brown*.

vol. 3, no. 1
the love of music

Publication: summer 1996.

Editors: Timothy S. Murphy, Roy Sellars and Robert Smith

Music surrounds us today. But as our range of choice in musics has widened, our power to choose to hear or not and our ability to listen have narrowed. In moving out of the concert hall and the shrine into the home, the workplace and the market, music has taken on a series of contradictory and unstable determinations: soundtrack to everyday life, assertion of ethnic or social identity, testament to taste, 'pure' aesthetic, Edenic language, commodity, and so on. The difference between music and noise is no longer clear.

In the midst of this polyphony or cacophony, what can it mean to love music? What is the place and time and voice of music, and how does music find its way into our domestic lives and intellectual work? How do we use music, whether as alibi, idea, marker of status, ur-language, or Other? Is the appropriation of music inevitable, impossible, or both?

The editors invite contributions from all critical perspectives (musicological, philosophical, psychoanalytic, literary, social) addressing any field of music. Submissions should be sent to one of the following:

Timothy S. Murphy, 3614 Faris Drive #31, Los Angeles, CA 90034-7544, USA.

Roy Sellars, Dépt. d'anglais, Univ. de Genève, CH-1211 Genève 4, Switzerland.
(e-mail: SELLARS@uni2a.unige.ch)

Robert Smith, All Souls College, Oxford, OX1 4AL, UK.

CALL FOR SUBMISSIONS ON

THE DISCURSIVE ECONOMIES OF KNOWLEDGE AND CULTURE
with constant reference to the work of
BILL READINGS

A special issue of the journal *Surfaces*

The electronic journal *Surfaces*, published by the Comparative Literature Department of the Université de Montréal, is devoting a special collection of essays to the issues and concerns present in the critical work of our friend and colleague Bill Readings.

As you know, Bill's interests were very broad, ranging from Renaissance literary theory to the role of the university and to questions of culture and the politics of knowledge. The general theme of *The Discursive Economies of Knowledge and Culture* simultaneously gives the project a unifying focus and permits a wide range of these concerns to be represented. This focus, inspired by Bill's work, offers a context for vigorous and provocative debate of the issues his work addressed.

We welcome proposals on any aspect of this general theme. The deadline for proposals (which should be limited to 250 words) is September 1st; the final essays are due by January 1st.

Surfaces currently accepts submissions in French and all other Romance languages, English, and German. Proposals and inquiries should be addressed to:

SURFACES
Département de littérature comparée
Université de Montréal
C.P. 6128, succursale Centre-ville
Montréal (Québec) H3C 3J7
tel.: 514 343 5683   fax: 514 343 2211
e-mail: <cochrant@ere.umontreal.ca>   or
<valleej@ere.umontreal.ca>

fragmente

a magazine of contemporary poetics

6

New poetry   Bob Perelman, Sheila E Murphy, Tony Lopez, Ken Edwards, Peter Middleton, Harriet Tarlo, Ray DiPalma, Drew Milne, Spencer Selby, Roberto Smith, Gavin Selerie, Johan de Wit, John Welch, Nicholas Piombino

Gary Banham	on Jacques Derrida, *Aporias*
Antony Easthope	'Prynne's Imaginary'
Anthony Mellors	'Out of the American Tree: Language Writing and the Politics of Form'
Nicholas Royle	'Mollusc' (on Les Murray)
D S Marriott	'Signs Taken For Signifiers: Language Writing, Fetishism and Disavowal'
Gavin Selerie	on Robert Duncan's *Selected Poems*
George Hartley	'Silence from Babel: On Nick Piombino'
Ken Edwards	'Ten British Poets'

fragmente

edited by Anthony Mellors
University of Durham, Dept. of English Studies,
Elvet Riverside, New Elvet, Durham DH1 3JT
EMAIL A.M.MELLORS@DURHAM.AC.UK

Subscription: £4,95 for one issue, £9 for two issues (including p&p)
Institutions £10 per issue

OXFORD LITERARY REVIEW

16 (1994) On India: Writing History, Culture, Post-Coloniality
edited by ANIA LOOMBA and SUVIR KAUL

ANIA LOOMBA and SUVIR KAUL *Introduction: Location, Culture, Post-Coloniality*
URVASHI BUTALIA *Community, State and Gender: Some Reflections on the Partition of India*
SUSIE THARU *Rendering Account of the Nation: Partition Narratives and Other Genres of the Passive Revolution*
RAVI VASUDEVAN *Dislocations: The Cinematic Imagining of a New Society in 1950s India*
SUVIR KAUL *Separation Anxiety: Growing up Inter/National in Amitav Ghosh's* The Shadow Lines
RAJESWARI SUNDER RAJAN *Ameena: Gender, Crisis and National Identity*
TANIKA SARKAR *Bankimchandra and the Impossibility of a Political Agenda*
SUMIT SARKAR *Orientalism Revisited: Saidian Frameworks in the Writing of Modern Indian History*
DILIP SIMEON *Tremors of Intent: Perceptions of the Nation and Community in Contemporary India*
PURUSHOTTAM AGRAWAL *'Kan Kan Mein Vyape Hein Ram': The Slogan as a Metaphor of Cultural Interrogation*

17 (1995) The University in Ruins
Essays on the crisis in the concept of the modern university
edited by TIMOTHY CLARK and NICHOLAS ROYLE

BILL READINGS *Dwelling in the Ruins*
BARRY HINDESS *Great Expectations: Freedom and Authority in the Idea of a Modern University*
IAN HUNTER *The Regimen of Reason: Kant's Defence of the Philosophy Faculty*
MAY JOSEPH *Dystopia, Promise and the Imagined Citadel: The Citizenship of Education*
THE COMMITTEE OF PUBLIC SAFETY *Heidegger High School*
J. HILLIS MILLER *The University of Dissensus*
DIANE ELAM *Literary Remains*

Individuals 1 volume £7.95 (U.K.), £11.00 or $19.00 (foreign)
Institutions 1 volume £20.00 (U.K.), £23.00 or $40.00 (foreign)
Prices include postage. For airmail add £4.00 or $8.00 per volume. Payment: US: by personal cheque or US Postal Order in US $. Other overseas orders: in £ or US $ by International Money Order, or cheque drawn on UK (£) or US ($) bank, charged prepaid. Make cheques payable to *Oxford Literary Review*. Send to Oxford Literary Review, Dept of English Studies, University of Durham, Elvet Riverside, Durham DH1 3JT, UK.

WARWICK STUDIES *in* Philosophy & Literature

WARWICK STUDIES IN PHILOSOPHY AND LITERATURE
General Editor: **Andrew Benjamin**, *University of Warwick*
In both philosophy and literature, much of the best original work being done today exploits the connections and tensions between these two disciplines. The books published in this series present the work of the Centre for research in Philosophy and Literature at the University of Warwick. They combine a sense of new direction with traditional standards of intellectual rigour.

Walter Benjamin's Philosophy
Destruction and Experience
Andrew Benjamin and **Peter Osborne**

This collection explores, in Adorno's description, Benjamin's 'philosophy directed against philosophy.' The essays cover all aspects of Benjamin's writings, from his early work in the philosophy of art and language, through to his concept of history.
November 1993: 216x138: 312pp Hb: 0-415-08368-0: £40.00 Pb: 0-415-08369-9: £13.99

Judging Lyotard
Edited by **Andrew Benjamin**

The first collection of papers devoted to the work of Lyotard, it provides an estimation and critique of his work and in particular considers how the subject of judgement was of supereme importance to his thought.
July 1992: 216x138: 224pp Hb: 0-415-05256-4: £37.50 Pb: 0-415-05257-2: £12.99

The Problems of Modernity
Adorno and Benjamin
Edited by **Andrew Benjamin**

A collection of original papers tackling the problems arising from the use of the concept of modernity and covering a wide range of topics from feminism to music.
April 1991: 216x138: 232pp Pb: 0-415-06029-X: £12.99

Abjection, Melancholia and Love
The Work of Julia Kristeva
Edited by **John Fletcher** and **Andrew Benjamin**

Opening with a previously unpublished essay by Julia Kristeva, this collection offers profound insights into work central to linguistic and psychoanalytic thought.
January 1990: 216x138: 224pp Pb: 0-415-04190-2: £12.99

Post-Structuralist Classics
Edited by **Andrew Benjamin**

An exciting and important collection revealing both the diversity of approaches that mark the post-structuralist endeavour, and the challenge it poses to the conventional practice of classical studies and ancient philosophy.
September 1988: 216x138: 256pp Hb: 0-415-00922-7: £40.00

Available through booksellers. For further information or a FREE Philosophy catalogue, please contact: Kevin Waudby, Routledge 11 New Fetter Lane, London EC4P 4EE.
Tel: 0171 842 2011 Fax: 0171 842 2306. Email: kwaudby@routledge.com

ordering information

Angelaki, Volume 2 (1995/96)
(3 Issues) ISSN: 0969 725X

Subscription rates per volume (inc. p+p)

	UK	Overseas*
Individuals:	£12.00	£14.00/US$24.00
Institutions:	£21.00	£23.00/US$38.00

Single issue/sample copy rates (inc. p+p)

	UK	Overseas*
Individuals:	£5.00	£5.00/US$10.00
Institutions:	£8.00	£8.00/US$15.00

Please make cheques payable to Angelaki. Send your order with payment to:
Angelaki 44 Abbey Rd
Oxford OX2 0AE UK

Please ensure that you provide us with your full address.

If you have bought home and family **and you would like to subscribe to the remaining issues in the current volume,** authorizing culture **and** intellectuals and global culture, **individuals can do so at a cost of: £8.00 / £9.50 (overseas*); US$16.00* – inc. p+p. Send your order, with payment, to the above address.**

* Overseas prices subject to change. Other nationalities please apply for own-currency prices.